# Psychology in Utopia

# Psychology in Utopia

*Toward a Social History of Soviet Psychology*

*Alex Kozulin*

The MIT Press
Cambridge, Massachusetts
London, England

This book was set in Baskerville by The MIT Press Computergraphics Department and printed and bound by Halliday Lithograph in the United States of America.

**Library of Congress Cataloging in Publication Data**

Kozulin, Alex.
  Psychology in Utopia.

  Bibliography: p.
  Includes index.
  1. Psychology—Soviet Union—History.  2. Psychology—Soviet Union—Philosophy.  3. Psychology—Soviet Union—Social Aspects.  I. Title.  [DNLM: 1. Psychology—History—U.S.S.R.  2. Psychology—U.S.S.R.—Biography. BF 108.R9 K88p]
BF108.S65K68   1984     150'.947     83-22264
ISBN 0-262-11087-3

# Contents

4191 Bauer +Taylor 25.00

## Acknowledgments

The origin of this book is typical: It emerged out of a chain of coincidences and the good will of a number of different people. For several years I worked at a historical study of Soviet psychology, convinced that my efforts would interest only the closed circle of Soviet scholars anxious to reconsider the recent past of their discipline. My acquaintance with the members of "Cheiron," the International Society for the History of the Behavioral and Social Sciences, and my affiliation with the Boston University Center for the Philosophy and History of Science helped to change this point of view. Gradually I realized that a socially informed study of Soviet psychology might be of interest to the general American community of social and behavioral scientists. At this crucial moment I was approached by Sharon Basco of The MIT Press, who convinced me that my studies should take the form of a book and as soon as possible. She also generously agreed to supervise my writing, since English is not my mother tongue. Later on Josef Brozek and James Wertsch volunteered to examine the manuscript and to make specific comments and suggestions. It is entirely my fault if I did not care to comply with all of their remarks.

Reidel Publishing Company has allowed me to include in this book material drawn from articles published in *Studies in Soviet Thought.*

I am especially grateful to Alexander and Nora Samarov, whose material assistance and moral support helped me to start this project. Discussions with fellow scholars greatly enhanced my understanding of modern philosophy of science and history of psychology. I would like to thank all of them, especially Thomas Blakeley, Arthur Blumenthal, Josef Brozek, Sigmund Koch, David Leary, Marx Wartofsky, and James Wertsch.

Alex Kozulin
Brookline, Massachusetts

# Chronological Table

**1885**
Moscow Psychological Society established.

**1889**
The first psychological journal, *Problems of Philosophy and Psychology*, founded by Nikolai Grot (1852–1899); closed in 1917.

**1907**
Psychoneurological Institute established by Vladimir Bekhterev (1857–1927) in St. Petersburg.

**1912**
Moscow Institute of Psychology founded by Georgy Chelpanov (1862–1936).

**1917**
The Bolshevik Revolution.

**1922**
Moscow Psychological Society disbanded; members of Moscow Psychological and Petrograd Philosophical Societies exiled to the West.

**1923**
Ivan Pavlov (1849–1936) publishes *Twenty Years' Experience of Objective Study of Higher Nervous Activity (Behavior) of Animals*.

**1923**
The First All-Russia Psychoneurological Congress, with principal speakers Georgy Chelpanov, Vladimir Bekhterev, and Konstantin Kornilov (1879–1957).

**1923**
Georgy Chelpanov dismissed and Konstantin Kornilov appointed director of the Moscow Institute of Psychology.

**1924**
Lev Vygotsky (1896–1934) forms his research group in the Moscow Institute of Psychology.

**1928**

Several new psychological periodicals established: *Psychology* (closed in 1932), *Pedology* (closed in 1932), and *Psychophysiology of Labor and Psychotechnic* (closed in 1934).

**1930**

Congress on Human Behavior features discussion on the "reflexology" of Bekhterev's school.

**1930**

Dmitri Uznadze (1886–1950) publishes the first sketch of his psychology of set.

**1931**

Discussion of Kornilov's "reactology"; Kornilov dismissed as director of the Moscow Institute of Psychology.

**1934**

Posthumous publication of *Thought and Language* by Lev Vygotsky.

**1934**

Sergei Rubinstein (1889–1960) publishes "Problems of Psychology in the Works of Karl Marx."

**1936**

State decree promulgated against testology and pedology.

**1947**

Alexei Leontiev (1903–1979) publishes the first sketch of *Problems of the Development of Mind.*

**1950**

"Pavlovian" Session of the Academy of Science; Pavlovian teaching pronounced the official doctrine of Soviet behavioral science.

**1955**

*Problems of Psychology*, the first psychological periodical of the postwar years, established.

**1957**

Soviet Psychological Society established.

**1960**

*Development of Higher Mental Functions* by Lev Vygotsky published.

**1962**

Meeting on Philosophical Problems of the Physiology of Higher Nervous Activity and Psychology partially restores non-Pavlovian approaches in psychophysiology.

**1965**

Department of Psychology, independent from that of Philosophy, established at Moscow University, chaired by Alexei Leontiev.

**1966**

International Congress of Psychology takes place in Moscow.

**1966**
Nikolai Bernstein (1896–1966) publishes *The Coordination and Regulation of Movements*.

**1971**
The Institute of Psychology of the Academy of Science founded in Moscow, directed by Boris Lomov.

**1974**
Alexander Luria (1902–1977) publishes *Cognitive Development*, based on field studies undertaken in 1932.

**1979**
International Symposium on the Unconscious held in Tbilisi.

**1980**
*Psychology Journal* established.

*Introduction*

Anyone who has ever approached the study of Soviet psychology knows that the subject is intrinsically paradoxical. Certainly psychological scholarship in modern Russia resembles its Western counterpart in all essential details. Soviet psychologists are trained at first-rate universities; a number of research centers have healthy budgets and facilities for a variety of experimental and theoretical studies; and books and journals on psychology have large and receptive audiences. Yet at the same time the political climate, ideology, and norms of everyday life of Soviet society scarcely have any resemblance to those in the West.

Vaguely familiar psychological concepts, such as the conditional reflex, or names, such as Ivan Pavlov or Alexander Luria, emerge from a social context that is almost utopian. The conceptual systems of Soviet authors turn out to be buried under layers of ideological verbiage. Published papers and official records must be taken not at face value but rather as rough material for subsequent distillation and decoding. The task of a scholar interested in Soviet research thus takes on an almost hermeneutical character. Like a historian studying a culture remote in time and space, the specialist in Soviet psychology must reconstruct the subject starting with fragments and adopting a mentality that has little in common with his or her own.

The author of this book has enjoyed the rare opportunity of being involved in psychological research in both the USSR and the United States. The following essays attempt to give a hint as to how the history of Soviet psychology might be decoded by a Western reader. Such a narration must inevitably be syncopated. The author must offer the viewpoint of a "native" brought by a time machine from the age of Soviet mentality, but at the same time he must use language comprehensible to his Western colleagues. This "double vision" is intended to provide close contact with the material while securing that measure of distance which is a sine qua non for critical analysis.

The work of Soviet psychologists is, of course, not entirely unknown in the West. A number of texts, particularly those edited by Michael Cole and Irving Maltzman (1969) and by Josef Brozek and Dan Slobin (1972), as well as a journal of translations, *Soviet Psychology*, provide a rich selection of the original texts of Soviet authors.[1] The major problem is that most of these sources remain "Greek" to Western readers.

In *The Concept of Activity in Soviet Psychology* James Wertsch points out that Western psychologists tend to misunderstand and misinterpret Soviet research mostly because of a lack of information about its philosophical foundations.[2] It seems, however, that the problem is more fundamental than a mere lack of knowledge about Soviet Marxism. Soviet philosophical texts are no less cryptic than the psychological ones, and they must also be decoded and interpreted.

There are two equally misleading tendencies in the interpretation of Soviet research. One focuses on the points of coincidence between Soviet psychological doctrines and the official ideology, trying to explain the development of the former in terms of conformity with the latter.[3] Raymond Bauer in his book *The New Man in Soviet Psychology* warned against such an attempt, pointing out that "the mere fact of points of consistency between a given school of psychology and a given social system may be coincidence. . . . One must focus his attention on the specific reasons why certain trends were facilitated and others discouraged, and not be content with the mere discovery of the uniformities."[4]

It would be equally misleading to portray the development of Soviet psychology purely in terms of intellectual history.[5] Removed from their specific sociohistorical context, the ideas and categories of Soviet psychology appear as deceptive linguistic forms, incoherent and misleading.

That leaves us a third way—a socially informed study of Soviet psychology that would distinguish between the actual conditions of its development and those secondary interpretations that are invented in order to present these conditions in ideologically coherent form. Soviet ideology itself appears in two different perspectives: once as an existing body of ideas and beliefs, but also as a censored version of these beliefs produced by official ideologists.

The first chapter of this book offers a general survey of the social and intellectual contexts of the development of Russian psychology from the pre-Revolutionary period to the present. Special emphasis has been placed on the distinction between the actual conditions of the production of knowledge and the appearance of these conditions in the false consciousness of ideology.

The remainder of the book provides specific case studies examining different styles of confrontation between psychological scholarship and ideological requirements.

A chapter dedicated to the work of Ivan Pavlov and Vladimir Bekhterev shows different patterns in the transition of pre-Revolutionary scholars into the realm of Soviet science. The contrasting fates of the work of Pavlov and Bekhterev will help us understand the mechanism of selection that endorsed one set of ideas and condemned the other.

While the Pavlovian strand in Soviet behavioral science is relatively well known in the West, the same cannot be said of the alternative concept of the "psychophysiology of activity" suggested by Nikolai Bernstein. It is impossible, however, to understand the emergence of the non-Pavlovian psychophysiology in the 1960s without recognizing the important role played by Bernstein. The story of Bernstein's resistance to the expansionist claims of the Pavlovian school offers a spectacular example of scientific integrity successfully withstanding the advances of an ideologically endorsed doctrine.

As noted earlier, the mere existence of points of coincidence between a psychological doctrine and an official ideology can be quite misleading. One and the same set of ideas can at one moment be considered dialectical and materialist, only to be condemned as "bourgeois" and pseudoscientific a few years later. The history of the rise, fall, and rehabilitation of the concept of the unconscious in Soviet psychology demonstrates this point. In the 1920s psychoanalytic studies were readily adopted by Marxist psychology as a plausible basis for a materialist behavioral science. In the 1930s psychoanalysis fell victim to the struggle against "bourgeois" ideas. In the 1970s the unconscious was rehabilitated as a valuable, though still controversial, therapeutic method. The wandering of the concept in the labyrinths of Soviet psychology gives some impression of the complex chain of engagements and separations that exist between psychological ideas and their social and institutional counterparts.

If the history of research on the unconscious in the Soviet Union remains practically unknown in the West, the works of Lev Vygotsky are relatively well publicized. Since 1962, when *Thought and Language* was first published in English, Vygotsky's name has become quite familiar to most English-speaking psychologists. This does not mean, however, that Vygotsky has been adequately understood or that his writings have been fully comprehended. First of all, the existing English translations of Vygotsky are either abridged or concocted from papers drawn from different periods of Vygotsky's career. Furthermore the analytic comments accompanying the translations have been prepared under the strong influence of Vygotsky's students, Alexei Leontiev and Alexander Luria, who have offered a biased interpretation of Vygotsky's theory, sometimes substituting their own ideas for those of their teacher.

After Vygotsky's death in 1934, his theory was interpreted in several ways, reflecting not only the great potential of his ideas but also the changing demands on theoretical scholarship in Soviet psychology. Against such a background it seems only natural to dedicate a special case study to an elaboration of the origins of Vygotsky's theory and also to its later development.

The chapter on Pavel Blonsky responds to a number of the objectives of this book. It portrays an exemplary transformation of a pre-Revolutionary scholar into one of the "founding fathers" of Soviet psychology. It also gives some impression of the psychological "software" that supported the utopian social and educational projects of the 1920s. Ironically, the concepts used by Blonsky were borrowed from John Dewey, and this connection will allow us to examine the mechanism of adoption of Western ideas by Soviet scholars.

The book concludes with a chapter describing recent developments in Soviet educational and theoretical psychology. Soviet psychology acquired its present features after a "revolution" in the late 1950s and early 1960s. Freed from the most nonsensical of the ideological bonds imposed in the Stalin era, Soviet psychology faced the task of restoring the profession both as theoretical scholarship and as an applied discipline. The struggle for advanced curricula and flexible methods of instruction in primary schools offers an excellent example of the interplay of social, intellectual, and ideological forces in present-day Soviet psychology.

This book is intended as an account of events that are crucial for the understanding of Soviet psychology. It is not meant to be a comprehensive history encompassing all trends and figures. A number of existing studies might therefore be suggested as useful complements. Among these is Levy Rahmani's book on the conceptual apparatus of Soviet psychology. Certain aspects of the development of Pavlovian school have been elaborated by Luciano Mecacci. Those who are interested in the theory of Sergei Rubinstein can consult Ted Payne's book, so far the only existing monograph in English dedicated to one particular Soviet psychologist. Finally, Alexander Luria left a memoir published in English under the title *The Making of Mind: A Personal Account of Soviet Psychology.*[6]

# 1

*Four Generations of Psychologists*

## The European Period

The first and truly the most distinctive generation of Russian psychologists was the pre-Revolutionary one. These were scholars and practitioners who grew up in the atmosphere of Russian Europeanism of the late nineteenth and early twentieth centuries. In all essential ways the universities in Moscow and St. Petersburg resembled their institutional counterparts in Vienna and Berlin. The influence of European, and especially German, science and philosophy was decisive. There was no limit to travel abroad, and so most Russian scientists were apt to spend a year or two in European universities.[1]

Nevertheless, Russia was just at the beginning of the process of westernization. Serfdom had been abolished only in 1861, and democratic institutions had barely started to gain ground. Academic liberties did exist, though, and Russian psychologists took these liberties for granted, unaware that they were destined to be the last generation of scholars enjoying such opportunities.

Pre-Revolutionary psychologists came generally from two different academic backgrounds: philosophy and medicine. On the whole such features as methodological pluralism, ideological tolerance, and an eagerness to match European studies were characteristic of pre-Revolutionary Russian psychology. This should be emphasized, since certain Soviet historians picture that period as an uncompromising struggle between "good guy" materialists and "bad guy" idealists.[2] Such a view results from a biased "presentism" that projects later ideological clichés onto an entirely different period of history.

The Moscow Psychological Society, founded in 1885, quickly became an interdisciplinary forum for both philosophers and physicians interested in psychological problems. Leading roles were played by

Nikolai Grot (1852–1899) and Georgy Chelpanov (1862–1936), who successively occupied a chair of psychology at Moscow University. Among the active members of the society were philosophers of various orientations: Vladimir Soloviev, Sergei Trubetskoi, Sergei Bulgakov, Lev Lopatin, Vladimir Preobrazhensky, Gustav Schpet, and Pavel Blonsky. Physicians were represented predominantly by psychiatrists: Sergei Korsakov, Ardalion Tokarsky, Georgy Rossolimo, Yuri Kannabich, and Alexander Bernstein. Other professionals, including the mathematician Nikolai Bugaev, the lawyer Anatoli Koni, and the sociologist Eugene De-Roberti, also presented papers at meetings of the society. Novelist Lev Tolstoy once delivered a talk "On the Concept of Life."

The establishment of the Moscow Psychological Society was followed by the founding, in 1889, of a journal called *Problems of Philosophy and Psychology*, which published most of the theoretical papers pertaining to psychology.[3] In 1904 the neurologist Vladimir Bekhterev (1857–1927) founded *The Herald of Psychology, Criminal Anthropology, and Hypnosis*, which covered a wide range of experimental and clinical analyses of behavior.[4]

Although Moscow and St. Petersburg continued to be the major centers of behavioral research, psychological laboratories were also established in Kazan (founded by Bekhterev), Kiev (founded by Chelpanov), and Odessa (founded by Nikolai Lange).

Scholars invested an enormous amount of effort in translating the leading Western psychologists. As a result, on the eve of the Revolution, the Russian-speaking audience had in its possession a whole library of psychological classics. To give an idea of the work that had been done and the seriousness with which Russian scholars regarded the exchange of ideas, here is a sample list of some of the most important translations: From German came the work of Wilhelm Wundt (five titles), Hermann Ebbinghaus (two titles), and Hermann Helmholtz (collected papers in five volumes). Translations from the French included seven books of Teodul Ribot and two of Pierre Janet. Anglo-American psychology was represented by William James (*The Principles of Psychology; Pragmatism; The Varieties of Religious Experience*), Edward Titchener (*An Outline of Psychology*), William McDougall (*Introduction to Social Psychology*), and John Dewey (*The School and Society*). Updated reviews of European and American behavioral research appeared in the issues of *The New Ideas in Philosophy*, edited by Nikolai Lossky and Ernest Radlov.[5]

Without question the most important pre-Revolutionary development in Russian psychology was the establishment of the Psychoneurological Institute in St. Petersburg and the Moscow Institute of Psychology. The Psychoneurological Institute, founded in 1907, was directed by Vladimir Bekhterev, a well-known neurologist and educator. A man of enormous erudition and organizational talent, Bekhterev established a multidisciplinary institution that included students, scholars, and physicians studying the human subject from all possible perspectives. It was a private university with a faculty for general instruction and graduate schools in medicine, education, and law. The research program of the Psychoneurological Institute and affiliated laboratories was centered on an empirical study of human behavior, development, and personality under normal and pathological conditions. The faculty included such distinguished scholars as the physiologist Nikolai Vvedensky, the sociologist Maxim Kovalevsky, the comparative psychologist Vladimir Vagner, and Alexander Lazursky, one of the first Russian specialists in mental testing.

The institute soon became the nucleus for a whole cluster of behavioral programs, including a neurosurgical clinic with a neuropsychological laboratory, an antialcoholism center, and a laboratory of child and educational psychology. Close ties were established with the St. Petersburg Philosophical Society, a headquarters for adherents of speculative psychology. There was a rich mixing of approaches. Psychologists of the philosophical persuasion argued but also collaborated with empiricists. For example, Bekhterev used the neo-Kantian ideas of Alexander Vvedensky in his own critique of introspectionism. The empiricist Alexander Lazursky collaborated with the philosopher-psychologist Semen Frank in studies on personality. The physiologist Nikolai Vvedensky was invited to be a commentator when Nikolai Lossky defended his thesis in intuitionist psychology at St. Petersburg University.[6] The picture was much more complex than a mere division into materialists and idealists; indeed it could not have been that simple because there was then no obligatory ideology to provide a basis for establishing rights and wrongs.

If Bekhterev's enterprise was in fact a well-balanced one in which there was room for alternative approaches and techniques, the same could not be said of the public sentiments shadowing it. Spectacular advances in the scientific understanding of behavior aroused the belief that human conduct would soon be completely explained in terms of reflexes and reactions and that all other schools of psychology would become useless and disappear. Scientific popularizers were eager to foretell the decisive victory of physiological methods and the emergence of a unified theory of human and animal behavior. Certain programmatic statements of Ivan Pavlov (1849–1936), who at that moment was working only with dogs but was applying his findings to humans, also inspired the belief that a physiology of neural processes would soon replace psychological research. This general mood prepared the ground for the mechanistic metaphor of human behavior that became popular in the first years after the Revolution. The adherents of scientific psychology had been prepared to accept some behavioral doctrine as the one and only correct one. They saw no possibility for their discipline to be scientific and pluralistic at the same time. In chapter 2 this theme is discussed at some length in connection with the work of Bekhterev and Pavlov.[7]

While Bekhterev started with experimental and clinical approaches to human behavior, Georgy Chelpanov, the founder of the Moscow Institute of Psychology, came from philosophical quarters. He studied philosophy at Novorossijsk University in Odessa and psychology in Germany under Wilhelm Wundt and Carl Stumpf. In 1907 he accepted a chair of philosophy and psychology at Moscow University. Chelpanov was an outstanding advocate of psychology as an independent discipline. His lectures attracted crowds of students and professionals to whom he argued that psychology should become a self-contained subject, connected with but not absorbed by philosophy or physiology. Even those like Pavel Blonsky who refused to consider Chelpanov an original thinker, admitted that he was an excellent lecturer and popularizer.[8]

Chelpanov taught three courses at Moscow University: methods and tools of psychological experimentation, general psychology, and experimental psychology.[9] Besides theoretical works—*The Problem of the Perception of Space* (vol. 1, 1896; vol. 2, 1904) and *Brain and Soul* (1900)—he published a number of textbooks, including an *Introduction to Experimental Psychology* (1915) that presented the most up-to-date methods of experimental analysis for perception, memory, and motor reactions, with special attention paid to the use of the theory of probability and statistics in the quantitative analysis of research data.[10]

Unlike the proponents of a unified physiological psychology, Chelpanov stuck to the pluralistic approach. He promoted a Wundtian experimentalism; but he also mentioned favorably the method of systematic introspection, and he did not hesitate to involve himself in epistemological polemics as well. His principal objective was the establishment of a psychological scholarship that would enable its practitioners to develop their subject independently.

Chelpanov's efforts toward professionalization resulted in the establishment in 1912 of the Moscow Institute of Psychology.[11] If Bekhterev's Psychoneurological Institute was established as a challenge to the existing institutions of higher education, Chelpanov's was simply an academic research unit affiliated with Moscow University. Financial assistance for this project came from a merchant family called Schukin, and the institute was initially named in their honor. There would be more than one name change: In the 1920s it was the State Institute of Experimental Psychology, and by the 1970s it was known as the Institute of General and Pedagogical Psychology. To avoid confusion I shall always call it simply the Moscow Institute of Psychology.

Chelpanov's institute produced a small but impressive crop of young researchers. Among them were two future directors of the institute, Konstantin Kornilov and Anatoli Smirnov. Chelpanov's students included the philosopher and educational psychologist Pavel Blonsky, the psychophysiologist Sergei Kravkov, and the cognitivist Peter Shevarev. On the eve of the Revolution Chelpanov started to publish a new journal, *Psychological Survey*.[12]

Besides establishing psychological institutions, translating psychological classics, and undertaking routine experimental work, Russian psychologists were engaged in substantial epistemological polemics. This was not just a topical argument between neo-Kantians and intuitionists, or between positivists and Hegelians: Russian scholars in fact debated the classical issues of psychology such as the psychophysical problem and the scientific validity of psychological experimentation. At the beginning of the century both problems revealed themselves in a discussion on the place of objective behavioral experimentation in psychology.

The centuries-old psychophysical problem reflects the evident dissimilarities between physiological processes in the brain and the contents of consciousness. Introspective psychology has traditionally appealed to self-observation, focusing on the sensations, images, and "feelings" of consciousness. Physiological psychology, on the contrary, centers on neurological processes, avoiding or denying the functions of consciousness. With the development of the experimental method in psychology, the duality of physiological and ideational approaches ceased to be merely a philosophical question and became a methodological dilemma.

In his paper "On Experimental Method in Psychology" (1913) Chelpanov outlined all the major arguments on psychophysical duality.[13] He pointed out that those who (like some of Bekhterev's students) tried to discredit the notion of consciousness in an attempt to establish a purely objective psychology, only deceived themselves. Clearly they could avoid mentalist terminology by replacing it with that of reflexes, but to be consistent they should then abandon the very idea of psychological research and confine themselves to the framework of physiology. Reflexologists, of course, continued to pursue both behavioral and physiological objectives. In this respect they did not differ from other psychologists using the experimental method, and they therefore needed some concept of a central apparatus that developed elementary physiological functions into purposeful behavioral acts.

Chelpanov himself considered the idea of psychophysical parallelism a plausible working hypothesis. He assumed that neurophysiological processes and the contents of consciousness could be studied as parallel realms, each with the help of appropriate experimental methods.

Discussing the ostensible opposition between introspection and experimentalism, Chelpanov pointed to the systematic introspection of the Wurzburg School and the intelligence testing of Alfred Binet to show how fine is the actual distinction between so-called introspection and experimental data based on the reports of subjects.[14] This problem may at first seem obsolete for contemporary psychologists, but not if viewed in light of the recent discussions between American behaviorists and phenomenologists on what can and should be taken as legitimate material for behavioral research.[15]

The eagerness of Russian psychologists to mesh experimental studies with philosophical analyses was quite in keeping with the divided professional loyalties of pre-Revolutionary scholars. Vladimir Preobrazhensky is a case in point. An active member of the Moscow Psychological Society, Preobrazhensky was known for his studies in the epistemology of Arthur Schopenhauer and the moral philosophy of Friedrich Nietzsche. He developed an original theory of perception as well, presaging some of the principles that a quarter of a century later were developed in Gestalt psychology.[16]

The combination of philosophical issues and psychological experimentation was obviously not unique to Russian psychology. William James, John Dewey, and George Mead certainly belonged to the same breed of scholars, since they pursued both empirical psychology and philosophy. However, while in Europe and the United States the two lines diverged, in Russia they fused, and under the Soviets psychology took the form of a philosophical ideologization of behavioral research.

Pre-Revolutionary psychology, however, remained an almost exclusively academic discipline. The few psychologist-practitioners who existed before the Revolution all had medical training. Russia never experienced the boom of psychological testing of military personnel that drastically altered American psychology during World War I. For that reason the Russian psychologist preserved the self-image of a scientist-as-scholar seeking the ultimate truth of human conduct, not that of a practitioner performing professional duties as a matter of business.

*Psychology in the Age of Bewilderment*

With the outbreak of the Bolshevik Revolution in 1917 and the Civil War that followed it, academic life in Russia was largely suspended. The years between 1917 and 1922 were a time of martial law. There was famine and massive devastation of industry. Fabulous social projects were suggested, including the total collectivization of property, personal belongings, and even spouses, only to be overtaken by even more utopian and ephemeral programs.[17] With the end of the Civil War and the proclamation of the New Economic Policy in 1922, the country recovered to a somewhat more rational organization that allowed small-scale private business, reestablishment of the institutions of higher learning, and some restraint on extravagant social experiments.

It was at this time that Russian science acquired its split structure. On the one hand, there were the Academy of Science, the universities, and short-term establishments such as the Free Philosophical Academy in Petrograd that employed pre-Revolutionary scholars and preserved academic rather than ideological guidelines. On the other hand, the new regime was eager to raise intellectuals of the communist persuasion who would replace those "unreliable" scholars who did not share the ideals of Bolshevism. To fulfill that goal institutions such as the Communist Academy, the Institute of Red Professors, and the Academy of Communist Education were established under the direct supervision of the Communist Party.[18]

For a while it seemed that these two lines in the development of learning could coexist harmoniously. Whatever reservations they felt toward the Bolshevik dictatorship, pre-Revolutionary Russian psychologists had not been engaged in political opposition. The first acts of the new rulers also seemed conciliatory: Bekhterev was allowed to establish the Institute for Brain Research in Petrograd; Pavlov retained his facilities at the Institute of Experimental Medicine, receiving a generous grant from the government in hard currency; and in 1921 Chelpanov was reappointed head of the Moscow Institute of Psychology.

The years 1922 and 1923 brought the first astounding changes. A large group of Russian intellectuals, among them members of the Moscow Psychological and the Petrograd Philosophical Societies, were briefly imprisoned and subsequently exiled to the West. Among them were Nikolai Berdiaev, Sergei Bulgakov, Nikolai Lossky, Ivan Lapshin, and Semen Frank.

Official Soviet historiography suggests a morally questionable but ideologically consistent rationale for this action. In his *History of Soviet Psychology* (1967) Artur Petrovsky claimed that the members of these societies had waged "a militant struggle against materialism and the new life," that they had "attacked new Soviet science," and that their journal *Thought (Mysl)* advocated "militant obscurantism and reaction." He concluded that "idealism was defeated in open struggle with the new ideology" and "a large group of militant reactionaries was exiled."[19]

The very idea suggested by Petrovsky—that a discussion on the place and value of materialism and idealism might result in the exile of one of the parties—seems strange if not ominous. It hints that under the new regime both political and theoretical opposition could be unsafe. However, if we consult the actual rather than the official record, we learn that, contrary to Petrovsky's assertion, pre-Revolutionary scholars suffered no defeats and had no "militant struggle" with the new science. The journal *Thought*, which was founded in 1922 but survived for only one year, published very tolerant reviews of Bekhterev's *Collective Reflexology* and Lazursky's *Classification of Personalities*, together with a brief survey of "Progress in Contemporary Experimental Psychology." Beyond these papers nothing was published either for or against the materialist trend in psychology. Among the eighteen full-length articles only one by Alexander Vvedensky—who was not exiled—could be regarded as manifesting a definite political ideology. Its title, "The Fate of Religiosity in Its Fight with Atheism," would shock a contemporary Soviet scholar brought up in an atmosphere of total atheism. However, the first Soviet constitution, unlike the later ones, explicitly allowed the propagation of both atheism and religion.

The meetings of the societies usually included talks by experimentalists ("materialists") such as Alexei Severtsov, who lectured on the evolution of behavior in animals and man, as well as by "idealists" such as Ivan Iljin, who analyzed the phenomenon of religious experience.[20]

Thus it is quite clear that the exile of Russian intellectuals was not the final act in a struggle between militant idealists and materialists, as Petrovsky would like us to believe. It seems that Petrovsky confused several different historical periods. In the period from the 1930s to the 1950s it was quite common to imprison or exile a scholar for nonorthodox views, but such a practice had no place in the early 1920s, when nothing like a clear-cut scientific ideology yet existed.

The exile of Russian intellectuals in 1922 was most probably a political act, perhaps even an act of revenge. More than a few of the exiled scholars had at one time been Marxists but then changed their position and turned toward intuitionism or religious or existential philosophy. Nikolai Lossky even suggested that the expulsion of his colleagues and himself was a gesture of "good will" addressed to Western governments concerned with the well-being of pre-Revolutionary intellectuals in communist Russia.[21]

The exile of the psychologists was in some sense just one more act of the "class struggle." But it provided a clear sign of the erosion of scientific ethics. While their colleagues were exiled, the rest of the psychological community remained silent, expressing no protests and no objections.

Further confrontation came in 1923. Georgy Chelpanov was not only fired as director of the Moscow Institute of Psychology but "purged" from the institute he had founded and led for a decade. His former students and colleagues, Pavel Blonsky and Konstantin Kornilov, who enjoyed full academic privileges before the Revolution despite their communist views, did nothing to prevent or protest the dismissal of their teacher. Kornilov was soon after appointed director.[22]

A few months before Chelpanov's dismissal, in January 1923, the First All-Russia Psychoneurological Congress took place in Moscow. The principal speakers were Georgy Chelpanov, Vladimir Bekhterev, and Konstantin Kornilov. Each presented his own program for the development of behavioral science in Russia. Chelpanov pointed out that "in contemporary world science we observe the steady tendency toward developing psychology as an exact empirical discipline, free of any philosophy. . . . It may have a philosophical superstructure and a philosophical, physiological, biological, or other substructure, but in itself it is neither philosophy nor physiology of the brain . . . but an independent empirical science like physics, chemistry, or mineralogy."[23]

Bekhterev, on the contrary, emphasized the biological foundation of behavioral research. "An objective biological approach to personality must replace currently widespread subjectivist studies."[24]

Kornilov, in turn, made a bid to reconcile the principles of empiricism with those of Marxist ideology. He claimed that psychology must follow the natural sciences and focus on the materialistic processes that have evolved into behavior. Proceeding from this scientific understanding of behavior Marxist psychology would seize and reshape the minds of men. "Marxism fundamentally breaks ties with the mentalism that has infiltrated the whole body of modern psychology. Marxism aims not only at the explanation of the human mind but also at its mastery."[25]

Although numerous critical references to "subjectivist methods" and "idealist psychology" were made during the 1923 Congress, it was nevertheless clear that the fight against "idealism" was dated. Not one paper submitted to the congress actually proposed introspectionist views or metaphysical explanations. Those who allegedly stuck to idealism had been either exiled or subdued. No questions were raised concerning the fate of the exiled scholars; it was as if they had never existed. Only a short time earlier, in 1916, the Petrograd Philosophical Society played host to both Pavlov and Bekhterev, and it seemed quite natural that persons with opposing views should have a chance to discuss problems of common interest.[26] Now, in 1923, the stage was half empty: there were no philosopher-psychologists who could argue with the enthusiasts of physiological and Marxist approaches. The new Soviet psychology from its very beginning abandoned dialogue and therefore lost the invigoration that comes with pluralism. Later on it started to "discover" idealists within its own number and treated them accordingly.

If we look beyond the case of the philosopher-psychologists and consider the theses proposed by Chelpanov, Bekhterev, and Kornilov, the picture is stranger still. In fact, practically nothing had changed in the positions of these psychologists since pre-Revolutionary times. Chelpanov, as ever, advocated empiricism; Bekhterev had always fought against subjectivist methods; and Kornilov, who proposed the study of reactions as a central thesis of his doctrine, had fairly well developed a "reactological" version of behaviorism even before the Revolution. What had changed was the perception of these programs. Chelpanov's refusal to start with philosophy was now perceived as a challenge to Marxism. Bekhterev's attack on subjectivism, however traditional that was for him, appeared as an act of breaking ranks with the pre-Revolutionary psychological establishment. Kornilov's reactological program, peppered with Marxist terminology, was perceived as a promise to develop an entirely original Marxist psychology.

In 1923 there were no psychological periodicals to report on the work of the congress, but the leading Bolshevik newspapers paid close attention to this event. They reprinted the papers of Bekhterev and Kornilov (skipping that of Chelpanov, who was one of the organizers of the congress) and made it clear that communist ideology must become a framework for further behavioral studies. Psychology had clearly ceased to be mere scholarship and was now seen as a socially laden and ideologically engaged field of "revolutionary practice."[27]

This changing social attitude was clearly revealed by Alexander Luria (1902–1977) in his memoirs written in the 1970s: "I began my career in the first years of the great Russian Revolution," explained Luria. "This single momentous event decisively influenced my life and that of everyone I knew. . . . My entire generation was infused with the energy of revolutionary change—the liberating energy people feel when they are part of a society that is able to make tremendous progress in a very short time."[28]

There is good reason to take this statement seriously and not as an obeisance to official ideology. Paraphrasing Karl Popper's words on Marx, one cannot do justice to Luria and his generation without recognizing their sincerity.

The first generation of post-Revolutionary scholars largely shared the utopian program of their time. In their minds the Revolution was more than a political turnover that changed the ruling class and the economy. They envisaged it as a cosmic event that would transform everything from technology to the very nature of people, their conduct, and culture. Behavioral science therefore had to become a social instrument aimed at the dissection and transformation of human personality in a manner that might at once implement and realize the communist vision.[29]

Several ideological beliefs contributed to this state of mind. Among them was a faith that rationalized and fair interpersonal relations would be a hallmark of the coming communist society. The elimination of the nobility and bourgeoisie was to guarantee the appearance of a new kind of person—the liberated proletarian, with new morals, culture, and rules of conduct. Unlike the allegedly chaotic and oppressive bourgeois society, the proletarian community would be ruled by scientific rationality and materialism. The rational planning of social and private life would prevent not only economic crises but also the personal delusions that had once been provoked by religion and idealistic philosophy. The human mind, liberated from the false concepts of the bourgeois past, would be treated in an absolutely objective, scientific way.

However fantastic these beliefs might seem today, they were a vital force in Soviet intellectual life in the 1920s. Striving for social justice, enchanted by the progress of science and technology, and armed with vaguely attractive formulas extracted from Marx, young scholars sincerely believed that they would comprehend and transform human nature within a few years time.

The idea of the transformation of human nature took a pronounced mechanistic form in the intellectual movement known as Proletcult (Proletarian Culture). Among the theorists of this movement was Alexei Gastev, whose program might be taken as a characteristic product of the 1920s. A promising young poet, Gastev had broken ranks with the literati and been appointed director of the Central Institute of Work, which was to become the cradle of Soviet industrial psychology.

Gastev called for the transformation of nonproletarian classes by a total "technologization" and proletarianization of their life and behavior. "Engineering," he claimed, "is the apex of wisdom in science and art."[30] The extent of his dedication to mechanism is suggested by the following: "It is essential for mankind to discover that the human being is nothing but a perfect machine . . . and that the technical progress of this machine is unlimited.[31]

Although Gastev's position seems an exemplary embodiment of mechanistic utopianism, the actual development of industrial psychology took a rather unexpected course. Isaak Shpilrein and Nikolai Bernstein, who worked in Gastev's institute, clearly escaped the bounds of utopian phraseology. Shpilrein picked up on the utilitarian aspect of Gastev's program, which called for the rationalization of the labor processes. Widely borrowing ideas and techniques from German (bourgeois!) industrial psychology and the differential psychology of William Stern, he developed an impressive variety of applied studies and established a system of professional testing. The success of his studies was so obvious that the Soviet "psychotechnicians," as industrial psychologists called themselves, were chosen to play host to the International Psychotechnic Congress in 1931.

But the most impressive transformation of the Proletcult form of mechanism occurred in the case of Nikolai Bernstein. Beginning with the biomechanics of work movements, Bernstein gradually developed an entirely antimechanistic concept of human behavior. Eventually he became the most serious challenger of Pavlovian psychophysiology. Bernstein's ideas and the history of his argument with the Pavlovians are elaborated in chapter 3.

One of the most prominent advocates of a new proletarian psychophysiology was Aron Zalkind. Physician, psychotherapist, and an active Party member, Zalkind emerged on the psychological scene in the early 1920s holding senior positions at the Institute of Communist Education and the Communist Academy. In his *Essays on the Culture of the Revolutionary Age* (1924), Zalkind went so far as to claim that human psychophysiology is directly conditioned by the social class to which people belong. As a concrete illustration of his approach Zalkind outlined a psychogram (psychophysiological pattern) of an average member of the Communist Party. Zalkind's psychogram seems almost grotesque and yet exemplary of the behavioral projects of the 1920s. It included the following characteristics: (1) revolutionary monoideologism (a concentration solely on revolutionary activity); (2) dynamic activity (a communist is constantly busy and only reluctantly switches to abstract, nonpractical thought); (3) avantguardism (the habit of being a leader); (4) emotions of constant risk; (5) a pioneering attitude; (6) control (a communist ceaselessly keeps watch on his subordinates, whom he can never trust wholeheartedly); (7) generality of conclusions (a recognition that any particular fact must be linked to the general content of events with the absolute goal of revolution); (8) high degree of sublimation (communists channel their libido into social activity to a much higher degree than ordinary citizens); (9) sociocentrism (a complete absorption by social activity, in contrast to the traditional self-centered attitude of the intellectual).[32]

Zalkind mentions no special method or experimental technique that allowed him to compose this psychogram. It is almost certain that it reflected nothing but personal impressions summarized in quasiscientific form. The psychogram was meant not only as a collective portrait of the existing Party members but also as an ideal for the general population. Zalkind strongly supported the idea that human behavior is plastic, and he assumed that reflex therapy and Marxist psychoanalysis would soon form a new, communist personality. Zalkind thought that psychotherapy should become a major instrument in the education and transformation of personality. The term psychotherapy here meant an educational technique that included reflex therapy, suggestion, indoctrination, and psychoanalytic treatment directed toward social catharsis—the establishment of adequate attitudes toward the social goals of revolutionary society. These psychotherapeutic methods were to become the core of pedology, the term used in the 1920s for research and testing in child and educational psychology.

Zalkind's program, however simple-minded it may seem, had a great impact on the development of Soviet psychology in the 1920s. Zalkind was editor of the journal *Pedology* and the main organizer of the Pedological Congress in 1928 and the Meeting on Human Behavior in 1930.

Zalkind's psychological views can be observed from two different perspectives. On the one hand, they are certainly eclectic, superficial, and vague, resembling ideological rantings more than products of theoretical or empirical studies. If, however, one takes into account the development of Soviet psychology from the 1930s to the 1950s, when psychoanalysis, testing, and certain applied studies were banned, Zalkind's program could appear as an "acceptable" framework for legitimizing concrete studies in child psychology, psychoanalysis, and differential psychophysiology.

Unlike Zalkind, who was scarcely known before the Revolution, Pavel Blonsky had been a mature scholar when he joined the bandwagon of Marxist psychology and pedology. A former student and protégé of Chelpanov, Blonsky managed for a number of years to combine his interest in ancient and classical philosophy with studies in educational psychology. In the 1920s he proclaimed his adherence to the principles of radical behaviorism and fought against the concept of consciousness, which he regarded as a relic of bourgeois metaphysical philosophy.[33]

Also unlike Zalkind, Blonsky had a number of reservations concerning the plasticity of human nature. He emphasized the importance of testing to provide objective data on the limits of intellectual and moral development in students of various ages. Blonsky's educational program was largely copied from that of John Dewey and other promulgators of progressive education, but under the economic and ideological conditions of the 1920s Dewey's ideas could hardly be adequately implemented in Russia. As a result Blonsky's educational program remained a utopian, unimplementable blueprint. Its author confessed in 1928 that he wrote his program "as if the classless society of the future were already the reality of today."[34] Chapter 6 gives an account of Blonsky's psychological views and his attempts to establish a Soviet version of progressive education.

Most of the trends looming in the Soviet psychology of the mid-1920s stuck to the naturalistic interpretation of the mechanisms of human behavior. Even Zalkind, despite his explicit sociocentrism, considered reflexes a basis for the transformation of the human mind. What united all the trends in Soviet psychology, each of which claimed superiority over the others, was their reluctance to accept any taint of mentalism, especially in discussions of consciousness.

The only group opposing this collective resistance was headed by Lev Vygotsky (1896–1934), whose first public recognition as a psychologist occurred in 1924. Speaking before the Second Psychoneurological Congress, Vygotsky boldly challenged the mechanistic and naturalistic attempts to reduce the human mind to elementary reflexes and reactions. Alexander Luria, then secretary of the Moscow Institute of Psychology, was greatly impressed by Vygotsky's presentation and did his best to persuade Kornilov to offer Vygotsky a position at the institute. As a result Vygotsky was appointed a research fellow. Together with Luria and Alexei Leontiev, he established a unit for the study of higher psychological functions. Vygotsky's program rested on a number of theoretical premises. He assumed that specifically human, higher mental functions emerge in the course of mastering biological functions such as natural memory or attention. The primary tools for such mastery, that is, for the transformation of natural functions into culturalized, human ones, are symbolic systems and speech. To study the development of the human mind means, therefore, to trace the transformation of natural functions into culturalized ones through anthropogenesis, the historical development of the human race, and the individual development of a child.[35]

Large-scale experimental studies that included children, mental patients, and the primitive peoples of Central Asia were conducted by Vygotsky's students and colleagues, including Luria, Leontiev, Leonid Sakharov, Alexander Zaporozhets, Lidia Bozhovich, Natalia Morozova, and Zhozefina Shif.

Unlike most of his contemporaries Vygotsky refrained from ideological verbiage in his writings. His references to Marx were thoughtful and well-grounded. He did not hesitate to acknowledge his indebtedness to Western (and thus bourgeois) psychologists and philosophers such as William James, Paul Natorp, Pierre Janet, Heinz Werner, and Wolfgang Köhler. Early on Vygotsky recognized the importance of the developmental psychology of Jean Piaget. A number of Vygotsky's papers were experimentally supported polemics with Piaget. (Chapter 5 gives a fuller account of the views of Vygotsky and his students.)

Although the majority of Soviet psychologists shared the utopian objectives of their time and preached the mechanistic transformation of human personality toward a communist ideal, this ideal was itself extremely vague. No more clear-cut was the question of which methods of study could be regarded as Marxist and which were bourgeois. Only one thing was certain: that scientific, Marxist psychology must have a single correct methodology.

This belief had its roots in a misinterpretation of the nature of psychological knowledge—a misinterpretation based in part on an uncritical acceptance of the methods of the natural sciences and engineering, where there seemed to be only one correct solution for each given problem. Blonsky, for example, claimed, "Psychology conducts research on its subject with the help of the regular methods of natural science, that is, through the mathematical presentation of behavior as a function of multiple variables."[36]

But even radical scientism never questioned the possibility of different *approaches* to the same problem. It was this very pluralism that was disallowed by Marxism. Marxism, as interpreted by Soviet psychologists, was a deterministic social doctrine that was uniquely "correct" as a philosophy of the proletariat. Moreover, the idea of a rational society based on entirely scientific, and therefore unequivocal, planning was among the most enduring myths of the 1920s.[37] Thus the idea of one, and only one, correct methodology was a natural offspring of the intellectual atmosphere of that period.

No less natural was the struggle waged between rival groups of Soviet psychologists. Each of these groups claimed that its methodology was the most scientific and most purely Marxist. Pavlovians such as Alexander Lenz and Ivan Ariamov claimed that conditional reflexes provide the only genuinely materialist base for behavioral science. Kornilov, accusing Pavlovians of the physiologization of human mind, suggested that reactology—his own version of stimulus-response methodology—must be chosen as the correct one. Bekhterev's students, among them Alexander Schnierman and Boris Ananiev, rejected reactology and Pavlovianism and claimed that Bekhterev's reflexology had long ago established a real ground for a determinist and materialist behavioral science.

What was unnatural in these polemics was the usage of ideological allegations and political epithets. Struggles in the ruling quarters of the Communist Party and changes in the market of Marxist philosophy had immediate effects on the assortment of ideological accusations. The years from 1929 to 1931 were characterized by a fierce battle between the adherents of mechanistic materialism and the "dialecticians." In 1929 the dialecticians, led by Abram Deborin of the Communist Academy, celebrated a victory over the mechanists, who were accused of leftist perversions and departure from the Marxist-Leninist philosophical position. In 1931 the dialecticians, in their turn, were ruined by a group of militant young philosophers under the direction of Mark Mitin, who accused them of menshevizing idealism and, naturally, of departure from the principles of Marxism-Leninism.[38]

Soviet psychologists promptly picked up the allegations that evolved in the struggle among mechanists, dialecticians, and Mitin's group. Aiming at Kornilov, Zalkind wrote in 1931 that "Menshevizing idealism in psychology objectively set its 'Marxist Psychology' in opposition to the goals of socialist development. It was rotten at its roots and contributed nothing to the practice of socialism, but rather slowed down the socialist development with the help of its objectively reactionary, pessimistic theories."[39]

A group of young Party members at the Moscow Institute of Psychology, including A. Talankin, F. Shemiakin, T. Kogan, and A. Vvedenov, hastened to denounce not only Kornilov and Zalkind, but almost every active Soviet psychologist. Isaak Shpilrein, Vladimir Borovsky, Lev Vygotsky, and Alexander Luria were found guilty of ideological deviations. Marxist philosophers and Party functionaries associated with psychology, such as Yuri Frankfurt, Isay Sapir, and Nikolai Karev, were also labeled menshevizing idealists. Talankin and his Young Turks claimed that the journal *Psychology* reflected the non-Marxist views of the menshevizing idealists and resembled bourgeois periodicals. The Young Turks were quick to link the deviations of Kornilov and others with the activity of the faction of dialecticians.[40] As a result of this attack Kornilov lost his position as director of the Moscow Institute of Psychology. The editorial board of *Psychology* was revised.

Bekhterev's "reflexologists," among them Boris Ananiev, could not escape a similar fate. They were accused of mechanistic deviations and departures from Marxism. In his talk to the Congress on Human Behavior (1930) Ananiev boldly replied that, since a certified Marxist epistemology for the behavioral sciences did not yet exist, psychologists themselves must be responsible for theoretical definitions.[41] In a year's time, however, the situation became so tense that Ananiev chose to denounce reflexology as an ideological mistake. Neither did he forego the opportunity to denounce other groups as well. Ananiev asserted that the Vygotsky–Luria theory of historical-cultural development of the mind "objectively leads to the idealist revision of historical materialism." Kornilov, Zalkind, and Frankfurt appeared in Ananiev's paper as pseudo-Marxists.

At the conclusion of his paper Ananiev made a statement that was destined to become almost a motto for Soviet psychologists in the next quarter of a century: "The real founders of Soviet psychology as a dialectical-materialist discipline are neither schools nor trends . . . but the founders of Marxism-Leninism." As Ananiev proceeded to denounce himself and his colleagues, he noted "certain attempts to base Soviet psychology on different psychological trends which are, in their essence and origin, avowedly bourgeois, instead of founding it on the philosophical heritage of Marx, Engels, and Lenin, Bolshevik experience, and the works of Stalin."[42]

Ananiev's account rounded off an era in the development of Soviet psychology. After the early 1930s there were no more discussions of which methodology might best respond to the ideal of a Marxist behavioral science. As a result of mutual ideological accusations almost all Soviet psychologists had been found guilty of dangerous deviations from the Party line and therefore became easy prey for Party functionaries.

If in the 1920s the problem was to develop behavioral science within the *framework* of Marxist terminology, in the 1930s it was to derive the categories of consciousness and behavior directly from the works of Marx, Engels, Lenin, and Stalin. In the 1920s competing groups had their own journals: Kornilov's *Psychology*, Zalkind's *Pedology*, Shpilrein's *Psychotechnic*, and *Problems of Research and Education of Personality* by Bekhterev and his students. None of these journals survived the year 1934.

In the early 1930s leading psychologists were forced to admit their "mistakes": Luria denounced his involvement with psychoanalysis; Shpilrein, his indebtedness to William Stern and German industrial psychology; Zalkind and Blonsky recanted their interest in intelligence testing.[43]

In 1936 a State decree condemned those educational psychologists who had been engaged in pedological studies and testing. Zalkind and Vygotsky (who died in 1934) were put on a blacklist. Given that almost all work in educational psychology in the 1920s was called "pedology," one may imagine the consequences of this decree. All forms of intelligence testing were forbidden, and other applied studies fell victim to the subsequent witch-hunt.[44]

Stalin's purges of the 1930s did not spare Soviet psychologists. Leading Marxist philosophers earlier associated with psychology—including Yuri Frankfurt, Nikolai Karev, and Ivan Luppol—were executed in prison camps. The same fate awaited Alexei Gastev and Isaak Shpilrein. Those who survived lived in an atmosphere of total suspicion. The social situation actualized the world of George Orwell's Oceania. Mutability of the past, one of the main features of the Oceanic system, was applied in full strength. People who dominated their fields yesterday might be denounced today as traitors and enemies of the people, and by tomorrow their names might disappear from all public records. Books and newspapers were constantly being recalled from libraries to rid them of "obsolete" names and references.[45]

A low profile seemed the best strategy for survival. Two such low-profile schools even made significant scientific advances during the period of terror. Both were located far from Moscow and Leningrad, and both published their research in obscure local proceedings. One of these was the Georgian school founded by Dmitri Uznadze (1886–1950). Uznadze developed an original theory of unconscious "set conditions" that reflected a holistic intentionality directed toward a subject's activity. He used perceptual illusions as his principal experimental material in an extensive study of the effects of set conditions in sensory-motor tests.[46] Only in this somewhat esoteric form did any sort of study of the psychodynamics of the unconscious survive in Soviet psychology from the 1930s to the 1950s. (For further discussion of Uznadze's theory see chapter 4.)

The other school that survived the 1930s and early 1940s was the Kharkov school of developmental psychology.[47] The core of this school was a group of former students and colleagues of Lev Vygotsky who decided to leave the turmoil of Moscow for the Ukrainian city of Kharkov. Among them were Alexei Leontiev, Alexander Zaparozhets, and Lidia Bozhovich. In Kharkov they were joined by Peter Zinchenko, Peter Galperin, V. Asnin, and Yuri Lukov. As a general framework for their developmental studies, the Kharkovites used Vygotsky's concept of internalization—the transformation of external actions into internal psychological functions. They were eager, however, to emphasize their disagreement with Vygotsky about the role of signs in the internalization process. Vygotsky's emphasis on signs as means of mediation between objects of experience and mental functions was replaced by the thesis that physical action must mediate between a subject and the external world. The work of the Kharkov school established an experimental base for Leontiev's theory of the psychology of activity, which was recognized in the 1960s as an official Soviet psychological doctrine.

While the Uznadzeans and Kharkovites avoided ideologically sensitive matters, a more intrepid psychologist, Sergei Rubinstein (1889–1960) of the Leningrad Teachers College, ventured to derive psychological categories directly from the works of Marx and Lenin.[48] Rubinstein had earned his doctorate in philosophy from Marburg University in 1913. His professors were the famous neo-Kantians Hermann Cohen and Paul Natorp. In the 1920s and early 1930s Rubinstein taught in Odessa and Leningrad, publishing nothing and taking no sides in psychological disputes. In 1934 he published his first psychological paper, entitled "Psychological Problems in the Works of Karl Marx."[49] Viewing his very successful career in the years of terror, one may guess that Rubinstein chose his moment of publication carefully. He became the first Soviet psychologist to realize the goal of deriving psychological categories literally from the works of Marx.

Starting with an analysis of the crisis of bourgeois psychology, Rubinstein proceeded to analyze Marx's notions of consciousness, human nature, and social practice. To be sure, Rubinstein offered nothing like a definite psychological methodology based on these Marxian concepts. What he offered instead was a highly professional (compared with the work of Soviet psychologists other than Vygotsky) presentation of Marxist philosophical anthropology, which he tried to pass off as the theoretical foundation of behavioral science.

The content of this paper and the moment of its publication left no doubts that it was a direct response to the changing market of Soviet ideology. This is not to imply that Rubinstein was just a shrewd opportunist. His knowledge of psychology and philosophy was profound, and he was a skillful theorist. His essay-reviews of Western psychology that appeared in the late 1930s bear all the signs of thoughtful work. Nevertheless, Rubinstein's papers, however professionally written, fell short of free theoretical discourse. The point of arrival was predestined irrespective of the path of narration: as expected, the categories of Marxism turned out to offer the only plausible concepts for psychological theory.

Rubinstein's career followed an impressive track. In 1943 he was elected a member-correspondent of the Academy of Sciences—the first psychologist to receive such an honor. In the mid-1940s he was simultaneously chairman of the Department of Psychology at Moscow University and director of the Moscow Institute of Psychology. In 1945 he was appointed head of the Department of Psychology in the Institute of Philosophy at the Academy of Sciences.

In the postwar years, in the shadow of military victories and in the nascent chill of cold war, the antibourgeois rhetoric of Soviet ideology became increasingly chauvinistic. Proletarian internationalism, a concept popular in the 1920s, was replaced by the doctrine of Russian superiority. In application to science this meant that any reference to Western scholars was cause for suspicion. Simultaneously, a search for "great men" of national science was launched. As a result, as an anecdote says, Russia was pronounced "the native land of elephants," since everything from the steam engine and the telephone to modern methods of agriculture was claimed to be an invention of Russian nationals.[50]

Special meetings of the various disciplines were called to teach the new chauvinism and to reassert with new passion the slogan of a "rotten Western science." During the meetings on philosophy in 1947, on genetics in 1948, and on linguistics in 1950, those scholars who used methods or developed theories originated by Western authors were condemned. As a theoretical rationale for xenophobia, the following thesis was offered: "In a class society nothing like universal, international science can exist."[51]

Research in genetics and cybernetics was declared unpatriotic, laboratories were closed, and a number of scientists were arrested or exiled.

The outburst of Russian chauvinism coincided with the start of an anti-Semitic campaign. In 1948 the members of the wartime Anti-Nazi Jewish Committee were arrested as "American-Jewish spies" and later executed. In 1953 the same charges were brought against a number of well-known physicians who had allegedly poisoned Party leaders. Stalin's death saved the lives of all but two who had died under torture during the investigation.[52] The Soviet government eventually admitted that all the anti-Semitic trials had been fabricated. The victims were acquitted posthumously.

The trials and executions were accompanied by a press campaign against "cosmopolitans." Soviet psychologists had been absolutely unprepared for such an ideological turn. It happened that in the 1920s scholars of Jewish ancestry—including Vygotsky, Luria, Zalkind, Shpilrein, and Schnierman—were among the leaders of the discipline. In some fields the picture was impressive indeed: In 1929, among the twenty-three members of the Russian Psychoanalytical Society, only one, Ivan Ermakov, was Russian, while all others had Jewish or German names.[53] In those years, however, xenophobia was termed an old-regime superstition, and nobody was supposed to care about the ethnic origin of his or her fellow scholars. In the 1940s, as we have seen, the situation changed abruptly, and Rubinstein, Luria, Bernstein, and others suddenly discovered the potential danger of their family names.

Rubinstein was singled out for especially severe criticism.[54] In 1949 the journal *Soviet Pedagogics*—in an editorial, "Raising High the Banner of Soviet Patriotism in Education," and a paper by P. Plotnikov, "To Purge Soviet Psychology of Nationless Cosmopolitanism"—accused Rubinstein of "worshiping bourgeois science" and "insulting Russian and Soviet psychology."[55] In the next issue of *Soviet Pedagogics* Leonid Zankov claimed that Rubinstein had deliberately suppressed studies by Russian authors and advocated the decadent views of bourgeois psychology. Zankov maintained that there was no need for critical reviews of such authors as Piaget, for "it is well-known that the 'theory' of Piaget is a militant attempt to depict child intelligence in an absolutely distorted form."[56]

As a result of this campaign Rubinstein lost all his administrative positions, continuing on only as a research fellow at the Institute of Philosophy. Alexei Leontiev was appointed chairman of the Department of Psychology at Moscow University.

The condemnation of Rubinstein and other so-called cosmopolitans was balanced by the hero worship of Pavlov as an exemplary Russian scientist. "How was it possible," wrote Rubinstein's critic, "to compare the great Russian scientist Pavlov . . . with an obscurantist and reactionary like Thorndike?"[57] Pavlovian hero worship was in fact a well-planned ideological action that had been started earlier, in 1943, by chief Party philosopher-ideologist Mark Mitin, who sought to exalt Pavlov as the father of Russian science.[58] Boris Teplov, in his 1947 essay on the history of Soviet psychology, pursued this theme, while simultaneously attributing ideological mistakes to Kornilov, Bekhterev, Vygotsky, and others.[59] In 1950, on the occasion of a special Joint

Session of the Academy of Science and the Academy of Medical Sciences, Pavlovian hero worship reached its climax.[60]

Physiologists led by Alexander Ivanov-Smolensky challenged the very right of psychology to exist as an independent discipline. They reasserted the Pavlovian claim that the physiology of higher nervous activity is the only materialistic doctrine that can serve as a basis for behavioral science. Even within physiology, all the most original concepts, such as those of Peter Anokhin and Iosif Beritov, were denounced as a departure from the main line of Pavlovian teaching.

Faced with the threat of a total physiologization of behavioral research, Soviet psychologists adopted a defensive position. Most admitted their "mistakes" and promised to pay more attention to the Pavlovian heritage. Boris Teplov, for example, tried to head off the invasion of physiologists, claiming that his research group had already begun a program of studies based on the Pavlovian notion of the properties of the higher nervous system and that there was therefore no reason for direct supervision of their research by physiologists.

The attack against psychology launched during the Pavlovian session was reinforced by an editorial in *Pravda*, the leading Party newspaper, on February 5, 1951, which severely criticized Soviet psychologists for having had an insufficient impact on the socialist development of the country. To make the situation more complicated, Stalin, who had suddenly discovered his gifts as a scholar, published a paper in 1951 entitled "Marxism and the Problems of Linguistics." Soviet psychologists were ordered forthwith to incorporate Stalin's ideas into their research.

An All-Union Meeting on Psychology was called in 1952 to set up a detailed program for the Pavlovianization and Stalinization of Soviet psychology.[61] Once again, Soviet psychologists had a chance to acknowledge their former mistakes and to take an oath of loyalty to a Pavlovian heritage and to Stalin's concept of linguistics. Sergei Rubinstein, Anatoli Smirnov, Alexei Leontiev, Alexander Luria, Peter Galperin, Boris Teplov, and Boris Ananiev all hastened to accuse each other of the serious "deviations" from the prescribed scientific ideology. At the same time, at the disciplinary level, there was a considerable effort to create a unified defense against radical Pavlovians who envisaged the abolishment of psychology as an independent study.

Psychologists did succeed in preserving their autonomy, but at the price of a Pavlovization of their research. Only one group, the Georgian school, stood firm, rejecting all accusations of idealism as groundless.

The year 1956 brought great relief to most Soviet psychologists. Party leader Nikita Khrushchev exposed the atrocities of the Stalin era and rehabilitated the victims of purges. Although Khrushchev focused on Stalin's political mistakes and his violation of law and justice, it was actually the entire legacy of that epoch that was revised. Once-forbidden names such as Vygotsky and Shpilrein now reappeared in the pages of books and articles.

The period between the late 1950s and the 1960s was something of a renaissance for Soviet science. Studies that had earlier been suppressed—in genetics, cybernetics, linguistics, and other "bourgeois" disciplines—reappeared in public view. Psychology, too, underwent its share of liberalization. Almost every psychologist of the second generation published his magnum opus in these years. *Problems of the Development of Mind* by Alexei Leontiev, published in 1959, won the highest state award, the Lenin Prize, in 1963. Peter Zinchenko published a book on involuntary memory, Peter Galperin a programmatic paper on the formation of mental actions, and Alexander Zaporozhets a monograph on voluntary movements. Starting in the late 1950s, Alexander Luria published dozens of books in neuropsychology. Two volumes of Vygotsky's papers were published in 1956 and 1960. Sergei Rubinstein, who was reappointed chairman of the Department of Psychology at the Institute of Philosophy, published three volumes of his theoretical papers in 1957, 1958, and 1959. *The Experimental Basis of the Psychology of Set* by Dmitri Uznadze appeared in Russian in 1961. After years of political pressure, forced confessions, and cross-allegations, psychologists of this generation, now in their sixties, at last occupied solid and unshakable positions in the universities and research centers of Moscow, Leningrad, and Tbilisi. One can only imagine how they felt about themselves after all these years.[62]

*Crystallization of the Profession*

The generation that came after that of Leontiev, Rubinstein, and their colleagues undoubtedly enjoyed the great opportunity provided by the relatively mild ideological climate of the early 1960s. Although they grew up in the intellectual tradition of the previous generation, the younger psychologists did not suffer the nightmares of their teachers. Several factors contributed to the complex mixture of sober pragmatism and high theoretical aspiration that characterized the third generation of Russian psychologists.

The research of the third generation appeared in the late 1950s and early 1960s—a unique period at the height of destalinization when a subtle consensus emerged between the policy of pragmatists within the Party leadership and the aspirations of Soviet intellectuals. The blind chauvinism of the early 1950s was officially rejected as an offspring of Stalin's rule. To use Western technology and scientific methods turned out to be more practical in the long run than to insist on Soviet superiority in every field of knowledge. As a result references to bourgeois authors were legitimized, and a flow of translations rushed onto the book market.

If in 1949 even a critical assessment of the work of Jean Piaget was considered an ideological mistake, in the 1960s that work was treated with all possible respect. Translations of Piaget were followed by those of Jerome Bruner and Karl Pribram, and by collections of papers in applied psychology, psycholinguistics, artificial intelligence, and other once-forbidden topics.

In order to bridge the gap between Western and Soviet studies in applied psychology, especially in those fields that had an immediate impact on training pilots, astronauts, and workers in high-risk jobs, Soviet authorities established a number of programs in so-called engineering psychology. Some of the prominent psychologists of the third generation, notably Vladimir Zinchenko of Moscow University and Boris Lomov of Leningrad University, started their careers in such programs, only later becoming involved in more fundamental research.

The pragmatic attitude toward applied research could not be institutionalized without confronting the Pavlovians, who still obstructed all modern trends in psychophysiology. The first clash took place in 1962 at the All-Union Meeting on Philosophical Problems of the Physiology of Higher Nervous Activity and Psychology. The hard-line Pavlovians, led by Esras Asratian of the Institute of Higher Nervous Activity, tried to convince the participants that any departure from their version of Pavlovian teaching was a surrender to idealism.[63] This strategy was, however, slightly dated. The majority of psychophysiologists felt that some modern notions, such as the circular reflex suggested by Nikolai Bernstein or the acceptor of actions proposed by Peter Anokhin, could safely coexist with a moderate version of Pavlovianism. The meeting became a real landmark, for it was the first time that such scholars as Nikolai Bernstein could openly present their own alternatives for the development of psychophysiological research. It does not matter that Bernstein and his collaborators were, for a while, a minority faction. The principal goal had been achieved: A new generation of behavioral scientists received an elaborated concept that could successfully and legitimately compete with Pavlovianism.

The results of this remarkable breakthrough were not long in coming. Bernstein's notions of the active, rather than reactive, nature of human psychophysiology were promptly incorporated into applied research by Vladimir Zinchenko and Lev Chkhaidze, and they were used by

Alexander Luria to shed new light on neuropsychology. Bernstein's research in probabilistic behavior was continued by Josif Feigenberg. (The work of Bernstein's students and followers is the subject of chapter 3.) Even those psychologists, like Boris Teplov, who had willingly accepted the Pavlovian doctrine in the 1940s, now sought a compromise between modern neurophysiological methodology and the conceptual apparatus of certified Pavlovianism. The work of Teplov's students, Vladimir Nebylitsyn and Inna Ravich-Scherbo, on the influence of the nervous system on human performance followed this reconciliatory line.[64]

The practical objectives of engineering psychology exercised some influence even on such well-established fields as Alexei Leontiev's psychology of activity. Leontiev's student, Vladimir Zinchenko, showed that the methods of the psychology of activity needed to be revised if they were to be applicable to the microstructural analysis of work. Operations lasting only milliseconds and yet leading to important decisions could not be explained by the "macro" concepts of this predominantly qualitative field. The categories used by Western cognitive psychologists such as George Sperling and those of Nikolai Bernstein turned out to be more plausible. Zinchenko, however, did not reject the idea of a unified theory that would encompass the macro- and microanalyses of behavioral acts. Working in this direction, he suggested a somewhat extravagant theory that included notions borrowed from phenomenological psychology, the psychology of activity, and modern cognitive studies.[65]

Another remarkable breakthrough occurred in the field of philosophy. The destalinization of Soviet society did not of course mean abandonment of the idea of the primacy of Marxism-Leninism, or the deideologization of the social and behavioral sciences. But now the ideological verbiage that had for decades substituted for a more professional philosophy was no longer considered adequate for the explication of Marxism. This temporary vacuum was filled by a number of younger scholars who ventured to establish a philosophy that would be both Marxist and professionally competent. The first achievements in this direction were made by Alexander Zinoviev and Evald Ilienkov, who devoted their doctoral dissertations to elaborations of the logical structure of *Das Kapital.* Known to the Soviet public only as a source of ideological quotations, *Das Kapital* appeared in the works of Zinoviev and Ilienkov as a highly sophisticated attempt to bring the structure of Hegelian dialectics into concordance with the needs of a concrete empirical discipline of economics.[66]

Other philosophical works dealt with the structure of scientific knowledge (Vladimir Bibler, Anatoli Arseniev, Alexander Zinoviev), the critical reassessment of classical German philosophy, and the educational implications of the development of philosophical ideas (Evald Ilienkov, Felix Mikhailov). The 1960s witnessed a gradual restoration of philosophical scholarship as a professional, and not just an ideological, sphere of activity. Themes that had been abandoned earlier, notably alienation and the reification of human culture, appeared in the works of Merab Mamardashvili and Eric Soloviev. A fresh look at the philosophical problems of anthropogenesis was offered by Mark Turovsky. The classics of Western philosophy—from antiquity to the nineteenth century—were translated and commented upon with great care. The rise in standards of philosophical scholarship is fairly obvious just from a comparison of the *Encyclopedia of Philosophy* published in five volumes between 1960 and 1970 with the *Dictionary of Philosophy* produced in 1954.[67]

A central feature of Soviet social and behavioral sciences in the 1960s was their interdisciplinary development. A new brand of scientific epistemology emerged at the crossroads of logic, philosophy of science, and structuralism in biology, psychology, and linguistics, acquiring the name of systems research.[68] This approach, based largely on the general systems theory of the Austro-American Ludwig von Bertalanffy, attempted to overcome the atomistic notions still dominating most of the disciplines by presenting such complex phenomena as behavior as structures of mutually related elements whose net effect is organic and holistic rather than mechanistic.[69]

In behavioral science, systems research brought new understanding to Piaget's structural epistemology and led to a number of original concepts in child psychology (Nelli Nepomniaschaja), the structure of consciousness (Vladimir Lefebvre), man-machine systems (Vitali Dubrovsky), and engineering psychology (Vladimir Zinchenko).[70]

Georgy Schedrovitsky, who is currently at the Moscow Institute of Psychology, can be singled out as the most prominent theorist working in the context of systems research.[71] Schedrovitsky's concept of complex behavioral phenomena rests on a number of epistemological premises. First is a distinction between naturalistic and activity approaches to human behavior. The naturalistic view assumes that objects of the surrounding world are independent entities involved in interactive relations with humans. The principal theoretical categories of the naturalistic approach are the subject and the object, where the subject is always a human being. The activity approach starts with human *activity* as an all-embracing principle within which objects and relations are revealed as concentrations, or embodiments, of the activity itself. Objects of the external world now appear only as secondary constructions dependent for their existence on the activity that is applied to them. As for the subject, the concept of activity is in this approach superior to the humans involved in the activity. This is Schedrovitsky's second major thesis: Activity should not be regarded as an attribute of the individual but rather as an all-embracing system that "captures" individuals and "forces" them to behave in a certain way. This approach may be traced back to the assertion of Wilhelm Humboldt that it is not man who has language as an attribute, but rather language that "possesses" man.

Activity thus appears as a complex system, whose structure can be viewed from different perspectives and grasped by different means of analysis. What follows from this is the third of Schedrovitsky's theses, namely, that an essential distinction exists between an object of study and its presentation as a particular scientific subject. A single complex object such as behavior might be analyzed as a number of different scientific subjects, depending on the epistemological and methodological positions chosen. The scientist's task therefore includes not only the study of the object within the framework of a chosen scientific subject but also the choice of theoretical procedures that mark this subject as a distinct component of scientific knowledge. Schedrovitsky suggests considering several scientific subjects that correspond in a complementary way to the same object. Establishing this complementarity and finding an adequate means for its theoretical presentation are the tasks of the behavioral theorist.

Schedrovitsky's activity approach has been applied successfully to the design of man-machine systems and to the evaluation of human factors in urban planning.[72] Schedrovitsky himself has devoted his energy largely to epistemological studies, convinced that the inadequacy of current theoretical means for analyzing complex behavioral phenomena are a principal obstacle to the development of behavioral theory.

Dissatisfaction with the current state of psychological theory is also revealed in the writings of Vasili Davydov, the present director of the Moscow Institute of Psychology.[73] Davydov has pointed out that for decades Soviet educational psychology has been based on an empiricist doctrine of concept formation that has prevented students from acquiring a broad-scale theoretical foundation in science and the humanities. Using Schedrovitsky's distinction between the object of study and the scientific subject, Davydov has argued that the acquisition of knowledge in a form of theoretically constructed scientific subjects is the only coherent way to learn. Educational psychology must therefore revise a methodological apparatus that has for a long time focused on the gradual development of quasiscientific concepts based in the everyday experience of the child.

Davydov has suggested starting in primary school with specially designed scientific subjects that provide students with a basis for theoretical concept formation relevant to the epistemological standards of modern science and the humanities. Special curricula in grammar and mathematics designed by Davydov and his collaborators have shown that a seven-year-old child can in fact handle highly abstract concepts.[74]

One might distinguish two constituents of Davydov's program. The more practical of the two foreshadows a new education that would encourage creativity and bring children closer to the actual methods of modern scientific thought. The other is of a more philosophical nature and centers on the relation of empirical knowledge and formal logic to dialectics. Davydov adopted the version of dialectics developed in the 1960s by younger Soviet philosophers, including Evald Ilienkov and Felix Mikhailov. In his view the method of dialectics has much in common with the most advanced methodologies of modern science, in contrast to the method of empiricism and the naive assumption that science is a mere systematization of lay experience. In modern scientific theory as well as in dialectics, according to Davydov, empirical objects and their relations appear in a purposefully contradictory form as theoretical constructs and philosophical categories. Mastering these contradictions must be set as a goal for the student. In this light, dialectics appears as an integral component of the educational process. (Davydov's theory of learning is a major theme of chapter 7.)

As we have seen, the practical tasks of engineering psychology or education soon confronted Soviet psychologists with problems of a theoretical or philosophical nature. One peculiarity of this period of Soviet psychology, stemming from the lack of theoretical work in the Stalin period, has been the rediscovery of many studies conducted in the 1920s. The work of Lev Vygotsky has been central to this movement. New light has been shed on the Kharkov school, which not only developed Vygotsky's ideas but also revised some of his principal theses. The revisionist version established by Alexei Leontiev and his colleagues was for a while considered a genuine continuation of Vygotsky's program. In 1979, however, at a colloquium dedicated to the theoretical legacy of Vygotsky, Georgy Schedrovitsky pointed out a number of discrepancies between Vygotsky's and Leontiev's concepts of the cultural-historical development of the mind. In discussions and publications that followed, Vasili Davydov and Vladimir Zinchenko offered their own versions of the controversy. Despite the variety of approaches all the participants emphasized the extraordinary vitality of the questions raised by Vygotsky in the 1920s.[75]

Thus Soviet psychology came full circle, and a later generation of psychologists had to face anew many of the problems considered in the early years. One might guess that the peculiarity of the development of their discipline actually helped Soviet psychologists to recognize the perennial character of some behavioral problems, ones that cannot be solved once and for all time, even if there were a single correct method that could be applied to them.

*The 1970s*

Of the youngest generation of Soviet psychologists, by which I mean those who joined the profession in the 1970s, it would be premature to make any assessment or to single out any individuals. What we can do is to take stock of the social and intellectual circumstances in which the latest generation has been trained and oriented. Chapters 3 and 7, which deal with contemporary research, must be viewed in the context of the institutional and intellectual conditions outlined here.

Soviet and American systems of higher education differ in important ways. First of all there is from the Western standpoint an enormous degree of centralization in the Soviet system. It is reasonable that education and research should be consistent with the general pattern of Soviet life and economy, characterized by centralization and tight control from above. There are no private universities or colleges; all schools operate under the supervision of the Ministry of Higher Education, which decides how much money will be allocated to each university, what courses will be taught, and what their enrollments will be.

There are a number of scientific councils in universities and research centers that can grant Ph.D. ("candidate of science") degrees, but there is only one governmental organization empowered to control the activity of the councils and to issue the actual diplomas. This organization can annul the decision of a council on the grounds, for example, of insufficient "ideological reliability."

Much of the fundamental research in the Soviet Union is conducted outside universities, in research centers and laboratories affiliated with the Academy of Sciences, the Academy of Pedagogical Sciences, and the Academy of Medical Sciences. These centers have their own Ph.D. programs and employ a large portion of the graduates. The structure of the research centers is even more rigid than that of the universities. Each has a state-approved program based on a teamwork scheme which assumes that junior research fellows must contribute to projects designed by heads of departments and laboratories. In the universities as well the department head is empowered to control the work of his or her subordinates. Since all senior teaching and research positions are part of a tenure track, the mobility of faculty is insignificant. It is not rare for a department head to occupy the position for twenty years, exercising a powerful influence on an entire generation of scholars.

Students must decide at the time of entry into a university which discipline they will study. All undergraduate courses within a given discipline are required, and it is practically impossible to change one's course of study. For that reason departments in Soviet universities play somewhat the same role that individual colleges, or schools, play within American universities. A department of psychology provides all the required courses for those who enroll to study psychology, with the exception of ideological subjects, such as Marxist philosophy and the history of the Communist Party, and of mathematics.

The normal course of study takes five to five-and-a-half years and leads to a degree roughly equivalent to a master of arts or master of science. No bachelor degrees are awarded for shorter-term study. Only a limited number of optional courses are offered in the two years of graduate study.

Education is free, and employment is guaranteed, with state authorities deciding which position and institution suit the graduate. In this respect Ph.D. programs can be considered more a place of temporary employment than one of study. Only with the appropriate authorization from a university council may a graduate enter a Ph.D. program, even at another university or research center. Once employed, graduates are required to spend two to three years in one place before they are given an opportunity to continue their studies. If one takes into account that the number of Ph.D. scholarships is limited, it is not strange at all that many graduates spend three years as research or teaching assistants before they can seriously expect to compete for postgraduate programs.

There is one feature peculiar to Soviet life that seriously influences the institutional context of learning, namely, the idea of proper residence (*propiska*). The exclusive legitimate residence of Soviet citizens is their place of birth. To change one's place of residence, one must obtain permission from the authorities. Permission to settle in Moscow and other big cities is granted only in exceptional cases, usually to high-ranking officials who are promoted to the capital. The pretext for this system is that it provides an even distribution of manpower and prevents the overpopulation of big cities. In fact, of course, it is a consequence of the policy of centralization. In all respects, from the supply of food and consumer goods to the availability of libraries and research facilities, the big cities are much more attractive than are smaller towns. If people were allowed to move at will, many white-collar employees would leave the provinces for urban centers.

Even if one is admitted to the most prestigious universities in Moscow and Leningrad, one ultimately returns to one's native town, or, if the authorities so decide, to some provincial capital. Moscow natives may easily change their residence to a province, but they then abandon their right to return to Moscow. Now, imagine a gifted student, brought up in a small town in Siberia, who enters Moscow University and manages to earn a Ph.D. there. For all practical purposes, this young scholar will not be able to compete with Moscow natives, for his or her destiny is to return to Siberia or some other provincial place where the authorities offer employment and residence.

There are no private publishing companies in the Soviet Union, and all scientific papers accepted for publication must pass through state censorship. To submit a paper to an international journal one must clear it with a number of commissions that determine whether it is reasonable to permit such a submission. The same procedures apply to papers submitted to international meetings.

Soviet scholars, like other Soviet citizens, cannot travel to the West on a private basis. To attend a meeting that takes place in a Western country, one must be included in an official delegation and travel in a group. Since a trip to the West is regarded as a reward for prominence and reliability, younger scholars have little or no chance of being included in such delegations.

Up until the late 1970s there were no foreign bookstores, and those that have opened in the past few years do not carry many scientific books. Only full professors have the privilege of ordering books from abroad, but up to a limit of approximately $30 a year. Although first-class scientific libraries exist in Moscow and Leningrad, libraries in provincial centers are poor and receive no foreign books or journals. Sometimes bizarre ideological restrictions are imposed on the books permitted for circulation. For example, *Eros and Civilization* by Herbert Marcuse can be found in Moscow's Lenin Library, while *One-Dimensional Man* by the same author is branded as anti-Soviet and would be taken from a home library if discovered by authorities. There is, at the same time, a form of "closed publication," under which certain Western books are translated and published in limited numbers for restricted circulation among high-ranking Party officials and members of the scientific elite. Trusted scholars are permitted use of these books for writing critical reviews of modern trends in the political and social sciences. The ordinary reader, however, has no chance to compare such reviews with the original works in question. A striking example is *1984* by George Orwell, which was being discussed in many Soviet publications while it was officially prohibited from public circulation.

It is within this general framework that we must understand the lives and careers of the youngest generation of Soviet scholars. There are also events and circumstances that specifically relate to psychology. Until 1965 chairs of psychology in Soviet universities existed as subunits within departments of philosophy or education. A number of research centers in Moscow and Leningrad with no affiliation with universities offered their own psychology Ph.D. programs; among these were the Moscow Institute of Psychology, the Institute of Higher Nervous Activity, and the Institute of Preschool Education. In 1965 an independent department of psychology was established at Moscow University. Leningrad, Tbilisi, Tartu, and Jaroslavl universities promptly adopted this institutional pattern. In 1971 a new Institute of Psychology was established in Moscow under the auspices of the Academy of Science. Its director, Boris Lomov, was elected a member-correspondent of the Academy of Sciences. The new institute's mission is to carry out research in applied, mathematical, and physiological psychology. It has also absorbed a group of theoreticians, mainly the students of Sergei Rubinstein, who had earlier comprised the department of psychology at the Institute of Philosophy. The new institute has established its own Ph.D. program.

To get a sense of the scale of psychology in the Soviet Union, consider the fact that only the large university centers mentioned here have graduate programs in the behavioral sciences; just in terms of the limited number of students, Soviet psychology is certainly at a disadvantage.

Rigid centralization, bureaucracy, and the lack of hard currency have made it painfully difficult for Soviet psychologists to obtain modern research equipment. For example, there exists no Soviet-made encephalographic recorder to fit the modern standard, and it takes years of bureaucratic paperwork to obtain a Japanese or American one. Only the leading research centers employ current techniques used abroad; provincial universities must get along with obsolete equipment. These conditions slow down the practical implementation of scientific ideas, as does the fact that all contact between psychologists and clients is mediated by the state bureaucracy.

There are a number of differences in the professional opportunities available to Soviet and American psychology graduates. These differences rest on two factors, one of them quantitative, the other structural. In the 1970s psychology was a growing discipline in the Soviet Union, which meant that the demand for psychologists was greater than the supply. As a result a large number of graduates found employment at leading research centers or teaching positions in provincial universities.

Unlike their colleagues in the United States, Soviet psychologist-practitioners still constitute a tiny fraction of the profession. Only in the past few years have modest attempts been made to establish counseling centers affiliated with the outpatient departments of mental hospitals. Moscow and Leningrad, however, have a wide network of research institutions affiliated with the Academy of Pedagogical Sciences and the State Department of Education, and these provide positions for those who choose to become specialists in child and educational psychology. A growing number of centers of engineering psychology also absorb a portion of the graduates.

As noted above, the head of a department or a laboratory exercises tight control over his or her subordinates, designing research objectives that usually correspond to his or her own research program. Psychologists work full-time in research laboratories in teams rather than individually. For that reason young psychologists must be sure that their interests suit the program favored by the head of the laboratory or department they would like to join. The Soviets have a favorite proverb for this, which goes: "Tell me who your chief is, and I will tell you what your thesis is."

Under the conditions that prevail in Soviet science, it is sometimes easier for young psychologists to get an adequate job than to publish the results of their studies. Between 1955 and 1979 there was only one psychological periodical, *Problems of Psychology* (published bimonthly), to satisfy the needs of the profession.[76] Transactions published more or less regularly by universities and research centers do not cross regional and institutional boundaries, and thus cannot serve as an adequate means of scientific communication. Members of the editorial board of *Problems of Psychology* and editors of transactions exercise vigilant control over the content and scientific tendencies of submitted papers. Since there is no alternative place of publication, authors are forced to comply with the current editorial policy even if they disagree with it.

All these factors have helped to shape the Soviet psychological community. The numerous constraints imposed on the course of scientific thought from its conception to its practical implementation force its intellectual maturation to be much longer than it would be in the West. Certain ideas may be dormant for years or decades, with no chance of being published or implemented. But that does not mean that they are destined to go no further than their author's imagination, for chains of informal or semiofficial seminars and scientific meetings provide a secondary communications structure for Soviet behavioral science. There are both advantages and weak points to this secondary structure. The advantages lie in its informality. The search for truth and knowledge is the only moving force of such informal sessions, since they can do little to enhance the visibility of a participant. Moreover, they provide a forum in which the textbook authorities can be freely criticized or even ignored. Nevertheless their "underground" character bears the threat of sectarianism. In an attempt to counterbalance officially recognized doctrines, participants in informal seminars sometimes begin stewing in their own intellectual juices. It would be erroneous, of course, to consider the secondary structure as completely detached from the official doctrines of Soviet psychology. It does sometimes happen that ideas first conceived during the informal talks later appear as the respectable concepts of certified knowledge. This route, however, can take a decade or more.

Another result of the current situation is the phenomenon of subgroup solidarity. In the face of tight centralization, ideological restrictions, and the problems involved in implementing new ideas, psychologists almost instinctively cling to one another in an attempt to form groups that share a set of intellectual ideals and fight for them collectively. Certain past events have also contributed to this group structure. The students of Sergei Rubinstein, for example, form a cohesive group opposed to Alexei Leontiev and his school, not only because of the dissimilarity of their scientific approaches but also because Rubinsteinians feel that the Leontievites took unfair advantage of Rubinstein in the late 1940s when he fell victim to a witch-hunt against Jewish "cosmopolitans."

Finally, the same department or laboratory head who exercises powerful control over the work of junior research fellows also protects them from outside criticism. Since the work of these subordinates contributes to a common research program, the head is eager to help them in all possible respects, from the publication of papers to improvements in their housing conditions.

The youngest generation of Soviet psychologists therefore faces a complex reality that includes a rigid institutional structure, ideological restrictions, and authoritarian control by scientific bosses, but also group solidarity and high standards of scientific ethics developed within the secondary structure of their profession.

# 2

*Personalities and Reflexes: The Legacies of Ivan Pavlov and Vladimir Bekhterev*

*The careers of Vladimir Bekhterev (1857–1927) and Ivan Pavlov (1849–1936) form a good starting place for an attempt to make sense of the history of Soviet psychology. On the surface they had much in common. Both had achieved fame and honor before the Revolution. Both chose to stay in their homeland in hopes of proceeding with their studies. Both succeeded in this and were later praised as leaders of Soviet science. And both were devoted to the epistemology of the natural sciences and sought so-called objective methods for the study of behavior.*

*At this point the similarities between the two cease. Bekhterev left hundreds of disciples who, on the eve of the Revolution, filled most of the departments of psychiatry and neurology in Russia (except for those in Moscow). Within a decade of his death, however, there were only a handful left who dared to call themselves Bekhterev's students and to develop his theories. Pavlov, in contrast, was always reluctant to call anybody a disciple, yet today his self-proclaimed protégés occupy most of the top positions in Soviet psychology. In contemporary texts Pavlov is lavishly praised as the founder of modern neurophysiology and the most profound theorist of the behavioral sciences; Bekhterev is simply mentioned in historical surveys as a prominent neurologist. Pavlov's writings can be found in any library or bookstore; Bekhterev's books, especially the ones published in the 1920s, have been rarities for many years. It is perhaps not surprising to find that the two scientists were extremely hostile toward each other, forever searching for weak points in the other's studies, forever embroiled in arguments concerning priority.*

*Pavlov*

The early careers of the two scientists are similar. Both were born in provincial towns to lower-middle-class families. Pavlov's father was a priest, Bekhterev's a police inspector. Both, owing to their abilities and persistence, managed to study in St. Petersburg, then the center of higher education in Russia. Bekhterev undoubtedly got off to a quicker start than his future rival. At twenty-four he earned his doctorate. Four years later, in 1885, he was invited to take a chair of psychiatry at Kazan University. Pavlov was thirty-four when he earned his M.D., and it took him another seven years to gain a professorial chair in physiology and pharmacology at St. Petersburg's Military Medical Academy.

It was traditional at the time for young scientists to spend several years abroad studying in European laboratories. Pavlov chose for his foreign training Rudolf Heidenhain's laboratory in Breslau and Carl Ludwig's in Leipzig, a clear indication of his early interest in the fine mechanisms of secretory processes and visceral innervation.[1] From the beginning of his career Pavlov saw himself as a physiologist; indeed his famous studies on conditional reflexes were in some sense a side result of his work on the visceral physiology of digestion.

Pavlov's first achievements were products of an elaborate surgical technique and painstaking laboratory work. In this period he induced permanent artificial fistulas in the pancreas of a dog, invented a form of "sham feeding" that allowed him to obtain pure gastric juice, and created an artificial pouch in the dog—a procedure that marked a milestone in the progress of experimental physiology. Ten years were dedicated to the study of the nervous mechanisms in the digestive glands, and in 1904 Pavlov was awarded a Nobel Prize for this research.

Until the Revolution Pavlov did all his work in one place, the Institute of Experimental Medicine in St. Petersburg, which was founded and supported by Prince Oldenburgsky. Neither organizational nor teaching skills were Pavlov's forte; he was a "laboratory man," unique as a hard worker and master of fine experimental methods.[2]

In 1903, on the occasion of an International Medical Congress, Pavlov delivered his "Madrid speech," the first sketch of reflex theory as the source of a methodology for the objective study of behavior. Pavlov began the speech with the premise that the need to adapt to changing conditions underlies all physiological functions in living organisms. He then conjectured a similarity between visceral physiological mechanisms, such as the digestive reflexes, and so-called mental phenomena, which he saw as nothing but "distant" and "condition-related" physiological reactions. This connection led him to introduce two new concepts: unconditional (*bezuslovnye*) and conditional (*uslovnye*) reflexes.[3] The former consist of reflexes that are the same all the time, including all the basic physiological reflexes. "But the data on the mind," emphasized Pavlov, "are also reproducible. There are simply a greater number of conditions that can influence the results of mental as compared with physiological experiments. That is, what we have in this case are conditional reflexes."[4]

A careful reading of this statement will reveal that Pavlov's point was directed toward methodology. He was interested only in reproducible data obtained with the help of the methods of the natural sciences, and these data alone he called conditional reflexes. He remained indifferent to the nature of the reality underlying these psychophysiological data. Pavlov stated: "For the natural scientist everything is in the method, in the opportunity to find a steadfast and reliable truth; from this point of view, which is obligatory for the scientist, the notion of 'soul' as a natural-scientific principle is not only unnecessary but even harmful because it might restrict the depth and challenge of the naturalist's analysis."[5] Clearly Pavlov was a true child of his time—the late nineteenth century—when only the truth of the natural sciences seemed undeniable; objects existed for him exactly to the extent that they could stand up to experimentation.[6]

Curiously, Pavlov's posthumous reputation as well as the special destiny of his teachings in post-Revolutionary Russia were not due to a victory of the principles outlined above but rather to their overextension. Only specialists could have become excited at the discovery of the fine mechanisms of secretory or sensory-motor activity in dogs. The picture changed drastically when these same mechanisms were proclaimed the only possible way to analyze human mental functions. From the point of view of the social history of science, Pavlov's case was, however, not atypical. Worldwide acclaim came to Freud when he went beyond psychotherapeutic case studies and proposed a challenging new approach to individual and collective psychology. While Skinner taught pigeons, he was merely known to his pigeons and to behavioral specialists, but once he transferred the rules of pigeon training to human society he soon became a celebrity.

It is important to emphasize that Pavlov's suggestions for the use of reflex methodology to explain the human mind were almost entirely speculative. He had no appropriately designed methods for work with human subjects. Moreover, he had no data on human reflexes. Take, for example, his paper "General Types of the Higher Nervous Activity of Animals and Men" (1935). Throughout the paper Pavlov discusses the problem of balance between the processes of excitation and of inhibition in the nervous system of the dog. Despite the title, only the last two pages are dedicated to human subjects, and these are filled with conjectures that the human typology suggested by Hippocrates might coincide fairly well with the types that emerged from his own study of dogs.

To explain the shift in his interests from problems of visceral physiology to the physiology of the nervous system, Pavlov wrote: "The complex conditions of everyday experience require a much more detailed and specialized correlation between the animal and its environment than is afforded by the inborn reflexes alone. This more precise correlation can be established only through the medium of the hemispheres as temporary and interchangeable signals for the comparatively small number of agencies of a general character which determine the inborn reflexes, and this is the only means by which a most delicate adjustment of the organism to the environment can be established. To this function of hemispheres we gave the name of 'signalization.' "[7]

This remark might in itself be considered an explicit statement of his scientific position. But Pavlov hastens to generalize his thesis: "Conditional reflexes are phenomena of common and widespread occurrence: Their establishment is an integral function in everyday life. We recognize them in ourselves or animals under such names as 'education,' 'habits,' and 'training,' and all of these are really nothing more than the results of an establishment of new nervous connections during the postnatal existence of the organism."[8]

Pavlov's statements on the generality and omnipotence of reflexes go far beyond an obligatory reliance on the scientific method of study. There are constant lapses in his texts, with shifts from the scientific approach to behavior to generalized claims that reflexes are the essence of behavior. In his lecture before the members of the Institute for Advanced Medical Studies, Pavlov managed to include two unequal and in some sense contradictory statements in two successive phrases. He wrote that "behavior and higher nervous activity *coincide* and mean one and the same thing. Behavior *as* higher nervous activity may then be analyzed in a purely scientific manner."[9] In the first phrase Pavlov insists on the coincidence of behavior and nervous activity; then in the second he talks only about the opportunity to study behavior with the help of methods once designed for the study of animal reflexes. Unfortunately, Pavlov's followers stuck to the former version and inevitably proceeded toward neurophysiological reductionism in their studies of human behavior.

The history of Pavlov's involvement in psychology is quite curious. According to Soviet texts, Pavlov contributed substantially to the following fields of psychology: differential psychophysiology, which he enriched by his concept of types of nervous activity and the artists-thinkers classification; the theory of higher mental processes, in which he introduced the concepts of primary and secondary signal systems; and clinical psychology, in which he developed the concepts of experimental neuroses and neural mechanisms of hysteria.[10] Here we shall focus on Pavlov's ideas concerning signal systems and the artists-thinkers classification.

In his 1924 lecture before the students of Military Medical Academy, Pavlov used the term "signalization" to designate the function of cerebral hemispheres that connects sensory input to a motor or secretory output. Developing this approach, he began to call all agents of the environment that evoke a response from an organism "primary signals." The concept of "secondary signals" was introduced in the following context: "Then speech, chiefly the kinesthetic stimulation flowing into the cortex from the speech organs, [is] the secondary signals, the signals of signals."[11]

Thus, while environmental agents (all material stimulation) are primary signals, words play the role of secondary stimuli or signals of signals. It should be mentioned that, at least in the beginning, Pavlov's definition of secondary signals was nothing but a play on words. He merely extended his conditional reflex theory to the subject of verbal communication, disregarding practically all characteristics that qualify speech as a distinctive phenomenon.

This first incursion into the field of psychology was followed by papers on hysteria and human typology. Before examining these works, it is useful to consider a sample of Pavlov's psychological reasoning:

Life clearly reveals two groups of human beings: artists and thinkers. There is a striking difference between them. The first group, artists of all kinds—writers, musicians, painters, etc.—perceive reality without breaking it up or decomposing it. The other group, the thinkers, on the contrary, dismember it, thereby, as it were, killing it and making it a kind of temporary skeleton. Only afterwards do they gradually, as if anew, assemble its parts and try to revive it. But this they are unable to accomplish.[12]

Pavlov goes on to give a "photographic" analogy for the artistic type: "Evidently in this case the cerebral hemispheres receive the visual stimuli exactly as the variations of intensity of the light in a photographic plate, just as a phonographic record is made from sound. Indeed this is, some may think, a characteristic of all types of artists!"[13]

As soon as the concept of "types" was formulated, Pavlov claimed that the dominance of an artistic nature meant the prevalence of primary signals and the animalness of a person. The prevalence of secondary signals was linked with a reasoning nature and the humanness of a person.

As appropriate evolutionary support, he added this statement: "It is obvious that at first we had a million-year period of a purely animal world and, therefore, the first signal system alone. But then, above the first, the second one was built, in the human era. It was the system of words and speech movements. So we are composed of the two parts: the purely human and the animal."[14]

Pavlov related his notion of the animal aspect of the person and its dominance in the artistic type to some psychiatric observations: "The extraordinary fantasy and imaginative state of the hysteric, but also the dreams of everyone, are the activation of the primary signals with their imagery and concreteness. . . ."[15]

Pavlov has thus left us with two different definitions of the primary signals. The first takes into account the imaginative, fantastic, and symbolic character of dreams, while the second relies on photographic reality. Considering these further in relation to the artists-thinkers typology, we are confronted with the following problematical picture: Dominance of primary signals (which include everything but words) is associated with artistic persons (even writers!), who are said to grasp the world directly without analysis. This type is considered to be evolutionarily older and more animal-like. In contrast, the predominance of secondary signals (words) indicates a human, analytical, and incomplete view of the world.

Pavlov must have assumed that a piece of neurophysiological flesh— however hypothetical—would provide support for his signal systems theory. Consider: "In artists, the activity of the cerebral hemispheres, while developing throughout their entire mass, least of all involves the frontal lobes and concentrates mainly in other parts; in the thinker, on the contrary, it is intense in the frontal lobes."[16] But clearly this additional hypothetical precision failed to mend the breach between Pavlov's typology and the theory of conditional reflexes.[17] Thus the peculiarity of Pavlov's entrance into the field of human behavior: Although he advocated a rigorous scientific approach, that is, the methodology of conditional reflexes for the study of human psychology, he had no experimental data to back his hypotheses.

One may suppose that the desire to create his own theory of human behavior was so strong that Pavlov decided to adapt available psychological and psychiatric observations to his purpose. If that were so, then only one problem remained, namely, that these latter observations had nothing in common with the methodology of conditional reflexes. This fact was not unknown to Pavlov himself.[18]

Pavlov was thus faced with a major task: to connect the general principles of conditional reflexes with available psychological data. This issue goes far beyond the historical peculiarities of Pavlov's work. What we see is the classic conflict arising when an "old" theory is expanded to include "new" observations essentially alien to it. Similar conflicts have occurred within almost all scientific theories that have exceeded their original boundaries and attempted to invade related fields of knowledge.

The first step Pavlov took toward developing a theory of human behavior was to identify behavior with higher nervous activity. Because he had no experimental data to confirm this, adaptation of alien data became crucial. In other words, he had to borrow and assimilate available psychological observations and at the same time retain the premises of reflex theory. This second step required some fresh ideas on the manifestations of the human mind, for the "old" theory could not offer anything relevant in those days.

A problem Pavlov faced in trying to assimilate available psychological observations was his reluctance to acknowledge the value of ideas that were not his own. He ignored the reflexological studies of Bekhterev, he tried very awkwardly to ridicule Gestalt psychology, and he failed to recognize the importance of Pierre Janet's contribution to clinical psychology.[19] It is reported that he did find a couple of good words for Freud, but psychoanalysis as a method of study failed to impress him.[20] Neither Vygotsky nor anybody else among the Soviet psychologists of the 1920s attracted Pavlov's attention.[21]

From a study of Pavlov's writings, his scientific sympathies, and his antipathies, I have come to the conclusion that the source of Pavlov's ideas on the human mind was not scientific at all; they grew, rather, out of his own experience. Thus the building material used to bridge reflex theory and human psychology was not conceptual but personal, based not on data but on self-observation.

The very notion of involving private experience in the process of scientific work may be considered by some to be paradoxical. Nevertheless the investigation of such an involvement might help to clarify the complex phenomena concealed within the vague concept of intuition.

If in the so-called pure sciences one may produce numerous hypotheses in a strictly formal way—in accordance with logicomathematical schemes and without any concrete evidence—in the behavioral sciences this is not possible. Therefore it is not surprising that the nearest source—the self—insistently intrudes into psychological theorizing. It may be argued that it is somehow incorrect to allow this to happen, but it is clearly inevitable. One may assert, for example, that somewhere between the self-analysis of Viktor Kandinsky and the writings of Dostoevsky is the true ground of Russian descriptive psychiatry.[22] Many psychiatrist-practitioners admit that the nonscientific prose of Dostoevsky has provided them with more insight into the human mind than theories that pretend to be strictly scientific. Therefore, if on a theoretical level the validity of nonscientific self-analysis remains questionable, in practice it is a normal part of the process. Its acceptance, however, provides no assurance that its involvement will always prove fruitful.

In Pavlov's case the papers titled "Clinical Wednesdays" allow us to reconstruct the transformation of his private experience into a quasiscientific theory.[23] The strange and inconsistent definitions that appear in Pavlov's works on typology and signal systems find their roots in these texts.

"This is my case. I myself am psychasthenic, but you need not be surprised. I'll explain now what it means. One may say normal psychasthenic! There is nothing artistic in me at all."[24] Pavlov goes on to recall that in his youth, while attending a seminary, he was excused from singing lessons even though music was usually a required subject. Concerning painting, he notes that, though he remembers all his laboratory dogs, he cannot draw even an outline of them. It is characteristic that he mentions only performance skills and not more general creative abilities. His conclusion flows quite naturally from this account: "One may take images from reality only to synthesize them in one's own way: a head from one, a leg from another. Regardless of the manner, the constituent parts will be from real life. You can have nothing without this. You may have fantastic synthesis within the primary signal system, but its elements must be based on real visual images. And the same in music."[25]

It is thus clear that Pavlov's psychasthenia was the specific reason for his "scientific" human typology. The perceptual stimuli prepared in the laboratory and artistic creativity appear to have been one and the same in his mind. Pavlov linked artistic creativity with primary signals and the animal aspect of human nature because true artistic talent was simply unknown to him. His mind recognized only commonplace compositions of everyday objects. "I have told you that I cannot draw a dog or distinguish a note, but pictures I understand well. Everyday themes—that is what I understand."[26]

The strange contradiction between an "imaginative" and a "photographic" definition of the artistic type becomes "normal" in the context of Pavlov's abnormal psychasthenic view. He saw artistic creativity as nothing more than a process of summing sensory data; thus it is not surprising that he identified the artistic personality with primary signality. Since Pavlov apparently was weak in the symbolic arts, musical theory, and formal logic, he simply did not have these matters on his mind. So it did not trouble him that they cannot belong to either primary or secondary signals.[27]

The further development of the Pavlovian typology was as capricious as the typology itself. During the 1930s the concept of signal systems and the artists-thinkers typology were occasionally criticized as "unclear" and "mechanistic,"[28] but in the mid-1940s they were accepted as outstanding scientific achievements. The contradictions inherent in Pavlov's ideas were overcome by the method of partial rejection: Psychophysiologists put aside the "imaginative" version of signal systems theory and developed Pavlovian typology within the framework of conditional reflexes. Psychiatrists, in turn, keeping in mind the "imaginative" definition, developed descriptive methods of clinical analysis in which the dominance of primary signals indicated the animal, nonanalytical personality. While psychiatrists developed their descriptive methods, psychophysiologists—attempting to make the signal studies experimental—reduced the primary signals to simple flashes of light or the sounds of a buzzer, which were entirely meaningless outside the experimental situation.[29]

The concept of secondary signals also underwent a considerable transformation. The original definition given by Pavlov included only speech, and that only in its signal function. Such a definition was unsuitable for the problems addressed in both psychiatry and psychophysiology. This limitation was overcome by identification of the secondary signals with self-instruction, and even with the subject's cognition.

But, after all, why were there any proponents of these weak and contradictory ideas? The answer is both very simple and very complex. Since the mid-1940s Pavlov had been idolized as *the* hero of national science and as a materialist opponent of bourgeois psychology. (The latter term embraced almost all Western theories of behavior. Such different scholars as Charles Sherrington, Wolfgang Köhler, and Pierre Janet were sweepingly labeled bourgeois idealists.) Development of his scientific legacy, however contradictory, became a matter of great ideological importance and, at the same time, a good way to make one's career.

But why was it Pavlov who was chosen as the hero, given that hero worship seemed a necessity? In so-called Sovietological studies one can find the view expressed that the Pavlovianization of Soviet psychology in the late 1940s and 1950s was superimposed from the top down and reflected a whim of Stalin. Robert Tucker, for example, states that "there is abundant evidence to show that during the early postwar years, the professional psychologists in the USSR were quite oblivious of the impending revolutionary reorganization of their science on the basis of the reflex principle."[30] This perspective, however, fails to take into account the special position Pavlov occupied in Soviet science. With the help of "decoded" psychological texts, including the essay of Boris Teplov that Tucker uses to make his point, one sees that by the mid-1940s Pavlov was practically the only prominent scientist who had escaped severe criticism for "deviations," and the only one who was still accepted as a leader of national science.[31]

To understand Pavlovianization, one must take into account the general climate of the postwar years. It was a period of revitalization of Russian nationalism inspired by war victories and backed by an official propaganda that bore conspicuous signs of chauvinism. This led to xenophobia and to a search for "great men" of national science and culture to set in opposition to the "false achievements" of the bourgeois world. Physics, mathematics, and biology had already suffered under this chauvinistic campaign, and psychologists were quite aware that their turn would come next. In the race for a great man, Pavlov's name had scarcely a rival. He was 100 percent Russian, unlike Lev Vygotsky and Sergei Rubinstein; he had never been in real disfavor, unlike Konstantin Kornilov and others; and his scientific credentials were beyond question. The only plausible competitor was Vladimir Bekhterev, and, for reasons we shall now examine, Bekhterev was unsuitable for canonization.

*Bekhterev*

From the time of his travel abroad, shortly after graduation, Vladimir Bekhterev's scientific interests stood in sharp contrast to Pavlov's. Although both were trained in medicine, Pavlov never practiced and had no apparent experience in psychiatry or in the treatment of neural diseases. Bekhterev always considered himself a physician-practitioner. In his student years he volunteered to go to Bulgaria, then at war with Turkey, as a military paramedic. This firsthand experience of the pain and suffering of others greatly impressed the young man and convinced him that he had made the right choice for his life's career.[32]

Bekhterev studied neuroanatomy in Paul Flechsig's laboratory in Leipzig, but he also attended Wundt's seminars on psychology. In Paris his clinical work at the famous mental hospital of Jean Martin Charcot, Salpêtrière, drew him to the problems of hysteria and hypnosis. Personally of marked hypnotic abilities, Bekhterev promptly realized the clinical benefits of this new but, by Russian standards, suspicious method. In the following decades hypnotherapy became one of his favorite clinical techniques; Bekhterev cured dozens, possibly hundreds, of psychoneurotics and left interesting records depicting behavior in the state of somnambulism.

Unlike Pavlov, who began with visceral physiology and only gradually turned to brain research, Bekhterev was from the start preoccupied with neurological problems. His approach included laboratory experiments, observations, clinical work, and organizational efforts directed toward the establishment of special institutions for neurological research. It was during his professorship in Kazan, from 1885 to 1893, that Bekhterev succeeded for the first time in fulfilling this complex program. It later became his lifelong style of activity. Thus it would be erroneous to judge Bekhterev's achievements simply on the basis of his hundreds of publications, some of them premature and superficial. His observations, hypotheses, lectures, and conversations are an inseparable part of his legacy. While in Kazan, Bekhterev founded one of the first psychophysiological laboratories in Russia, established a hospital for nervous diseases, organized the Society of Neuropathologists and Psychiatrists, and established the journal *Herald of Neurology*. These same years were dedicated to a thorough analysis of the anatomy and physiology of the nervous system. This work resulted in his *Conductive Paths of the Brain and Spinal Cord* (1888), which was translated into French and German.

Bekhterev's neurological studies were continued in St. Petersburg, and between 1903 and 1907 seven volumes of *Bases for Teaching about the Functioning of the Brain* appeared, taking their place as an international encyclopedia of neuroscience. Bekhterev's erudition was so enormous that, according to an apocryphal story, one German professor used to say that "genuine knowledge of the brain is in possession of only two persons: God himself and Herr Professor Bekhterev."

Bekhterev never made a secret of his ultimate goal of establishing an objective science that would embrace all the phenomena of human conduct. In a metaphoric way he can be seen as a late child of Renaissance humanism. The human being appeared to him in its totality:

as a body structure, as neural and behavioral processes, and as a healthy or troubled personality. It is impossible to imagine Bekhterev satisfied with a "scientific" understanding of man; this could only be a step toward practical clinical applications, philosophical elaborations, or further studies. Bekhterev was aware of his own erudition and enormous energy and ventured to fill the whole explored area of the study of man. In contemporary philosophical slang one might call his efforts attempts to overcome the alienation of the science of man from the being of man.

Extending the metaphor, one might say that Bekhterev's legacy is as irreducible to any particular product of his activity as that of the Renaissance humanists. Some humanists, who left behind nothing of themselves but private letters, yet represent for us the very spirit of Renaissance life and culture.[33]

Here again is a drastic contrast to Pavlov. If Bekhterev was a humanist, Pavlov was obviously a specialist. Digestive glands in the beginning, higher nervous processes later—those were Pavlov's objects of study. Either insulated in the "tower of silence" or fixed to the laboratory stand, but always separated from real life and sealed off in a "space of experiment," Pavlov's subjects lived in a world designed by nineteenth-century naturalism. It is not strange, therefore, that at the height of their dispute Pavlov claimed that Bekhterev "debased" science and that he and his allies opposed Bekhterev "in the name of science."[34] Bekhterev's aims seemed to Pavlov strange and unscientific.

Probably most interesting is the fact that the humanist Bekhterev did once fall under the spell of scientific ideology and did try to focus his activity onto one basic scientific unit—the so-called associative reflexes. He failed, and the superficial unity of his reflexology went to pieces under the force of his own humanistic orientation. But the details of this story will come a bit later.

In 1893 Bekhterev left Kazan for St. Petersburg, where he was appointed professor of mental and nervous diseases at the Military Medical Academy. His organizational efforts in his new home yielded a neurological hospital with well-equipped laboratories, the start of the Russian Society of Normal and Pathological Psychology, and a new journal, *Review of Psychiatry, Neurology, and Experimental Psychology.* After the renovation of the neurological hospital, Bekhterev established the first special neurosurgery clinic in Russia, under his personal supervision.

The major themes of Bekhterev's research during this period were the localization of functions in the cortex; hysteria, hypnotism, and psychoneuroses; and mass psychology and "psychological contagion." In 1897, on the occasion of the anniversary meeting of the Military Medical Academy, Bekhterev delivered a lecture entitled "Suggestion and Its Role in Social Life."[35] In it he noted that apart from medical suggestion under hypnosis there was a whole domain of human conduct that could not be explained as rational and conscious behavior. Authoritative views, beliefs, and ideologies—all highly influential factors of social life—penetrate the mind beyond the control of consciousness. Bekhterev emphasized the importance of psychological contagion, the waves of excitation that can sweep from person to person, creating an endless chain of emotional reactions similar to a contagion of illness. He discussed cases of religious hysteria, then spreading in Russia, that included mass hallucinations and visions. He concluded that traditional mentalistic psychology was absolutely helpless in such cases, since it artificially secluded itself in a world of rational, conscious processes and had no objective methods for the study of complex and seemingly irrational phenomena.

By the turn of the century Bekhterev thought he had found an objective method for the study of human behavior in his work on reflexes. As early as the 1880s, studying the localization of functions in the cortex, Bekhterev had used the method of "natural reflexes," whose essence was to observe the natural reactions of an animal before and after the extirpation of an appropriate region of the cortex. For example, a dog approaching a cat undergoes a series of respiratory changes. Electric stimulation of cortical respiratory centers will evoke the same respiratory responses in the absence of the cat; but these changes disappear after removal of the centers.

Later on Bekhterev designed a method for the study of artificial, associative reflexes.[36] Electric stimulation of the sole of a man's foot was associated with other stimuli, both visual and auditory. After some trials the reflex of the sole was evoked in response to the artificial stimulus. Reactions were registered with the help of a paper-and-ink recorder. This simple and reliable method obviously had numerous advantages over the Pavlovian experiments with salivary reflexes, which required surgery and could not be applied to human subjects.

The advantages of the method of associative reflexes seemed so obvious that Bekhterev could not tolerate the growing fame of Pavlov as the "founder" of the method of reflexes. Disputes over priority and the validity of the results achieved by the rivals erupted with increasing frequency. Here is a characteristic case reported by the eyewitness Boris Babkin.[37] Belitsky, one of Bekhterev's collaborators, claimed that after surgical extirpation of the cerebral cortex in the region of the salivatory centers all associative reflexes disappeared. Because these experiments were connected with the physiology of digestion, they were repeated in Pavlov's laboratory. It was discovered that various natural conditional reflexes, as well as artificially formed ones, were fully preserved. It was also shown in a later experiment that extirpation of the cortical centers of gastric glands does not harm the formation of gastric reflexes. Responding to this experimentally proved criticism, Bekhterev pointed out that subcortical structures could rapidly compensate for the function of cortical areas. (This view eventually proved to be correct.) Pavlov dismissed this explanation as a groundless hypothesis and accused Bekhterev of negligence in his physiological experiments. The case made Pavlov suspicious of any result obtained in Bekhterev's laboratories.

This story gives us a clear-cut notion of the characters of both scientists. For Pavlov it was unthinkable to report experimental data without double-checking, collateral experiments, and supplementary studies. For Bekhterev the general picture of brain functions was much more important than the predictable details, which he depicted with the help of intuition. It is curious that Pavlov hastened to discard all of Bekhterev's reflexological experiments without any attempt to repeat those experiments using human subjects.

The wide program of studies on human associative reflexes that Bekhterev developed in the 1900s coincided with his grandiose new enterprise—the establishment of the Psychoneurological Institute in St. Petersburg. Here again he demonstrated his uniqueness. Bekhterev was already convinced that the method of associative reflexes would be a major tool for the behavioral sciences. This would have led an ordinary scholar toward the establishment of a reflexological laboratory. But for the humanist Bekhterev the climax of the experiments with associative reflexes was overshadowed by the establishment of the institute, whose goals greatly exceeded the bounds of reflexology. The Psychoneurological Institute, one might assert, was to be a substitute for Bekhterev's personal involvement in all aspects of the study of man—that is, an interdisciplinary body of students, scholars, and physicians studying the human subject from all possible perspectives. In a certain sense it was a "collective Bekhterev."

Administratively it was a private university (unlike other Russian universities, which were state-controlled) with a faculty for general instruction and graduate schools in medicine, education, and law. There were several affiliate laboratories and research units, such as the antialcoholism center, the neurosurgical clinic, and the laboratory of child psychology. The institute was unprecedentedly democratic:

no political loyalty certificates were required, and no nationality quotas were observed. It was also one of the first coeducational colleges in Russia. The ruling body of the institute was an academic council elected by faculty and staff. A student committee had wide responsibilities over the problems of everyday institute life.

All of these liberties might seem natural, but they must be observed against the background of the situation in other Russian universities. At Moscow University, for example, students were encouraged to take scholarships for study abroad. This was an attempt to reduce the number of students in Moscow and thus to diminish political unrest. The quota for Jewish residents in the big cities was vigilantly observed; this restriction forced some Jewish women who wanted to attend college to register as prostitutes in order to obtain temporary residence permits, as "self-employed" persons.[38] And unlike the Psychoneurological Institute the majority of Russian universities cultivated the characteristic arrogance of the European university establishment toward students and subordinates.

In February 1908, at the beginning of the new semester, Bekhterev delivered a speech in which he outlined the goals of the institute. He pointed out that, among the specialties of Russian higher education, there was none dedicated to the study of man. There were lawyers, engineers, and physicians, but no special training for those interested in human behavior, the development of personality, or the psychological causes of crime and delinquency. Filling this gap, he concluded, would be the task of the Psychoneurological Institute.[39]

Bekhterev's program attracted hundreds of students and also the most open-minded and gifted professors, among them the historian Eugene Tarle, the sociologist (one of the first in Russia) Maxim Kovalevsky, the psychologist Alexander Lazursky, the specialist in comparative animal psychology Vladimir Vagner, and the physiologist Nikolai Vvedensky.

For a while it seemed that Bekhterev's aim was nearly achieved. The institute worked efficiently and gained great popularity. The method of associative reflexes, beyond its scientific significance, promised interesting practical applications. Bekhterev reported in 1912 that associative reflexes cannot be suppressed by an individual's conscious efforts. This finding led him to apply the reflexological method to the detection of simulated (or "functional") blindness, deafness, and anesthesia: When electric stimulation followed flashes of light, a subject simulating blindness could not help but form the associative reflex, and when the flash was used without electric reinforcement, he responded to the stimulus. This method was demonstrated during the Physiological Exhibition in Dresden and won first prize.[40]

In the field of psychiatry, Bekhterev introduced a behavioral therapy for alcoholism in which associated defense responses were attached to the sight and smell of vodka. He also popularized a form of group therapy in which hypnotic suggestion was amplified by the effect of psychological contagion. This later became the classical method for alcoholism clinics.

Neither Bekhterev nor his institute was secluded from the political unrest of the times. The 1900s were a period of rapid and sometimes feverish growth of political activity. Legal, illegal, and semilegal parties and groups flourished in colleges and universities, and the police establishment grew more inquisitive and repressive in response. (There is a French saying applicable to the Russian scene: "For each monsieur there is a dossier.")

Here, for example, are some lines from the dossier of "academician Bekhterev" later discovered in the police archives: "Institute Assembly, more than 150 professors and lecturers, has obvious antigovernmental attitudes. . . . In the tearoom of the institute a library of illegal literature was seized. . . . All political parties without exceptions have their members in the institute. . . . Huge crowd of students organized a meeting and were being dispersed by cossacks when academician Bekhterev appeared in his general of medical corps uniform and ordered withdrawal of the forces. . . ."[41]

Bekhterev's abhorrence of chauvinism and nationalistic oppression showed clearly in his reaction to the Mendel Beilis case. In 1911 educated Russia was stunned and drawn into dispute by this Russian equivalent of the Dreyfus trial. A Jewish citizen of Kiev, Beilis was accused of the ritual slaying of a Christian boy in order to obtain blood for some mysterious Jewish ceremony. All the details of the investigation, including contradictory statements and much outright nonsense about Jewish customs, indicated that the case had been fabricated; but it was also clear that powerful political forces were behind the prosecution.

When Bekhterev was invited to participate in the case as a psychiatric expert, he recognized that it was not only the case but the investigation itself that required a professional psychological perspective.[42] Anti-Semitic hysteria had clearly distorted the testimony and the analysis of evidence. For example, one prosecution argument was that the number of wounds, thirteen, was not accidental but reflected a "magic number" in the Jewish ritual of sacrifice. Bekhterev resisted the atmosphere of prejudice and ordered a reexamination of the body, which revealed that the true number of wounds was fourteen. This simple fact halted many of the speculations about magic rituals. On the basis of his experience and his work in psychiatry, Bekhterev hypothesized that the murder could have been committed by a group of psychopaths in a state of emotional excitement.

Later, after Beilis had been acquitted, it was shown that Bekhterev's hypothesis was correct. But this success was not to bring Bekhterev much happiness. After the Beilis trial he was labeled a philo-Semite who had "spoiled" an important political action. To make his relations with the government even worse, Bekhterev published essays in which he deplored the policy of confining Jews to a pale of settlement and argued against quotas for Jews in universities.[43]

All these actions angered Bekhterev's superiors, and he was discharged from the Military Medical Academy under the pretext that he had already exceeded the twenty-five-year term required for retirement. Simultaneously, the Minister of Education refused to approve Bekhterev's nomination for the next term as a director of Psychoneurological Institute. In a few years the institute itself was to be closed, but by now it was 1917, the eve of Revolution.

Given the bad relations between Bekhterev and the bureaucrats of the old regime, it is not strange that he welcomed the abolition of autocracy and greeted the democratic reforms proclaimed by the February Revolution. When the Bolsheviks seized power in October 1917, Bekhterev chose to stay in Russia. He explained his decision to Anatoli Lunacharsky this way: "Considering that Russia will retain this new image for a long time, probably forever, I would like to provide continuation for the field of study that I have served for the whole of my life in this new Russia."[44]

The early post-Revolutionary years seemed to justify Bekhterev's decision. He was allowed to organize an Institute for Brain Research in which he continued the studies he had initiated at the Psychoneurological Institute. He continued to publish extensively, to found new journals, and to deliver public lectures.

It was in the 1920s that Bekhterev yielded to the temptation to reduce all behavioral phenomena to one fundamental process: the associative reflex. At first glance his program could scarcely be distinguished from that of Pavlov; but a careful examination of Bekhterev's *General Principles of Human Reflexology* (1918) reveals important differences. First of all, while Pavlov, who was weak in philosophy and in the epistemological problems of science, simply took the objectivist position in the study of behavior for granted, Bekhterev approached reflexology only after substantial thought and a demonstration of the pitfalls of traditional introspective psychology. His own work with neurotics, together with data from Janet and Freud, convinced him that the study of conscious processes alone cannot satisfy an "objective" behavioral science. He also realized that, given our knowledge of the unconscious and of subconscious psychophysiological regulation, there is little point in attempting to rely solely upon self-reports by human subjects.

Bekhterev proposed the total reflexological study of man as the only method that could guarantee objective results. Stimuli, according to his thesis, could play an internal or an external role. "Therefore it is clear that the new science which we call reflexology has for its aim the study of personality by means of objective observation and experiment, and the registration of all its external manifestations and their external causes, present or past, which arise from the social environment and even from the framework of inherited character. In other words, the aim of reflexology is the strictly objective study, in their entirety, of the correlations of the human being with the environment through the mediation of man's facial expression, his gestures, the content and form of his speech, his behavior, and, in general, everything by means of which he manifests himself in the environment."[45]

Certainly Bekhterev would have been happy to explain human conduct as a complex of reflexes, yet he was wise enough not to try to reduce the variety of human behavior to a sum of the artificially formed motor reflexes he had been studying in his laboratory since the turn of the century. As a result he achieved a strange compromise: Terminologically all of his work in the 1920s was reflexological, but essentially it was as eclectic as ever, combining systematic observation, clinical methods, questionnaires, and reflexological studies in the strict sense.

One might say that due to, rather than in spite of, the inconsistency of his reflexological position, Bekhterev succeeded in developing important psychological studies under reflexological labels. The Institute for Brain Research included departments in general, individual, genetic, and collective reflexology. In the laboratory of individual reflexology, studies in differential psychophysiology combined individual profiles of associative reflexes with anthropometry, clinical observations, and even biochemical analyses. Genetic reflexology developed Bekhterev's early work on the localization of functions in the cortex but also included the study of child performance during the first months of life and the problem of interaction between hearing and vision in infancy. And the department of collective reflexology, though they used objectivistic terminology, in fact carried out the first socio-psychological studies concerning the interaction of individuals with different types of groups.[46]

As an example of a psychological study carried out under the label of reflexology, we might consider the 1924 paper of Figurin and Denisova, with the characteristic title "Experimental Reflexological Study of Early Discrimination of Combinative Reflexes in Infancy."[47] In this study an infant chose among objects on the basis of color, with the choice of an object of a certain color reinforced by food. The authors found that the infant was able to discriminate bright colors when only two objects were present at once. A fine experiment, but why call it reflexology? The connectionism of Edward Thorndike, for example, would seem to suit the experiments fairly well.

Bekhterev died suddenly in 1927. According to official statements, he had eaten unfresh canned meat; in one of the obituaries a heart attack was mentioned. Rumors called attention to the fact that Bekhterev had been a neurologist-consultant for Kremlin rulers and thus knew a great deal about their real mental status. In any case, in 1927 Bekhterev's school found itself without the direction and help of its leader.

Bekhterev had left an empire of learning that included half a dozen research institutions, such as the Institute for Brain Research, the State Institute of Medical Knowledge, and the Institute of Pedology and Special Education, and legions of former students and colleagues. In some places, such as Kharkov, then the capital of the Ukraine, the very term "psychology" was replaced in college curricula by "reflexology."

This thriving field was, however, already impregnated by the seeds of future decline. Being eclectic, Bekhterev had allowed very different, and sometimes contradictory, methodological and theoretical premises to coexist in his writings. When the struggle for theoretical orthodoxy was launched at the end of the 1920s, his theories thus became easy prey for anyone searching for a target.[48] What is worse, Bekhterev's own disciples promptly adopted the current ideological style and immersed themselves in uncompromising and unfair disputes with Pavlovians, Kornilovians, and others, accusing their opponents of all the sins of which they themselves had been accused. Instead of holding the ground that practical results were the one and only possible measure of their achievements, Bekhterev's disciples waged a struggle with the help of an arsenal of epithets like "menshevizing idealist" and slogans like "class struggle in the field of theory."[49]

To trace the transformation of Bekhterev's school, consider the career of Boris Ananiev, one of Bekhterev's most prominent disciples.[50] Like almost all of Bekhterev's students Ananiev began with the objectivist version of reflexology that considered the phenomena of consciousness beyond the scope of study. In 1929, however, Ananiev revised his position and suggested that "psyche and consciousness should not be left beyond the sphere of correlative activity [associative reflexes]; they should be examined within the framework of this activity."[51] Reflexology, according to Ananiev, should be treated as a "biosocial" discipline and should employ the objective methods of both the natural and the social sciences.

Expanding on this thesis, Ananiev suggested that reflexology should embrace the social genesis of behavior in its historical as well as individual dimensions. This social dimension is what decisively separates reflexological studies, in Ananiev's view, from the Pavlovian theory: "Associative reflexes in their essence are sociogenetic, whereas the conditional reflexes are biogenetic."[52]

At the 1930 Congress on Human Behavior Ananiev presented his program for study of the social origins of associative reflexes and simultaneously rejected the criticism that this approach was not Marxist. He argued that no certified version of Marxist methodology existed for specific disciplines, and that it should be left to scientists themselves to elaborate appropriate dialectical and materialist approaches in the behavioral sciences.

Only a few months later Ananiev was forced to acknowledge his "mistake" and to admit in the course of self-accusation that "the real founders of Soviet psychology as a dialectical-materialist discipline are neither schools nor trends . . . but the founders of Marxism-Leninism! Nevertheless we have witnessed certain attempts to base Soviet psychology on different psychological trends which are, in their essence and origin, avowedly bourgeois, instead of founding it on the philosophical heritage of Marx, Engels, and Lenin, Bolshevik experience, and the works of Stalin."[53] In the decades that followed this statement became the motto of Soviet psychologists.

What caused this reversal in Ananiev's position? Just consider the panoply of battle raging in the field of scientific methodology at the end of the 1920s. This was a period when the boundary between Party functionaries and psychologists was fairly open: Aron Zalkind, Yuri Frankfurt, and others were at the same time active Party members, Marxist-practitioners, and Fellows of psychological research institutions. For a short time a strange consensus had been achieved between political ideas and scientific problems. Scientific ideas were held to be unthinkable in separation from ideological issues. For that reason it was considered erroneous to talk separately about scientific theory and its ideological and social applications. Almost all psychological concepts were accepted as fraught with social implications from the very start. Psychologists themselves might be unaware of the impact their theories could have, but the *Zeitgeist* authoritatively suggested its own "reading" of scientific ideas.

It is not necessary to point out how artificial, if not malignant, this consensus was. It was rooted in a very special view that in any field there exists a single global, comprehensive methodology that derives from the correct sources and leaves no room for rival ideas. This approach went hand in glove with the general principle of planning that governed post-Revolutionary Soviet thought.[54] It was, in a sense, an extension of the nineteenth-century natural science paradigm imposed on all spheres of life, including ones that had nothing in common with the objects of science. The doing of science was thus replaced by the search for methodology. A glance at the special psychological journals of those days, such as *Psychology* or *Pedology*, reveals that methodological disputes occupied at least half of each volume. Obviously, the eclecticism and methodological versatility of Bekhterev's ideas were inappropriate in such circumstances.

Political and ideological struggles between different factions within the Party were tightly interwoven with methodological issues. In this ideological drama, which in a few years was to become a tragedy for Soviet science, each faction played a role. The Party chiefs tried to overtake each other, the philosophers and methodologists tried to find and possess the one true method of study, and the scientists tried to exhaust the enigma of human behavior with the help of objectivist methods. The cumulative effect of the aspirations of all these groups was the emergence of two major trends: "materialists" and "dialecticians." While the materialists were eager to stick to the natural-scientific and deterministic version of Marxism, the dialecticians tried to develop a "philosophical" or Hegelian Marxism.[55]

In the spring of 1929 the dialecticians, led by Abram Deborin of the Communist Academy, celebrated a pyrrhic victory over the materialists, who were accused of departing from the Marxist-Leninist philosophical position. Shortly thereafter the Central Committee of the Party issued a decree instructing the Communist Academy to implement the introduction of the dialectical point of view in science. Thus it is difficult to be sure whether the shift to problems of the social genesis of behavior within Bekhterev's school at this time was a result of the logical development of Bekhterev's ideas or just a response to the changing market of methodology.

The dialecticians had a very short honeymoon period, however. In a few months they were overtaken by a group of militant young philosophers under the direction of Mark Mitin, who accused them of menshevizing idealism and, naturally, of departure from the principles of Marxism-Leninism. By 1931 it had become clear that attempts to build a scientific methodology that would be self-sufficient and yet would not contradict the general principles of Marxism was doomed to failure. It is in the context of these desperate circumstances that one should view Ananiev's confession.

To see what would be left after the battle, consider finally Ananiev's paper on "The Psychology of Educational Assessment," which appeared in the mid-1930s. This paper clearly reveals its author's retreat from the dangerous grounds of reflexology.[56] It includes obligatory but minimal references to Marxism, but it turns out to be purely descriptive; it contains no hint of methodology in either the ideological or the plain scientific sense of the word. In a way it marks a return to prescientific psychology with its loosely collected observations and trivial, commonsense conclusions.

# 3

## Nikolai Bernstein: In Revolt against Pavlovianism

*In the minds of Western scholars the term Soviet psychophysiology was for many years synonymous with the Pavlovian doctrine. This seemed only natural. The defeat of Bekhterev's school in the early 1930s and the suppression of the "inner opposition" in the 1950s left the orthodox Pavlovians firmly in control of psychophysiological studies in the Soviet Union. Thus when research based on non-Pavlovian premises started to appear in the 1960s, it was greeted with surprise. Where had it come from? The answer is to be found in the work of one man, Nikolai Bernstein (1896–1966).*

*In the early 1930s Bernstein examined and rejected conditional reflexes as a sole basis for the study of human behavior. The Pavlovian doctrine seemed to him deficient and out-of-date. In its place he proposed a study of feedback mechanisms in the physiology of body movements. This was cybernetics a decade before Norbert Wiener coined the term. Bernstein was courageous enough to pursue his thesis through the 1940s and 1950s, when cybernetics was being denounced in the Soviet Union as a "bourgeois pseudoscience." When in the early 1960s most Soviet psychophysiologists were attempting to reconcile reflex theory with modern neurophysiology, in order to avoid a decisive break with the "great legacy" of Pavlov, Bernstein resisted this temptation and called for a total abandonment of the reflex ideology.*

*Bernstein was a brilliant man, equally learned in physiology, mathematics, and musical theory. Unfortunately only a few details of his life are known. Those who were acquainted with him remember him, though, as a person of deep scientific integrity, a dedicated scholar for whom intellectual compromise was unthinkable. This chapter is devoted to an exploration of his legacy.*

### The Psychophysiology of Activity

Bernstein's scientific career began at the Central Institute of Labor, where a wide range of psychophysiological studies was conducted in the 1920s. The very subject of his investigations—the complex body movements of workers and craftsmen—put Bernstein outside the mainstream of the methodological debates of the day. While Pavlovians occupied themselves with elementary forms of behavior common to animals and humans, Bernstein started with a complex phenomenon, manual work, which in principle had no analogue in the world of animals.

At first his studies centered on biomechanics rather than psychophysiology. The word "mechanics" suggests a parallel between the movements of the human body and those of machines. From the beginning, though, Bernstein emphasized the differences between a body and a machine. Even if we reduce the body to a structure of rigid units and joints, we must deal with no less than fourteen such units, each of which has some freedom of movement in relation to the others. Most artificial mechanical systems have just one or two degrees of freedom, whereas a finger tip has no less than sixteen if we take the chest as the center of a system of coordinates. (To grasp the complexity of active body movements, consider that only two degrees of freedom allow a system to move along countless paths on a two-dimensional plane.)

Because of the large number of degrees of freedom, coordination is the foremost problem in any motor act. Since the living organism is always in motion, producing unforeseen constellations of its parts, Bernstein proposed the following definition: "The coordination of a movement is the process of mastering redundant degrees of freedom of the moving organ, in other words, its conversion to a controllable system."[1] External factors, moreover, such as uneven ground or resisting material, add to the complexity and unpredictability of movement even in automatized acts such as walking or running.

Bernstein concluded that human biomechanics required a method of study different from reflex methodology or simple observation. He and his colleagues designed the cyclographic method to fill the gap between the complexity of movements and the simplicity of available techniques. Small sources of light were attached at various points to the subject's body, usually at the joints. Body movements were then recorded on slowly moving film. Even complex circular movements that are hardly detectable to the eye appeared on film in the form of smooth, "readable" curves. In order to add "flesh" to the picture, masses and centers of gravity of different parts of the body were measured. This method, with some later modifications, remained Bernstein's favorite scientific tool for decades and provided the experimental base for almost all his studies.[2]

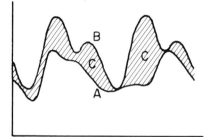

**Figure 1**

Bernstein's findings on the coordination of complex movements could not be reconciled with the prevailing views of the brain's motor functions. Since the research of Gustav Fritsch, Eduard Hitzig, and David Ferrier in the nineteenth century, classical neurophysiology had adopted the principle of one-to-one reciprocity, according to which every organ and muscle of the body has a singular representation in the cortex. Applied to body movements, this principle suggested a direct correspondence between the contraction of a particular muscle and the excitation of that muscle's center in the motor area of the brain. In other words, scientists viewed the motor areas as a kind of "keyboard," so that if they could locate the neuronal "keys," they should be able to draw exact tables or maps representing the projections of body movements onto the brain.

The principle of one-to-one reciprocity accorded well with the ideology of conditional or associative reflexes and with the schema of the "reflex arc," which depicts afferent (sensory) impulses flowing from receptors to the brain, where they "find" the motoneuron that can produce the efferent (motor) impulse that, in its turn, causes a particular body movement. The conditional-reflex model suggested a deterministic reduction of the complexity of motor actions to a simple sequence of central commands.

In his studies on the organization of body movements Bernstein proved that the principle of one-to-one reciprocity oversimplifies the processes of motor behavior and fails to explain much of the experimental data. He showed that a central impulse can produce completely different muscular movements depending on the interplay of external factors and variations in the initial conditions.

Figure 1 shows the course of a single central impulse during a regularly repeated movement. Here *A* indicates the external forces, *B* the resulting movement, and *C* (cross-hatched area) the central impulse that must be produced to achieve result B under the given circumstances.[3] If at a particular moment the required forces at the joint are represented by the curve *B*, and the resultant forces in the external field by the curve *A*, then the central impulse provides only the additional fraction *C*, which can have no similarity with the contours of *B* and is much smaller in magnitude than *A*. The findings indicated in the figure led Bernstein to the following programmatic thesis:

1. A one-to-one relationship between central impulses and movements does not and cannot exist.

2. The more complex the kinematic chain, the further away from being one-to-one are the relations between impulses and movements.

3. A movement can be accomplished only if there is a fine adjustment— unforeseen in advance—of central impulses to the events occurring at the periphery of the body. The conditions in the peripheral kinematic chains are sometimes less dependent on central impulses than on the forces of the external world.[4]

The rejection of the principle of one-to-one reciprocity and the keyboard model of the motor cortex led Bernstein to two new problems: determining the principles of interaction of center and periphery and uncovering the organization of the motor centers in the brain. As a tentative solution to the first problem he offered the model of the "reflex circle" as a substitute for the simplistic schema of the reflex arc.

The reflex circle was the first application of a feedback mechanism to complex behavioral acts.[5] It grew out of a realization that external stimuli alone fail to guide body movements and that only a closed circuit of impulses flowing from the proprioceptors situated in muscles, tendons, and joints can provide information crucial to the accomplishment of kinematic activity.[6] According to Bernstein, body movements cannot be explained as a sequence of separate reflex actions delivered by a cortical center because they involve cyclical processes of action and sensory correction that have internal (proprioceptive) as well as external constituents.

Bernstein suggested the servomechanism as an elementary prototype of the reflex circle. Today, when feedback and programming have become household words, such an analogy seems natural and unimpressive, but it was a quite radical approach in the mid-1930s, thirteen yers before Norbert Wiener gave life to the new science of cybernetics. Bernstein therefore was not only challenging reflex theory but also anticipating one of the most influential trends in Western psychophysiology. It was not until 1960 that George Miller, Eugene

Galanter, and Karl Pribram offered a model (TOTE) that could match what Bernstein had developed nearly thirty years earlier.[7]

Because of its cyclical nature and the involvement of the closed-loop mechanism of sensory corrections, a movement cannot be decoded, as was assumed by the adepts of reflex theory, through an analysis of the efferent impulse, which in fact brings only an additional fraction of motor efferentation. This fact transforms our mode of understanding the cortical localization of motor functions. We must now account for the coexistence of uncertainty in the relationship between an efferent impulse and the resultant movement with the predictability of the general contours of movement.

With his innovative methods, Bernstein in fact pioneered a new field. His study of rhythmical movements, which he modeled within an accuracy of a few millimeters as the sum of three or four harmonic oscillations (the so-called Fourier trigonometric sums), formed the basis for the mathematical theory of movements, a discipline that was recognized and appreciated in the Soviet Union only in the 1960s.[8]

The fact that accurate mathematical interpretations of movements are possible means that all the details of movement must be organized in advance. Since the efferent impulse has nothing in common with the resultant movement, which must nevertheless be prepared in advance, perhaps somewhere in the central nervous system there are movement "engrams" that contain a "script" of the whole process over the course of time. Thus at the moment when the movement begins, the whole group of engrams necessary for its accomplishment would already be in operation. This idea was later confirmed in direct neurophysiological experiments.[9]

It must be emphasized that engrams, in Bernstein's conception, have a dual nature: They contain in a compact form the formulas of movement, but they also govern the realization of those formulas. One might imagine the engram as a gramophone and a record at one and the same time. The speed of rotation of the record and the sequence of its musical pieces are determined by the work of a motor. Thus, besides the formulas of movement, engrams must contain a special mechanism—Bernstein called it an "ecphorator"—that will unfold the program in real time.

Between the central representations of movements in the form of engrams and the efferent impulses that produce only excess values necessary for a particular phase of movement, there are various intermediate blocks. One block of prime importance is the coding of messages from the central apparatus in such a way that they can become operational.

Approaching the problem of localization, Bernstein suggested as a working hypothesis a principle of simplicity. When we are dealing with a system whose structure is unknown but whose functioning we can observe, it might be useful to analyze the "cost" of performance depending on each of the variables. With the help of such a methodology we would be able to separate "low-cost" and "high-cost" performances.

Let us return to the gramophone model. Changing records, we soon discover that the structure of the gramophone is independent of the content of the records—church chorales and jazz can be played with equal efficiency, requiring no changes in the structure of the apparatus. Playing different records turns out to be an example of "low-cost" performance and indirectly tells us something about the structure of the gramophone.

Observing automatized movements and applying the principle of simplicity, we can draw conclusions about the structure of brain motor centers. For example, it has been shown that the precision and quality of an individual's handwriting are independent of the position and means of fixation in the intermediate links of the arm. The same pattern of handwriting can be achieved with the body and hand in various positions that, in terms of muscular physiology, reflect absolutely different systems of innervation and self-correction. Thus, if we assume that handwriting style is a muscular habit, then every new posture of a subject would require the establishment of a whole new system of muscular regulations. However, the uniformity—that is, the equal simplicity—of writing in different postures indicates that the central formula of this habit is not connected to a particular muscular organization. The engrams of the habit resemble a final good—personal handwriting—rather than a muscular skill. Uniformity of performance under different circumstances indicates that in engrams we have formulas for objective results—lines of written words or the performance of a musical passage—that have no predetermined motor organization.[10]

This idea decisively transforms our approach to the problem of localization. Instead of searching for centers of particular movements, it suggests that we should analyze the functional organization of habits, the hierarchical system that unfolds the engram into motor actions under particular circumstances.

At this point Bernstein's studies, once directed toward problems of biomechanics, almost imperceptibly entered the sphere of psychology, for it turns out that the contents of the engrams reflect the psychological meaning of a movement instead of its physiological means.

During the decade from the mid-1930s to the mid-1940s Bernstein analyzed dozens of movements, from walking and running to piano playing and the locomotion of invalids. In 1947 he published a cumulative record of these studies under the title *On the Formation of Movements*.[11] The major achievement of this work was its elaboration of the hierarchical levels of movement formation. Each level corresponds to a system of sensory self-corrections that enables a given movement to be accomplished according to its goal. Each locomotional problem, depending on its content and aim, finds an appropriate level of movement formation, which controls a system of sensory self-corrections relevant to the purpose of the particular locomotion.[12]

There are clear-cut differences in the formation of similar movements if they belong to different levels of formation. The experiments of Alexei Leontiev and Alexander Zaporozhets on the rehabilitation of injured veterans showed that the amplitude of impaired movements vary significantly depending on the goal of the action. When an injured subject was asked to raise his hand as far as possible, the result was insignificant. But when the same subject was asked to touch a blot on a piece of paper posted on a wall, the result was four inches better. And when he was unexpectedly ordered to put on a cap hung even higher up, he succeeded in this task, performing a movement of considerable amplitude. Significantly, when the subject returned to the abstract task of raising his hand, he failed to repeat the achievements of the purposeful acts.

According to the hierarchical model, the act of raising a hand can occur on three different levels of sensory-motor coordination. The abstract, aimless gesture corresponds to level B, which represents the spatial field of proprioceptive corrections. The task of touching the blot requires visual corrections and therefore belongs to level C of spatiovisual coordinations. The act of grasping the cap requires the apperception of an object of action, and therefore includes a conscious analysis of its shape, form, and function; these objective coordinations are carried out at level D. This example does not include the extremes of coordinational hierarchy: level A, which harbors the simplest corrections in the form of proprioceptive reflexes, and level E, which embraces the highest symbolic coordinations such as writing and speech.

The "law of superior level" formulated by Bernstein states that only the superior level of coordinations involved in a given act enters a person's consciousness. Copying a circle (level C), a subject is aware of performing the act of drawing, but he is unaware of the gestural level B, which in its turn might become superior in a gymnastic exercise.

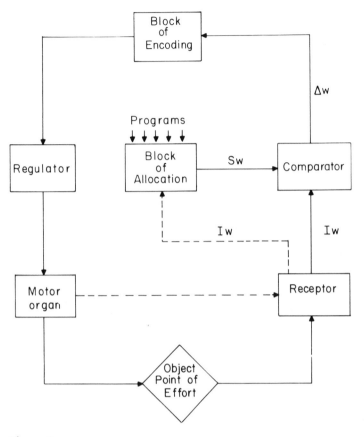

**Figure 2**

And when a subject draws a circle on a blackboard during the proof of a mathematical theorem, he will be quite indifferent to the quality of the drawing since he is consciously preoccupied with mathematical (level E) matters. In all of these cases the resultant movement will be circular, but in each of them the level of coordination and therefore the system of corrections will be different.

Given the idea of a multilevel system of coordination, the principle of the reflex circle proved too simple for the new model of the relations between center and periphery. In the mid-1950s Bernstein therefore developed a model that was to replace the reflex circle as a general principle, retaining it as an element of the more complex system.

This new model (figure 2) contains five blocks: *programs*, which contains the engrams of movement; *allocation*, which sets the required value of a given parameter of movement (Sw, from the German word

Sollwert); *receptor*, which assesses the actual value of the parameter (Iw, from the word Istwert); *comparator*, which calculates the discrepancy between the required and the actual values ($\Delta w = Iw - Sw$); and *encoding*, in which the impulses of discrepancy are transformed into the impulses of corrections.[13] Impulses of correction, with the help of the regulator, reach the motor organ that performs a movement.[14]

An important feature of the mechanism of programming and coordinating movements is its forecasting character. No complex action can be accomplished without a plan or model of the future situation. This "model of the future" is a flexible program that sets the required values of parameters according to a current assessment of the changing environment. Therefore only the objective aim of an action is deterministic, while the means of its achievement are, in principle, operational.

This model gives only a schematic representation of the organization of actions. It will vary in detail depending on the character and complexity of a movement and the number of levels of coordination that it needs. Bernstein emphasized that our knowledge of the physiological nature of some blocks is limited, especially the regulator and encoding mechanisms.

Up to this point the presentation of Bernstein's ideas may make it appear that he worked in a vacuum without contact with the rest of the community of Soviet behavioral scientists. In fact, his work received little publicity up until the late 1940s. His papers were published in obscure journals, he never taught in major universities, and the very subject of biomechanics lay far outside the center of psychological debates.

Alexei Leontiev, the future head of the psychology department at Moscow University, was probably the first psychologist to recognize the theoretical potential of Bernstein's ideas. In his *Essay on the Development of Mind* (1947) Leontiev paid tribute to Bernstein's multilevel system of movement coordination, suggesting that it could provide a psychophysiological basis for his own theory of activity, which involved a distinction between leading activity and subordinated actions and operations. It seems that Leontiev eventually abandoned the idea of building on Bernstein's ideas, and he significantly reduced the references to him in the later editions of the essay.[15]

By the 1950s Bernstein no longer simply stood outside the mainstream: He obviously went against the current. After the notorious Pavlovian Session of the Academy of Science, there was no room for non-Pavlovian studies.[16] It happened, however, that exactly in the years preceding the session, Bernstein collected enough data to prove that the ideology of reflexes not only failed to fulfill its promise but could be successfully replaced by the model of sensory-motor coordinations.

Bernstein pointed out that in reflex theory the objects of the external world are considered mere signals for reactions that are arbitrarily connected with them as stimuli. Such a model is absolutely inapplicable to even moderately complex motor actions, which are precisely adjusted to the objective properties of external agents.

Reflex theory attempted to study psychophysiological functions under inactive, artificial conditions. Pavlov built the famous "tower of silence" in an attempt to avoid external disturbances, but seclusion itself turned out to be a powerful stress factor. The artificially induced experimental reactions of animals were presumed to be proof of the homeostatic nature of behavioral functions. But all complex reactions, from simple locomotion to the finely regulated movements of crafts-men, reveal that behavior is active rather than reactive. It does not aim to achieve balance with the environment, but to change it according to purposeful goals.

The reflex arc not only failed to take feedback mechanisms into account, but also limited the reflexological experiments themselves to the study of sensory conditioning. The efferent (motor) part of the reflex arc had been unconditional under any circumstances. Therefore only reactions that had predestined results could be analyzed within the framework of reflex theory. Needless to say, such a model cannot encompass the reality of active behavior in a changing environment.

Pursuing their atomistic ideology, the adepts of reflex theory over-looked the fundamental fact that the conditional reflex is an elementary form of behavior; it cannot be the element, the universal building block of behavior.

The weight of Bernstein's challenge to the Pavlovians was amplified by the practicality of his ideas, which have been successfully imple-mented in designs of prosthetic appliances, in sports physiology, and in the training of Soviet astronauts.[17]

I have no reliable information on how Bernstein fared during the period of Pavlovianization. Those scholars who suffered as a result of the campaign against genetics, cybernetics, and non-Pavlovian phys-iology were not allowed the opportunity to tell their bitter stories even after the ideological "rehabilitation" of their disciplines. At least two things are clear, though: First, Bernstein did not admit his "mistakes." Second, not a single paper of his was published between 1949 and 1956.

The most explicit argument between the Pavlovians and Bernstein occurred in 1962 on the occasion of the All-Union Meeting on the Philosophical Problems of Higher Nervous Activity and Psychology.[18] The hard-line Pavlovians, under the direction of Esras Asratian, accused Bernstein of idealist deviations (as though nothing had changed since the 1930s). Asratian claimed: "As you know, certain groups of foreign and Soviet investigators obstinately defend the view that it is impossible to understand the essence and laws of the formation and realization of behavioral acts in the light of the theory of conditional reflex activity, not to speak of behavior as a whole. . . . Most of them are overt or disguised idealists and violent antagonists not only of Pavlovian theory but also of modern materialist reflex theory in general. They . . . ascribe the role of the behavior organizer to some unknown, mythological, endogenous principles which they term insight, goal set, or accumulation of specific energy (Köhler, Buytendijk, Lorenz, Tinbergen, and other gestaltists and ethologists) or to a 'model of the future' (N. Bernstein and his adherents)."[19]

This attack was, however, slightly out of date. The majority of reflex theory's proponents chose a moderate position, acknowledging Bernstein's achievements and agreeing that the principle of the reflex circle might be a good supplement to classical reflex theory. At the same time they decisively refused to abandon the theoretical framework and conceptual apparatus of Pavlovian teaching. Only three of the participants—Nikolai Graschenkov, Lev Latash, and Josif Feigenberg— joined Bernstein in his critique of Pavlovian theory in general and brought evidence that recent neurophysiological discoveries were incompatible with the idea of conditioning.[20]

In the mid-1960s the official attitude toward Bernstein was still ambiguous. It became ever clearer that he had foreseen a number of promising lines of neurophysiological research that emerged in the United States and Western Europe in the late 1950s. The TOTE model of Miller, Galanter, and Pribram used a servomechanism with feedback afferentation similar to that proposed by Bernstein.[21] A growing number of sophisticated neurophysiological explorations of the localization of brain functions confirmed Bernstein's hypotheses. In the climate of relative pragmatism that replaced the blind chauvinism of the 1950s, the confirmation of research data from abroad was considered the best proof of quality. Yet, at the same time, it was distressing that Bernstein's epistemological position—which was still expected to be Soviet, not Western—was so suspiciously akin to that of "bourgeois" scientists. Indeed, in his *General Systems Theory*, Ludwig von Bertalanffy practically echoed Bernstein's ideas on the active, nonreflexive nature of human behavior:

Even without external stimuli, the organism is not a passive but an intrinsically active system. Reflex theory has presupposed that the primary element of behavior is response to external stimuli. In contrast, recent research shows with increasing clarity that autonomous activity of the nervous system, resting in the system itself, is to be considered primary. In evolution and development, reactive mechanisms appear to be superimposed upon primitive, rhythmic-locomotion activities. The stimulus (i.e., a change in external conditions) does not *cause* a process in an otherwise inert system, it only modifies processes in an autonomously active system.[22]

On the domestic scene the response to Bernstein's theory was ambivalent. The mid-1960s were a "honeymoon" period for Soviet cybernetics, which had at least gained a secure position in mathematics and engineering. Cybernetists naturally praised Bernstein's pioneering ventures and propagated his ideas, sometimes radicalizing them beyond reasonable limits.[23] In psychology itself the growing interest in unconscious processes and the development of Uznadzean set theory created new theoretical perspectives that could employ the facts about unconscious sensory-motor coordinations as a factual basis for a nonpsychoanalytic theory of the unconscious.[24] The adherents of this trend took Bernstein's side in his polemics with Asratian.[25]

Pavlovian teaching, however, remained a grass-roots ideology in Soviet behavioral sciences. It seemed unthinkable to admit that for years hundreds of research projects had been conducted within a framework of obsolete doctrine and that scores of officially recognized scientists were pursuing false goals. Certain statements of Bernstein's theory were even perceived as a challenge to the very principle of determinism, which was inconvenient to say the least for some influential philosophers of science.[26]

In 1966 Bernstein's *Essays on the Physiology of Movements and the Physiology of Activity* was published.[27] This was to be his final message to the scientific community, for he died that same year.

*Models of the Future*

Some theories achieve the apex of their popularity during the lifetime of their authors, then fade away. But a few theoretical legacies become more impressive as time passes by; this is the case with Bernstein's work.

Since Bernstein's death the psychophysiology of activity has been developed in a number of directions. The first line of research is the more or less direct continuation of Bernstein's study in biomechanics and the mathematical theory of movements, including the work of Lev Chkhaidze, Israel Gelfand, and Mark Shik.[28] The second includes the few attempts to place Bernstein's theory within a broader theoretical context and to compare it with Western theories. The relationships among Uznadzean set theory, the "New Look" approach of Jerome Bruner, and Bernstein's theory were analyzed by Alexander Asmolov.[29] And I ventured to contribute to this theme, drawing some parallels and pointing out complementarities between Bernstein's theory of sensory-motor coordinations and Piaget's ideas about the sensory-motor stage in the development of child intelligence.[30]

The third and probably most promising line of Bernsteinian study centers on the development of models of the future. The idea of the anticipation of future actions, as we have seen, emerged from the fact that the "scripts" of movements seemed to be prepared in advance, before the actual movement began.

To gain some impression of the importance and power of the anticipatory mechanisms, consider an "up" escalator that is not in working order. If you step on it, you will "perceive" upward movement for a few moments. You might even feel the need to grab the arm rail to keep yourself from falling, since the discrepancy between anticipation and the real situation can be great. When at last you realize the situation, it can take another few seconds to mobilize your ability to climb the stairs.

This everyday example suggests some important conclusions regarding the role of anticipatory mechanisms. For example, it is clear that automatized skills such as using an escalator are based on an unconscious anticipation of regularly repeatable situations. Well-established locomotional models of such skills resist transformation on the ground of a "mere" fact of discrepancy between visual information (escalator does not work) and predicted situation (if the escalator is open, it works). It is also clear that the re-formation of a locomotional task takes time, requiring a conscious apprehension of the situation and a subsequent adjustment of sensory-motor coordinations to the new circumstances and locomotional goals.

Bernstein suggested the following model of complex motor action. The conceptual unit of any action is a "situation" that includes "circumstances" and a "person" who aims to fulfill some "task" under the given circumstances. The accomplishment of action requires the formation of a model of the future, which must anticipate changes in the situation. To become operational, a model must be unfolded into a set of goals ("What must be done?") and set of means ("How can this be done?").[31]

Naturally the presence of a discrepancy between predicted and actual events constitutes the best experimental condition for the study of anticipation and correction mechanisms. The simplest form of discrepancy occurs in the so-called orienting reaction. If a person hears a beep, he usually orients himself toward it; his electroencephalogram shows characteristic changes, as does the electric resistance of his skin and blood pressure. But if the beep is frequently repeated, all such reactions soon diminish. The person habituates to the stimulus. In terms of Bernstein's theory, he changes his model and starts anticipating stimuli.

For a long time it was a common assumption that the phenomenon of habituation rested upon the rising threshold of the neural system to a given stimulus. Observation and experiment showed, however, that orienting could occur in a situation without stimuli. Karl Pribram called this a "Bowery-el phenomenon," after the elevated railway line (the "el") on Third Avenue in New York. This line made a fearful racket, but when it was torn down, people who had been living in apartments along the line began to awaken periodically during the night. The times of awakening coincided precisely with the times when the trains had formerly passed. Their sleep disturbance was caused by the orienting reaction resolving the change between a long-time experience of periodic noise and the unexpected absence of "stimuli."[32] This orienting caused by absent stimuli decisively shows that a rising threshold cannot fully explain habituation. It must result from a reformation of the model and a consequent revision of anticipation.

In most behavioral situations the anticipation and therefore the model of the future cannot be unequivocal—they must include a certain degree of probability. For that reason the main trend in the development of Bernstein's ideas on anticipatory mechanisms acquired the name "studies in probability prediction" or "probabilistic prognostication."[33]

Almost incidentally, the initial locus of these studies was in the field of clinical psychology. Studying psychophysiological functions in schizophrenic patients, Josif Feigenberg realized that various reactions usually identified as components of orienting behavior were subdued or distorted. This fact, together with a number of clinical observations indicating that schizophrenics rely poorly on their former experience and sometimes ignore the statistics of the most probable events, led Feigenberg to hypothesize that a disorder in probability prediction stands behind all these symptoms. If a person does not produce fairly definite anticipatory models of the future, he naturally will not respond to discrepancies between the (nonexistent) model and actual events. This was precisely what was found in experiments and observations on the orienting reactions of schizophrenics.[34]

To establish his hypothesis, Feigenberg sought a phenomenon involving anticipatory activity that had nothing in common with the orienting reaction. If a schizophrenic patient failed to perform normal responses both to an orienting situation and to another task that required anticipation, it would prove that the prediction apparatus was impaired. Feigenberg eventually found the required phenomenon: Charpentier's illusion, in which two identically shaped objects of different volumes are presented, and the subject is asked to compare their weights. The weights are equal, but normal subjects usually claim that the smaller one is heavier. There are different explanations for this phenomenon, but all agree that previous experience and anticipation play a decisive role. Everyday experience suggests that two objects of seemingly identical matter but different volumes should have different weights. The subject adjusts his proprioceptive and motor system in accordance with this prediction before handling the objects. The actual weights of the objects create a discrepancy between anticipation and perceptual data whose net result is an illusory feeling that the smaller one is heavier.

In Charpentier's illusion, as in some other illusions, we encounter the phenomenon of taking a relative for an absolute difference. The illusory heaviness of the smaller object is induced by the discrepancy between its predicted and actual weight, whereas for the larger object the anticipation coincides with reality. Since the discrepancy occurs only in connection with the smaller object, the unconscious conclusion is made that it is in fact absolutely heavier than the larger one. These considerations about the relation between anticipated and actual weights of smaller ($s$) and larger ($l$) objects might be presented in a formalized way:

*Predicted weights (PW)*

$PW_s = n,$

$PW_l = N,$

$N > n.$

*Actual weights (AW)*

$AW_l = AW_s = N.$

*Discrepancy*

$$AW_l - PW_l = 0,$$

$$AW_s - PW_s = N - n = \Delta n.$$

*Illusory weights (IW)*

$$IW_l = \frac{AW_l - PW_l}{PW_l} = \frac{AW_l}{PW_l} - 1 = 0,$$

$$IW_s = \frac{AW_s - PW_s}{PW_s} = \frac{AW_s}{PW_s} - 1 = \frac{N}{n} - 1.$$

*Illusory effect*

$$IW_s - IW_l = \frac{N}{n} - 1 > 0.$$

If it is a probability prediction that is impaired in schizophrenics, we might expect that Charpentier's illusion would be absent in them— that in some way they would compare given objects more accurately than normal subjects. This makes the illusion especially advantageous for studying mental patients. When mental patients fail to perform a proper action, it might be attributed to their general mental deficiency, but if they perform with better accuracy than normals, this fact unequivocally confirms the hypothesis of disorganized anticipation.

In the experiments conducted by Feigenberg and Vladimir Levi it was indeed shown that schizophrenics with pronounced defect were less susceptible to Charpentier's illusion and compared the weights of given objects more accurately than the control group of normal subjects.[35]

The confirmation of Feigenberg's hypothesis encouraged further investigative interest in models of the future. A number of questions had been raised in connection with probabilistic behavior. Either there is one center of prediction that also regulates the sensory-motor adjustment or there are two different systems, one that estimates probabilities and another that prepares actions. Are there two independent functions of expectation, one for sensory stimuli and the other for responses, or just one? What does the neurophysiological mechanism of prediction look like?

To gain some impression of the concrete research being done to answer these questions, consider the following study on the neurophysiological mechanisms governing the anticipation of stimuli and proper responses according to the probability of their appearance.[36] Subjects were asked to expect dim and bright flashes and to respond with a motor reaction whenever a dim flash appeared. In the course of the experiment the pseudorandom equiprobable sequence of dim and bright flashes was changed twice without warning by the successive presentations of one type of flash. The times of motor reactions and averaged evoked potentials in the brain were registered.

Whenever an equiprobable sequence of stimuli was replaced by dim flashes only, the times of motor reactions increased for a short period but then decreased below the initial level. At the time of the study, it had already been proved that a correct expectation of stimuli shortens the reaction time. Thus the obtained data were considered an indication of a changing probabilistic model.

The measured evoked potentials showed that different components of the potentials responded differently to changes in expectations for stimuli. One component (P 300 msec) decreased whenever a single type of flash, either bright or dim, appeared successively. Other components (P 200 msec and N 200 msec) increased when dim flashes, which required reactions, appeared successively, and decreased when only bright flashes were presented.

This suggested an independent influence of stimulus and reaction probabilities on the information analysis of stimuli (reflected in P 300 components) and on motor preparedness (represented by N 200 and P 200). We thus gain some insight into the neurophysiological structure of anticipation. It might be suggested that there are two different levels or mechanisms of prediction. One is in charge of estimating the discrepancy between the probability of predicted events and the actual frequency of sensory events, while the other takes care of responses and is affected only when a motor response is required.

These data not only expanded the scope of probability prediction studies but also provided a link between Bernstein's research and similar Western studies. In the late 1960s and the 1970s the problem of probabilistic behavior was beginning to attract American psychologists who did not know Bernstein's work and proceeded from quite different scientific premises, in particular the mathematical theory of learning.[37] Simultaneously, in the field of electroencephalography, interest shifted from elementary to complex sensory functions and inevitably encompassed problems such as selective attention and decision making.[38] The latter studies could not avoid the question of anticipation of stimuli and responses. Thus very different lines of research have converged on common problems and paradoxes of behavior. One might only regret that this convergence has been mostly unilateral: While Bernsteinians have thoroughly studied the work of their Western colleagues, the latter have remained rather ignorant of Bernstein's models of the future.

Let us return now to the impairment of the mechanism of probability prediction. In the mid-1970s it became clear that Feigenberg's hypothesis that impairments of probability prediction stand behind almost all symptoms of schizophrenia needed revision. E. Bazhin, J. Meerson, and I. Tonkonogy, studying the predictive abilities of different groups of mental and neurological patients, showed that only those patients who suffered from frontal-lobe impairment failed to predict stimuli, while all others, including schizophrenics, behaved quite normally.[39] Even more intriguing were data obtained by Rebekka Frumkina and her colleagues, showing that patients with severe schizophrenic syndrome fail to classify a test sample of words according to the frequency of their occurrence in everyday speech.[40] These data suggested that schizophrenic patients are unable to form and/or use the statistics of speech elements and to predict their probabilities. Later on Frumkina and colleagues investigated the probabilistic behavior of the same schizophrenic patients in sensory-motor tests (using the Charpentier illusion) and speech tests. They found that while the probabilistic prediction of speech elements was impaired, the Charpentier test was not.[41] It seemed that only the anticipation of speech elements was disorganized by the schizophrenic process, while the sensory-motor function remained intact.

Almost simultaneously with Frumkina's studies, I conducted my own pilot study of Charpentier's illusion in patients with nonsevere ("neurosislike") schizophrenic syndrome. In this study the rates of nonillusory answers in schizophrenic patients did not differ statistically from those of normals and quantitatively coincided with those revealed in Frumkina's experiments. These findings suggested that "higher" (speech, verbal memory, etc.) and "lower" (sensory-motor) mental functions involve different mechanisms of probability prediction and that the impairment of one level does not imply disorder in the other. The model proposed by Feigenberg had, therefore, to be reconsidered.

A central apparatus of probability prediction might be regarded as a "soft" system that becomes operational only when incorporated into a particular form of activity (verbal, sensory-motor, etc.). For that reason it is inappropriate to talk about the impairment of the anticipatory mechanism in itself; we can speak only about disorders in predicting components of a concrete task or action. It is also evident that the anticipation of forthcoming sensory events and the preparation of future actions are independent of each other; this thesis implies that the disorders of probability prediction might occur in both of these systems, manifesting themselves in almost identical syndromes. And, finally, it must be admitted that we have no conclusive evidence

**Figure 3**

that the impairment of anticipatory mechanisms stands behind the idiosyncrasies of schizophrenic behavior. This problem still awaits experimental clarification.

In the course of studies of the probabilistic behavior of schizophrenic patients, a number of perceptual illusions were examined as possible material for test and control experiments. One of them, the Delboeuf illusion, although not part of the tests on probability prediction, nevertheless turned out to be useful for development of another of Bernstein's ideas.

Figure 3 shows the standard Delboeuf circles. The inner circle seems smaller than the solitary one although they are identical. There are numerous theories of why this illusion occurs, but only one thing is certain: The inner circle seems smaller only when it is embedded in the "context" of the outer one. When a subject compares the circles, he unconsciously takes the inner circle in the context of the outer. According to Bernstein's theory, only a superior level of action, in this case the action of comparison, is conscious, while the contextual perception of the inner circle occurs automatically.

It can be assumed that an absence of the illusory effect would reveal an extraction of the inner circle from the context of the outer one. This extraction or "decontextualization" could be either a consequence of the concentration of attention or an effect of idiosyncratic, noncontextual perception.

In my experiments the standard Delboeuf circles were shown to fifty healthy subjects. In eight cases (16 percent) the illusory effect did not occur. Of forty-four patients with nonsevere schizophrenia, fourteen (31 percent) experienced no illusion. Thus the difference was statistically reliable, suggesting two hypotheses: first, that schizophrenic patients have an idiosyncratic noncontextual perception as a result of their mental disorder; second, that in the schizophrenic patient the "law of the superior level" of actions is not sustained, and that it is the spontaneous concentration of conscious attention to an inferior level of action that disorganizes the illusory effect.[42]

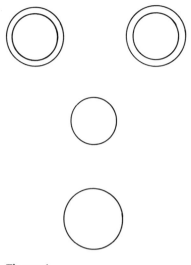

**Figure 4**

To test these hypotheses I modified the standard Delboeuf circles, arranging them to form a grotesque face (figure 4). Two pairs of concentric circles were placed as eyes, a smaller solitary one as a nose, and a larger one as a mouth. In conversation, the attention of subjects was drawn to the pictorial side of the face, and only after that were they asked to compare the circles.

I assumed that the semanticization of the Delboeuf figure would shift the superior level of action to the pictorial aspect and thus push the operation of comparison "deeper" into the levels of automatized skills.

In this experiment the same fifty healthy subjects participated along with those schizophrenics who had experienced no illusion in the first experiment. Only one healthy subject confirmed his illusionless answer, while seven others experienced the "nose" circle as smaller than the identical "eye" circle. Of eleven schizophrenic patients, eight perceived the illusory effect.

The hypothesis was thus confirmed that the introduction of meaningful features into the test picture leads to a "recontextualization" of the perception of both schizophrenics and healthy subjects. When the superior level of action is occupied by pictorial, meaningful information, patients exhibit a capacity for illusory perception. One might suggest that the spontaneous decontextualization that was observed in the first experiment takes place only when the level of conscious operation is insufficiently loaded. The operation of comparison is too simple to capture the entire attention, which spontaneously slips to a lower level and disorganizes the illusory effect. It was proved, therefore, that the schizophrenics' perceptions are quite contextual, but that they require more substantial tasks to keep their attention and awareness on a superior level of operation.

Beyond their importance to the development of the idea of levels of activity, these experiments suggest several methodological conclusions. A considerable portion of the available data concerning perception and its disorganization in mental patients has been obtained using experiments that offer subjects very easy tasks to perform. It is quite probable that in at least some of these experiments there are spontaneous shifts of attention from the test to other, perhaps imaginary objects. These shifts seriously influence the course of perception in directions that cannot be calculated by the investigator.

All of these examples simply show that Bernstein's ideas are still alive and that his legacy continues to motivate research even in areas far from his original focus of study.

# 4

## The Problem of the Unconscious

*When in 1979 an international symposium on the problem of the uncon-*
*scious was held in the Soviet Union, the most important feature of the event*
*was the fact that it took place at all.*

*The history of the attitude of Soviet science toward investigations of the*
*unconscious may be divided into three unequal stages. In the early 1920s*
*Freudian theory was popular among Russian psychologists. Most of Freud's*
*early papers were translated, and Soviet followers of his theory enjoyed equal*
*rights with their colleagues in the scientific community. But in the early*
*1930s this picture changed drastically. Publications on the unconscious*
*ceased, and psychoanalysts were forced (or chose) to acknowledge their "mis-*
*takes." Then began a thirty-year period of almost complete silence; only in*
*Georgia did some studies on the unconscious survive under the guise of the*
*"set theory" of Dmitri Uznadze. The beginning of the third stage coincided*
*with the general revaluation of methodologies for the behavioral sciences in*
*the early 1960s. Partly in the form of a fight against Freudianism, partly*
*in the context of discussions of contemporary neuro- and psychophysiology,*
*interest in the unconscious gradually rose to the surface of Soviet scientific*
*life. The three volumes of papers published for the* International Symposium on the Unconscious *(Tbilisi, 1979) commemorate the full rehabili-*
*tation of the problem.*

### Psychoanalysis in and out of Favor

The pre-Revolutionary development of psychoanalysis in Russia was
unspectacular, as might be expected given the country's relatively
strong religious tradition and rigorous standards concerning sexual
relations. In academic circles the classical German psychiatry of Emil
Kraepelin was dominant. Moreover, medical schools in Russia were
often attached to military academies. Such militarization of the profes-

sion of therapist could scarcely be favorable for the spread of a dissenting trend such as psychoanalysis. These conditions did not, however, prevent those who were interested in psychoanalysis from establishing a Russian branch of the International Psychoanalytical Society or from translating Freud's works into Russian.

Like the United States, Russia fell under the spell of psychoanalysis only after World War I. There were certain similarities but also obvious differences in how psychoanalysis conquered Russia and America. Among the similarities was an increasing general interest in the scientific explanation of all facets of life, including the relations between the sexes. The more or less educated public had become familiar with the idea that men and women are mere animals and that traditional moral codes have no universal validity. The state of mind that evolved in the aftermath of the war was also an important contributor to the readiness with which psychoanalytical revelations on the nature of sex and human relations were received. In Russia the outbreak was much more serious than in the United States, because of the Revolution and Civil War that followed the war against Germany. One did not have to be a proponent of the "biological" theory of human behavior to perceive the "animal" cruelty of people annihilating people; the animal metaphor came to mind unwilling.

While changes in the moral code in the United States were due to historical circumstances, in Soviet Russia these changes, in the period right after the Revolution, were purposely introduced as a part of the ideology of a newly liberated society. The following text gives a flavor of those ephemeral Sturm und Drang days: "Every girl above the age of eighteen is hereby declared to be state property. Every unmarried girl who has reached the age of eighteen is obliged, on pain of severe penalty, to register with the Free Love Office of the Welfare Commissariat. A woman registered with the Free Love Office has the right to choose from men who have reached the age of eighteen. Interested persons may choose a husband or wife once a month . . . . The offspring of such collaboration become the property of the Republic."[1] Of course, this incredible decree was issued not in Moscow but in some provincial town, by some obscure commissar; nevertheless it gives a colorful picture of the extent of social experimentation in the first years after the Revolution.

It would be erroneous to consider the "sexual revolution" of the early 1920s a mere revolutionary "happening." The idea of sexual liberation had in fact interested the liberal intelligentsia even before the Revolution. Consider, for example, the views of the famous philosopher, physician, and professional revolutionary Alexander

Bogdanov. Extremely gifted in a number of academic fields, Bogdanov became famous in Russia as a philosophical opponent of Lenin, who accused him of "Machism" and "positivist deviations" and made him a scapegoat for the sins of modern bourgeois philosophy. Bogdanov wrote a number of philosophical and methodological books, but it is to his utopian novels, particularly *The Red Star* (1907), a story about a community on Mars, that we turn for insight into the general mood of the Russian revolutionary intelligentsia on the eve of the Revolution. Speaking of an earthly lover, the narrator states: "Even more serious was our disagreement on the matter of our own relations. She considered that love requires concessions, sacrifices, but first of all fidelity as long as marriage exists. Actually I had no idea of seeking new liaisons, but I refused to accept the 'rule of fidelity' as a kind of ultimate principle. I assumed that polygamy as a mode of life is a superior achievement because it enables people to enrich their personal lives but also to improve the hereditary livestock."[2] Turning to life on Mars, which presumably had already reached this state of social harmony, the narrator notes with approval: "Netty has been a wife for both of her comrades simultaneously. I always considered that monogamy in our society [on Earth] was rooted exclusively in economic conditions which limited and ensnared us: here [on Mars] these conditions ceased to exist, and a polygamous society had been built which imposed no restrictions or limitations on personal feelings and liaisons."[3]

Similar ideas were propagated in more theoretical form by Alexandra Kollontai, a famous revolutionary feminist who peppered her writings with demands for equal economic rights, recognition of free love, abortion rights, and respect for unwed mothers and their children.[4]

Against such a background it is not at all surprising that psychoanalysis, as a theory that ventured to approach the forbidden but topical theme of sexual relations, was embraced by the newborn Soviet psychology. Psychoanalysis also attracted the interest of Soviet psychology as a materialist trend that had challenged the credentials of classical introspective psychology. The reluctance of the pre-Revolutionary establishment to propagate psychoanalysis also played a positive role in the post-Revolutionary years; it was a field uncompromised by ties to old-regime science. In other words, psychoanalysis still was a fresh discipline and thus suitable for adoption by Soviet psychology.

The story of Alexander Luria, a prominent Soviet psychologist of the second generation, provides a spectacular and instructive example of the fate of psychoanalytical studies in the Soviet Union.[5] In 1920 the eighteen-year-old Luria was a student at Kazan University. As he later recollected, his involvement with psychoanalysis initially took a fairly superficial form. Having acquainted himself with some psychoanalytical ideas, young Luria promptly decided to establish a Kazan Psychoanalytical Society. As a first step, he ordered stationery with an appropriate Russian and German letterhead. Then he informed Dr. Freud of Vienna about the establishment of the society. Luria was both surprised and pleased when, not long thereafter, he received a letter from Freud, who addressed him as "Dear Mr. President" and congratulated him on his initiative. Freud also authorized the Russian translation of one of his minor essays.

This humorous beginning of Luria's psychoanalytical career had an absolutely serious continuation. From Kazan, Luria moved to Moscow, where he joined the Moscow Institute of Psychology. In the mid-1920s the research themes of the institute were dominated by the "reactological" approach of the new director, Konstantin Kornilov. Luria acutely appreciated the fact that it was possible to reconcile his interest in the unconscious with reactological methodology. He started by attempting to synthesize the method of free association, which he had borrowed from Jung, with the registering of subjects' motor reactions, which was Kornilov's favorite methodology. In Luria's experiments subjects were asked to respond to a word by a verbal association and simultaneously by squeezing a small rubber bulb connected to a sort of paper-and-ink recorder. This simple method allowed Luria to compare the verbal association, which he analyzed psychoanalytically, with a motor reaction curve, which reflected the subject's psychophysiological status. He believed that hidden emotional complexes would manifest themselves in both verbal associations and a characteristic pattern of motor responses.

Although the first experiments gave interesting and promising results, Luria was dissatisfied with the artificial character of the emotions he was able to detect through this methodology. He looked for real emotions to study and found them close at hand. It was quite natural in those years to have purges from time to time in the university. Students were ordered to make reports to a special commission on their academic and ideological achievements. The commission was empowered to retain a student in the university or to purge him and force his expulsion. Luria realized the potential scientific benefits of these live experiments and began to test students prior to the purges.

Still searching for situations with strong and stable emotions hidden in the unconscious, Luria turned his attention to actual or suspected criminals. He thought that if he could study people just after their arrest, during interrogation, and on the eve of their trial, he would see real fear, aggression, and despair. As a control group Luria tested people who were later judged innocent but who for a while experienced general stress and fear of incarceration. Members of the latter group naturally had no knowledge about the details of actual crimes and thus had no specific complexes connected with such details.

Over several years Luria and his colleagues managed to collect experimental material on more than fifty subjects, most of them actual or suspected murderers. The experimental schema was roughly the following: A subject was asked to respond with verbal association and motor reaction to a list of word-stimuli that included both words connected with the crime and neutral words.

The first results gained in this study indicated that strong emotions usually prevent a subject from forming stable motor and verbal reactions. Subjects influenced by fear or by stress seemed to react to each presentation of a stimulus as if they had not heard it before, without forming a stable pattern of reaction. Subjects of equivalent intelligence, operating under normal circumstances, usually form stable responses after only a few trials.

This peculiarity of behavior under stress suggested to Luria that he compare individual responses to three different groups of stimuli. The first group included stimuli that were fairly certain to be neutral; the second, ones that were doubtful; and the third, ones that were closely connected with a crime situation. Comparisons in a single subject allowed Luria to distinguish the responses of actual criminals from those of other suspects.

This study did turn out to have practical value. Police officers directed criminal suspects to Luria. He then supplied the police with a list of the words that evoked the strongest emotional reaction and thus might be connected with the circumstances of the crime.

This study, like many other interesting scientific enterprises of the 1920s, was promptly forgotten, as it seemed then, for good. Nearly half a century later Luria realized that this study of his youth was a model for lie detection. He directed his archival notes to the State Institute of Criminology, and officers of this institution became very interested. Thus it is likely that contemporary Soviet lie detectors are designed in accordance with these studies inspired by Luria's early interest in psychoanalysis.[6]

The connection of Luria's experiments with psychoanalytical theory was rather loose. He picked up the method of free association and played a bit with the concept of "complexes," and that is all. In his theoretical writings of those years, though, Luria paid a more substantial tribute to psychoanalysis. He wrote: "Psychoanalysis decisively breaks with the metaphysics and idealism of the old psychology, and gives a new perspective in the understanding of psychological phenomena, namely, the perspective of an organic process which unfolds in the human organism taken as a whole. Psychoanalysis, together with the study of human reflexes and reactions, establishes a solid basis for the monistic theory of materialist psychology."[7]

It must be mentioned that the newborn Soviet psychology and philosophy were quite obsessed with the idea of monism as a key concept of Marxist dialectics. In the materialist interpretation of the whole continuum of life and nature they saw a possible remedy for the dualism of classical philosophy, which separated spirit and matter, mind and body, subject and object. While almost all Soviet psychologists agreed that the principle of materialistic monism should be their cornerstone, though, they argued fiercely about concrete methodology. During the height of these polemics, Luria proposed psychoanalysis as a concrete embodiment of the principle of monism in behavioral science. The teaching of Freud decisively abandoned the traditional splitting of human nature into a "high" spiritual part and a "low" physiological part. Luria and his colleagues saw in psychoanalysis a scientific reconciliation of social and biological perspectives in the study of behavior. Thus a chance was given for a unified, "monistic" theory of human behavior that proceeded from naturalistic, and thus "materialistic," premises. "In psychoanalysis," Luria wrote, "psyche is considered a part of the functioning of the entire human organism; it loses the image of an isolated entity which it had in traditional psychology."[8]

There is evidence that Luria was engaged in clinical psychoanalysis as well. At a 1925 meeting of the Russian Psychoanalytical Society he delivered an analysis of the free fantasies of a boy motivated by a castration complex and by the theme of birth.[9]

Until 1927 Luria served as secretary of the Russian Psychoanalytical Society, but in that year he resigned his position, and he later broke with the society. In 1932 he cunningly admitted his "psychoanalytical mistakes" in the Soviet journal *Psychology* while simultaneously authorizing publication of his studies on free association and hidden complexes in English. In *Psychology* Luria wrote: "The author himself in his early works shared the point of view that psychoanalysis is a monistic system that allows the laws of psyche to be traced back to their origins in elementary drives. This point of view, in its essence incompatible with Marxist psychology, was accepted in some of my works. It took a number of years for me to realize that these biologizing ideas are hostile to Marxism."[10]

In the same year, in the English version of his book *The Nature of Human Conflicts*, Luria preserved a limited psychoanalytical approach but deliberately dropped all clear references to Freud, Jung, or anyone else from the psychoanalytical movement.[11]

In his recollections, published in the late 1970s, Luria asserts that his separation from psychoanalysis was at least partially "forced." Luria claims that Kornilov refused to publish his article "The Experience of Objective Psychoanalysis," which was already in proofs, and after this their relations definitely cooled.[12]

In the late 1930s, in an article on "Psychoanalysis" published in volume 47 of the *Great Soviet Encyclopedia*, Luria got one more chance to express his view on the subject. He chose to give a more or less neutral description of the major concepts and methods of psychoanalysis, to acknowledge the limited success of psychoanalysis as a form of psychotherapy, and to reject it as a general methodology on the grounds of its incompatibility with the principles of Marxism.

From that time on Luria abandoned the theme of psychoanalysis and did not return to it until he set down his recollections in his mid-seventies.

Any assessment of the thoughts and deeds of Soviet psychologists almost inevitably faces the problem of "due to" versus "in spite of." It is axiomatic that Soviet scientists have always acted under the strain of ideological, political, and social restrictions. Thus any act or idea can be interpreted either as a form of obedience to these restrictions or as a hidden revolt against limitations. Such a state of affairs induces obvious ambiguity. One and the same act—for example, a criticism of psychoanalysis—can be interpreted as a coincidence of the theoretical position of the author with accepted ideological clichés, as the fulfillment of an ideologically prescribed obligation, or even as a concealed method of propagation of psychoanalytical ideas that might otherwise have no chance for exposure. More important, this ambiguity in interpretation exists not only for spectators but for the actor himself, who might first interpret his act as forced obedience and then later as hidden resistance. (In this regard it is instructive to recall that the rehabilitation of the problem of the unconscious, which had begun in the late 1950s, was inspired by a symposium dedicated to the criticism of Freudianism as a bourgeois trend in psychiatry.)

In the case of Luria, it is not quite clear whether his renunciation of psychoanalysis in the 1930s was a result of, or a form of resistance against, the silencing of the topic. Practically the same thing could be said of all the other participants in the psychoanalytical debates of the 1920s.

Let us turn to Bernard Bykhovsky, who in his later life became an orthodox philosopher who followed all zigzags of certified Marxism-Leninism in its struggle with bourgeois philosophy. The kind of struggle Bykhovsky waged can be easily understood from the charming titles of his books: *Debility of Contemporary Bourgeois Philosophy* (1947), or *Contemporary Idealist Philosophy Is a Weapon of the Imperialist Reactionary* (1954).

In spite of this (but perhaps due to this—who knows?), in his youth Bykhovsky fell under the spell of psychoanalytical theory and contributed to its popularization. It may be instructive to trace Bykhovsky's arguments in his appreciation of Freud. From the very beginning of his article on the theoretical aspects of psychoanalytical theory, Bykhovsky makes it clear that Freud is the leader of a dissent movement that broke with classical, "idealist" psychology. "Numerous fierce attacks," Bykhovsky wrote, "which bourgeois science had launched against psychoanalysis, failed to suppress its spread. Nowadays psychoanalysis has many influential supporters in all countries."[13] Further, with the help of appropriate references to Freud, Bykhovsky managed to secure a "materialistic" status for psychoanalysis. And in fact in his early writings Freud did unequivocally assert that the theory of psychoanalysis is a scientific superstructure that should be supplemented with the knowledge of the biophysiological substrata of the human organism and its neurological processes.

Developing his thesis on the materialistic nature of psychoanalytical theory, Bykhovsky pointed to the resemblance between Freud's ideas on the role of the unconscious psyche in the system of human behavior and those of Bekhterev and Pavlov, the recognized patriarchs of Russian materialist physiology.

Bykhovsky also noted the functional and dynamic character of psychoanalytical concepts; he was eager to conclude that this was a sign of the antimetaphysical position of Freud and thus proof of its "spontaneous dialecticity." This latter train of Bykhovsky's thought is so characteristic of the Soviet psychology of the 1920s that it deserves some attention. The specific circumstances under which the new Soviet psychology had been developed made it sensitive to the acceptance of Marxism as a scientific ideology; Marxism, however, proved incapable of producing an articulated epistemology that could serve as a basis for a reinterpretation of the concrete sciences. The endless "methodological" discussions of the 1920s on the place and scope of Marxism clearly confirm this thesis. As a result, in place of a Marxist renovation of the concrete sciences, a search for "elements of materialist dialectics" within existing scientific theories was launched.

Darwinism in biology, the theory of reflexes in psychophysiology, and, for a short time, psychoanalysis triumphed in this game of detecting elements of "spontaneous dialecticity" in scientific theories.

This state of affairs enabled Bykhovsky to conclude his article on Freud with the assertion that "despite its subjectivist appearance, psychoanalysis, in its essence, is a discipline infused with monism, materialism, and dialectics, that is, with the methodological principles of dialectical materialism."[14]

I have already noted that the problem of sexual liberation was undoubtedly among the major forces that brought psychoanalysis to the light of day in the Soviet Union. Curiously enough, that same issue caused the unfavorable attitude of Soviet officials toward followers of Freud.

As early as 1920, during his talks with Klara Zetkin, an activist of the Women's Chapter of the Komintern, Lenin criticized Freud's theory for its "exaggeration of sexual matters" and its "bourgeois views on women." For a while this comment had no consequences, but in 1925, in the midst of the power struggle between different groups of communists — a struggle that affected all ideologically important spheres — Zetkin's memoirs were reprinted in the central Party newspaper *Pravda*. The following remark acccompanied Zetkin's recollections: "Those who like to connect Freudism with Marxism and to use the 'achievements' of Freud, should think seriously about the words [of Lenin]."[15]

In 1925, however, the situation was still ambiguous. While some high-ranking Soviet officials criticized psychoanalysis, others, among them such influential persons as the State Commissar of Health, Nikolai Semashko, favorably mentioned the concept of the unconscious and supported Freud's theory of sublimation as a valuable practical approach.

An extremely interesting, and to some extent unique, report by Wilhelm Reich on the state of psychoanalysis in the Soviet Union was published in 1929. Reich was one of the first to attempt to combine the social aspects of Marxism with the method of psychoanalysis. During the 1920s he wrote and lectured extensively on "Marxist psychoanalysis" and tried to apply his ideas in a psychoanalytic clinic in Vienna. In 1929 he visited the Soviet Union and met with both followers and enemies of Freud. Because of his rebellious position, Reich was purged from the Communist Party in 1933, and he was expelled from the International Psychoanalytical Association in 1934.

Concerning the status of psychoanalysis in the Soviet Union Reich wrote: "Some statistics concerning the sexual life of the masses have already been obtained, the questions being formulated in a manner which could not even be dreamt of in Western countries where they would be considered 'shocking.' "[16]

However we assess the long-term results of the social experiments of the 1920s, the fact should be noted that a spirit of experimentation, sometimes with matters such as psychoanalysis that would be entirely alien to the future development of Soviet culture, reigned during this period. I have already mentioned the methodological premises of "monism," "materialism," and "determinism" that facilitated the infiltration of psychoanalysis into Soviet psychology. But in the peculiarly informal atmosphere that permeated the 1920s, when neither the ideological nor the organizational structure of the state had been completed, personal influences and interests played a no less important role than the so-called objective requirements of Marxist ideology.

It seems by no means accidental that, beginning in 1927, the position of secretary of the Russian Psychoanalytical Society was held by Vera Schmidt, wife of Otto Schmidt, a high-ranking communist and prominent scholar. In the 1920s people like the Schmidts enjoyed a unique opportunity to carry out their fondest ideas and whims.[17]

The pre-Revolutionary scientific establishment, with few exceptions, had either rejected the new regime or was persecuted by it. The resultant lack of intellectuals devoted to the new government threatened to ruin Russian science and education. Those few recognized scholars who were not just fellow-travelers, like Pavlov, but devoted members of the Communist Party enjoyed, for a time, unprecedented opportunites to foster particular fields of study. The case of the Schmidts is characteristic. Otto Schmidt, a mathematician and specialist in earth sciences, held a number of administrative positions during the 1920s. He was head of the State Publishing House, chairman of the Lenin Prize Award Commission, and editor of the *Great Soviet Encyclopedia*, to name some of his responsibilities. Vera Schmidt had worked in a children's home attached to the Psychoanalytical Institute. Both Otto and Vera Schmidt were members of the Psychoanalytical Society until it disbanded in 1933. In 1923 their privileged position allowed them to travel abroad, and the Schmidts visited Vienna and Germany, talking with Freud, Rank, and other psychoanalysts, who showed great interest in the work of the Russian Psychoanalytical Society and Institute and gave the Schmidts "many valuable hints" for further studies.[18]

But let us return to the problem of the development of psychoanalysis in the Soviet Union. However dangerous Lenin's warnings on the exaggeration of sexual motifs were for the further development of psychoanalysis, even more sensitive and dangerous were the social implications that Freud drew from his own work. If in the field of individual psychology and especially psychophysiology Marxists were ready to seek support in any doctrine pertaining to the natural sciences, within the domain of social phenomena they felt themselves at home and able to rely on their own concepts without borrowing from Freud, Jung, or anyone else. It must also be admitted that Freud's writings on social themes, in books like *Totem and Taboo* or *Group Psychology and the Analysis of the Ego*, were much more metaphorical and far less scientific than his clinical works.

It is not surprising that these Freudian ideas were promptly rebuffed by Marxist scholars when they appeared in the Soviet Union in the mid-1920s. However, there are different interpretations of the course of events and of the extent to which Freud's social writings were the fatal blow for the development of the Soviet psychoanalytical movement. Artur Petrovsky, the official Soviet historian of psychology, insists that, beginning in 1926, "the struggle against psychoanalysis was a topical goal of the Communist Party" and that "it was clearly stated that Soviet science has nothing in common with Freud and 'Freudism,' whatever guise these theories might take."[19]

There are serious grounds for considering this statement a mere reflection of the predominantly "presentist" position of contemporary Soviet history, which characteristically attempts to make early events fit later developments. It is true that, beginning in the mid-1930s, the struggle against "bourgeois" science, including not only psychoanalysis but also relativistic physics and cybernetics, did become a topical goal of the Party, but in the mid-1920s the social climate was quite different. For example, in his article "Geneonomic Views of Freud," Bykhovsky criticized the biologization of social problems in such works as *Totem and Taboo* and *Leonardo da Vinci*, but he did not argue the relevance of the psychoanalytical approach to the individual psyche.[20] Within the presentist view of Petrovsky, Bykhovsky's paper turns out to be an example of the total rejection of Freudian theory.[21]

It seems that Wilhelm Reich was not very far from the truth when he asserted that Soviet psychologists "had nothing against psychoanalysis as a psychological discipline, but are opposed only to so-called 'Freudism,' by which they meant a 'psychoanalytic view of the world.' "[22] It is also important to note that the hot discussions that emerged around the lectures Reich delivered in Moscow in 1929 resulted in an assertion that Reich had spoken of psychoanalysis as a science but not about Freudianism, and that while Reich's position was convincing, it was not Freudian psychoanalysis as the Soviets knew it.

It might be said that the Marxists overestimated the importance and the threat of psychoanalysis as a social worldview in competition with Marxism. But such overestimation seems only natural, since it was, after all, made by people who claimed excessive competence for their own theory and who dreamed of a total theory of human conduct that would encompass all the possible manifestations of human nature.

What exactly was the cause of the decline of psychoanalytical studies in the Soviet Union? In my view, it is essential to distinguish two phases in this decline. The first occurred from 1927 to 1930. During this period some of the most promising members of the Psychoanalytic Society left it as their research interests changed, but also, probably, because of pressure from colleagues and superiors. Among them were Luria and Vygotsky. The conditions of Luria's separation were discussed earlier. Vygotsky, who had once written a book on the psychology of art as a phenomenon of catharsis, in the late 1920s became entirely absorbed by his theory of the cultural-historical development of the psyche. Moshe Wulff, a former president of the society, had left the Soviet Union for Germany and later Palestine. On the institutional side the children's home, where a wide program of psychoanalytical studies had been conducted, was closed before 1929. Vera Schmidt, the supervisor of the home, explained to Reich that she herself closed it because she realized that "the requisite conditions for that type of work were not yet available." We can only guess what those "conditions" were. But we do know for certain that in 1928 Vera Schmidt wrote that "what the society chiefly lacks, however, are properly trained analysts with whom serious work might be undertaken in various fields of medicine and medical organization."[23] One may also speculate that the decline of private medical practice at the end of the 1920s had an unfavorable influence on analyst-practitioners.

The second phase of the decline, which began in the early 1930s and led to the complete removal of the psychoanalytical theme from Soviet life, had, in my opinion, no specific features. Psychoanalysis simply shared the common fate of all independent psychological movements. After the appropriate "methodological" or "ideological" discussions, all major groups of Soviet psychologists—reflexologists, reactologists, personalists, and pedologists—were silenced, their journals ceased publication, and all translations of "bourgeois" psychologists were banned.

*Interlude: On Uznadzean Psychology*

Whether as a specially selected target of ideological attack, or simply as a victim of the same fate that befell all independent trends in Soviet psychology, psychoanalysis in Russia deceased in the early 1930s. Curiously enough it was just at that time that there emerged a new trend in psychology that was later to be proclaimed a Soviet alternative to Western theories of the unconscious.

The author of this new approach was the Georgian psychologist and philosopher Dmitri Uznadze (1886–1950). It was in Germany, where he earned his Ph.D. in 1909, that Uznadze became acquainted with the problems and controversies of contemporary psychology. His prime interests, however, were more philosophical than psychological. As the topic of his thesis, Uznadze chose the philosophy of Vladimir Soloviev, the late-nineteenth-century Russian metaphysician; and after he returned to Georgia in 1920, he published a book on Henri Bergson.[24]

For a contemporary Soviet reader, the words "Uznadzean set theory" are associated first of all with a number of experiments demonstrating that certain attitudes or "sets" determine a subject's perceptual acts. In this simplified form set theory is considered a psychophysiological theory of expectation and predisposition to sensory-motor acts. This image has been reinforced by the fact that almost all of Uznadze's classical experiments were undertaken with sensory illusions as a principal experimental material.

Let me describe one of these experiments, known as the"Uznadze effect."[25] The subject is asked to focus his eyes on the screen of a tachistoscope and is told: "Two circles will be shown briefly. Each time you see the circles, I want you to tell me if they are equal in size or not. If you think they are unequal, tell me which circle appears larger to you." Then two unequal circles (20 and 28 millimeters in diameter) are shown several times. After these initial or "set" trials, two equal circles (24 mm) are flashed onto the screen. The effect usually obtained is the illusion that the circle shown at the former position of the 28 mm circle is "smaller," and the one that takes the place of the 20 mm circle is "larger."

Uznadze explained this phenomenon as the result of a "set condition" formed during the initial trials: "As a result of the initial trials a special condition is created in the subject, a condition that cannot be explained as any state of consciousness."[26] The interaction of the critical stimulus, equal circles, with this set condition causes the illusory effect.

Uznadze repeated the initial trials with the subject under hypnosis and then, with the subject awake, showed him the critical, equal objects. The effect was exactly the same as when the initial trials were conducted in a state of awareness—the illusory vision of equal objects perceived as unequal. Uznadze concluded: "Phenomena discovered in our experiments unambiguously show that in the psyche we have not only conscious but also nonconscious processes, which can be characterized as the domain of sets."[27]

In spite of their apparent simplicity, the interpretations suggested by Uznadze had deep epistemological roots. The concept of set clearly reflects an attempt to grasp the intentionality of human acts and thus to apply Edmund Husserl's phenomenological ideas to psychology.[28] Consider the following description: "Set is neither a partial content of consciousness nor is it an isolated content which could interact with other contents; it is a holistic state of the subject. . . . This is not one of several possible contents, but a moment of dynamic definiteness in the life of the psyche. . . . And it is, at least, a holistic intentionality directed toward a certain activity."[29]

The first sketch of the set theory appeared in Russian in 1930 in the journal *Psychology*,[30] and it obviously should be seen against the background of the methodological battles of those days. Unlike the "hawks" of reflex theory, Uznadze not only suggested that set should serve as an intermediate unit between stimuli and the central nervous apparatus, but also insisted on the psychological or at least the psychophysiological character of this unit. Unlike the "doves" of reactology, reflexology, and all the other brands of behaviorism, Uznadze rejected the atomistic approach to the human psyche and proposed a holistic and intentional theory. Within the framework of set theory, human acts appeared as active, intentional operations rather than the passive responses suggested by behaviorism.

When in the mid-1920s the discussion of the place of consciousness in a theory of behavior was launched, there were only two alternative positions. The first one suggested abandoning consciousness as a mentalistic superstition incompatible with the objective study of behavior. The second attempted somehow to save the concept. Uznadze argued that the concept of consciousness was needed in the psychological arsenal, but he also suggested considering the nonconscious set as a self-sufficient entity of psychic life. As was correctly emphasized by Philip Bassin, Uznadze "allowed" the unconscious psyche to have its specific content, whereas classical psychoanalysis took ordinary thoughts, drives, and emotions and endowed them with just one negative characteristic—to be nonconscious.[31]

One of the main targets of Uznadzean criticism and thus one of the principal justifications for introducing the concept of set was the so-called principle of immediacy. According to this principle, which Uznadze attributed to almost all theoretical constructions of traditional psychology including associationism and Wundt's psychology, external reality has an immediate influence on individual consciousness and behavior. From Uznadze's point of view this thesis is both theoretically and empirically groundless. The phenomena discovered in the experimental set studies clearly revealed the existence of mediatory mechanisms of an unconscious character situated "between" the stimuli of the external world and individual consciousness and behavior. These ideas are obviously congenial with Edward Tolman's program for the revision of primitive stimulus-response behaviorism, but they seem more radical and more theoretically promising.[32] Indisputably the attempt to grasp a specific content of the unconscious psyche was a step of great novelty and scientific ingenuity. But there are serious grounds for being more than cautious in assessing the real achievements of the Uznadzean program.

The first thing that strikes anyone who attempts to make a critical assessment of set theory is the discrepancy between its wide theoretical premises and its very narrow experimental base. Nearly all set studies revolved around visual, weight, and size illusions and thus did not exceed the sphere of elementary sensory-motor activity. The main effort of Uznadze and his students was directed toward the study of the so-called fixed set, that is, the set formed—as in the case of the visual illusion described above—through the repetitive presentation of the same objects or object relations. A great deal was also made of studying the fading of illusory effects as a result of the repetitive presentation of "critical," or test, objects; the transfer of set from one modality to another; and similar topics. Yet no really serious studies were undertaken to support the theoretically proclaimed thesis of set as a holistic, total, and intentional unconscious state of the individual psyche in general. Are we really meant to believe that the unconscious mechanisms of preparedness for sensory-motor acts exhaust the specific content of unconscious intentionality.[33] It must also be admitted that Uznadze's favorite experimental methodology—sensory illusions examined under laboratory circumstances—is hardly less artificial than that of the behaviorists. So far as I have learned, practically no attempt was made to include real-life experiments—which are typical of contemporary Western phenomenological psychology—in the methodology of set studies.

Uznadze's attempts to connect the concept of set with those of "drive" and "motivation" were abandoned at the stage of contemplative conjecture and did not acquire appropriate operational presentation.

There were a number of active forces leading to the reduction of set theory to the one-dimensional study of sensory-motor phenomena. In my opinion, the seclusion of set studies in Georgia and the lack of contact with the world phenomenological movement were primary factors. Between Uznadze's first publication on set theory in 1930 and the comprehensive posthumous publication of his work in 1961,[34] a good thirty years passed without publications in Russian and without durable connections between the Uznadzean group and the rest of the psychological community. Within Georgian psychology itself the Uznadzean line of research was accepted almost uncritically, and in time it became an object of national pride and also practically the sole permitted theme for study. Certain peculiarities of the "inner" fate of the development of set theory went hand-in-glove with its special standing among the trends in Soviet psychology. While all others suffered a decline in the 1930s and 1940s and underwent forced Pavlovianization in the 1950s, Uznadzean psychology happily survived the first period and was not seriously harmed during the second. One can only speculate on the extent to which the Georgian nationalism of Joseph Stalin influenced this fate.

## The Unconscious Regained

There were trends other than set theory in Soviet behavioral sciences that inspired, and eventually caused, the legitimation of studies on the unconscious. All the forerunners were collected and described in Philip Bassin's 1968 monograph, *The Problem of the Unconscious*, which commemorated the partial rehabilitation of the topic. Bassin's principal goal was to show that the problem is much wider than its psychoanalytical interpretations and that Soviet psychologists can therefore approach it without being compromised by alleged liaisons with psychoanalysis. It must be admitted that Bassin succeeded in this enterprise. He clearly demonstrated that all modern psycho- and neurophysiological studies—including those of the neo-Pavlovian Peter Anokhin, the anti-Pavlovian Nikolai Bernstein, and also Karl Pribram and other Western behavioral scientists—required a tentative theory of the unconscious, simply because the existence of unconscious psychical regulation had become an obvious experimental fact. Bassin emphasized the non-Freudian tradition in the interpretation of unconscious mechanisms in mental disorders represented by Pierre Janet and his students. He also mentioned the problem of psychosomatic disease as a topical medical field.

Bassin thus prophetically outlined practically all the major lines of study that were to develop in the 1970s. These are psycho- and neurophysiological analysis of unconscious sensory-motor regulation within the framework of the neo-Pavlovian approach, the cybernetic approach of Bernstein and the neuropsychology of Luria, the further development of set theory, and the gradual increase of interest in nondrug psychiatry and thus in various psychotherapeutic methods.

Only one important theme seems to have been overlooked by Bassin, namely a growing rivalry between Leontiev's theory of activity and Uznadzean set theory. During the 1960s and 1970s Leontiev's theory became virtually the official Soviet psychological doctrine, and all other trends were pressured to admit it as a general theoretical framework. The Georgians, who had managed to escape even the Pavlovianization of the 1950s and to maintain their own opinion on the subject of psychology and its proper methodology, naturally resisted this alien influence.

The tension between Georgians and Muscovites was clearly revealed during the 1979 International Symposium on the Unconscious, which was held in Georgia.[35] Most of the theoretical papers by Soviet authors avoided confrontation with psychoanalytical studies and directed their chief passions to domestic disputes. One of the leaders of the Georgian school, A. Sherozia, claimed that as concepts neither set nor activity could be derived one from the other; he argued that they are mutually conditioned by the general sphere of their relations, that is, by the sphere of personality. But he stressed that set, and only set, must be chosen as the initial point for the psychological analysis of the unconscious due to its "concreteness and at the same time its generality"! "Psychological set can be specified as the prime 'cell' of activity, consciousness, and personality. Psychological set thereby takes on the role of the initial point for the psychological analysis of these entities."[36] Vladimir Zinchenko, who shared some of Leontiev's theoretical premises but was attempting to establish his own variant of the theory of activity, took a reconciliatory position and gave evidence that "activity conditions the psychological set to the same extent as it is conditioned by it. . . . The exaggeration of either one of these two concepts can only delay the understanding of the realm of psychic life."[37]

What is probably most important, however, is the fact that both Uznadzeans and Leontievites at least confessed that "it cannot be concealed that in those years [1930s to 1950s] Soviet psychology made a mistake and threw the baby out with the bath water. The negative reaction of Soviet specialists to the defects of psychoanalytic methodology . . . was so strong that criticism of the weaknesses of psychoanalysis developed into a disregard for the very object of psychoanalytic studies. . . . Little by little, it becomes clear that insufficient elaboration of the problem of the unconscious and absence of appropriate methods of study retarded the growth of the most important fields of contemporary scientific thought within psychology as well as beyond it."[38]

This confession gave rise to a large stream of review papers on current psychoanalytical studies in the United States and Western Europe. The organizers of the symposium went so far as to include a paper by the French Marxist Louis Althusser on "The Discovery of Dr. Freud and Its Relations to Marxist Theory," in which he attempts— half a century after Bykhovsky and Luria—to show an obvious affinity between Freudian theory and Marxism.[39] Althusser asserts that this affinity is rooted in the dialectical character of the two theories and in their anti-ideological (!), scientific orientation.

One may regard the publication of the paper by the Soviet psychologist Tamara Florenskaya on "Catharsis as Consciousness: Sophoclean Oedipus vs. Freudian Oedipus" as another sign of the "new look."[40] The author revives the psychoanalytical motifs of Lev Vygotsky's *Psychology of Art*, compares them with the Freudian ideas on catharsis, and draws parallels with contemporary "culturalogical" interpretations of myth.

Aside from the publication of papers from this symposium (three volumes, 2,250 pages), some valuable institutional changes also occurred during the 1970s. At least one medical school—the Moscow Institute for Advanced Medical Studies—now offers a course that includes some instruction in the general principles of psychoanalysis and the elements of psychoanalytic psychotherapy. At the Moscow Institute of Neurology, Philip Bassin extended his studies on psychosomatic diseases. It now became evident that Soviet clinical psychologists had been "speaking prose" for many years and had been concealing their real abilities. The problems of neuroses and psychosomatic diseases had willy-nilly compelled Soviet specialists to introduce such concepts as "psychological defense," "unconscious motives," and so on, into their everyday practice, though they avoided them as far as possible in their textbooks and monographs.

Some general conclusions on the present state of the problem of the unconscious in Soviet science can and probably must be drawn. First, it has now become clear that the concept of the unconscious is essential for any approach to behavior, the Soviet approach included. Second, it seems to me that the variations of the theory of the unconscious that have been elaborated within the paradigms of the theory of activity (Leontiev) and the set theory (Uznadze) do not provide a genuine common ground for worldwide discussion on the problem of the unconscious. And third, Soviet psychologists have already faced the same phenomena and puzzles of the unconscious psyche as their Western colleagues, and they are prepared to discuss relevant topics; but at the same time they are not quite ready to develop a dialogue in psychoanalytic terms.

# 5

---

*Lev Vygotsky: The Continuing Dialogue*

*The fate of Lev Vygotsky's theoretical legacy belongs among the most pro-found mysteries of Soviet psychology. During his lifetime (1896–1934), Vy-gotsky was recognized as a promising researcher, but his cultural-historical theory of mind was clearly overshadowed by the more popular theories of Bekhterev, Pavlov, Blonsky, and Kornilov. Thirty years after his death, Vy-gotsky's ideas "suddenly" turned out to form a basis, probably the basis, of Soviet cognitive and developmental psychology.*

*Vygotsky had seemingly left behind a cohort of devoted disciples. From the 1930s to the 1950s, when his name was "blacklisted," they took risks to develop some of his ideas. After Vygotsky had been scientifically rehabilitated, they praised him publicly as a genius but were still unable or unwilling to publish his manuscripts. In the meantime their own books based on his writ-ings came off press one after another.*

*Vygotsky remains the most thoughtful Soviet interpreter of Marx's method in its relation to the problems of behavioral science. It was exactly this thoughtfulness that made Soviet scientific bureaucrats suspicious, prompting the ban that was imposed on his epistemological works for many years.*

*In recent years Vygotsky has attracted the interest of American psycholo-gists and philosophers, making him one of the best-known Soviet behavioral scientists. This is in itself a kind of mystery. Vygotsky's works are loaded with philosophical issues, literary images, and the once-topical arguments of European scholars. What could be more remote from the mainstream of American psychological thought? But perhaps it is precisely these "remote" ideas that are needed now.*

*Tools and Symbols*

In approaching Vygotsky's theoretical legacy it seems essential to retain several contrasting perspectives of analysis. A historical perspective would suggest placing Vygotsky's ideas in the scientific environment of the 1920s and early 1930s and treating them according to the measure of the times. A second perspective would embrace aspects of Vygotsky's theory that became "visible" only as a result of a half-century-long latent development and contemplation of his published and still-unpublished works. The historical perspective roughly coincides with what might be termed the official legacy of Vygotsky. The second perspective indicates the unused capacities of his heritage, which turn out to be much more up-to-date than one would expect. The two perspectives seem equally important; taken together, they provide valuable complementary images.

The facts of Vygotsky's biography take on differing value, depending on the perspective chosen. Let us begin with the first one. Graduated from Moscow University in 1917, Vygotsky joined the Moscow Institute of Psychology in 1924. In this and other research institutions, such as the Academy of Communist Education, he conducted his research until the time of his premature death in 1934.

In 1924 Vygotsky emerged on the psychological horizon for the first time as a participant in the Second Russian Psychoneurological Congress. Although practically unknown to the audience, he attracted attention by choosing a challenging and controversial topic for his presentation: the relationship between reflexes and consciousness.[1]

Aiming at the hawks of reflexology, he argued that while reflexes provide the foundation for behavior, we can learn nothing from them about the "building" that is constructed on this foundation. He pointed out that in their search for universal building blocks of behavior—animal as well as human—the adherents of reflex theory overlook the very phenomena that characterize the uniqueness of human behavior. "Any distinction of principle between animal behavior and human behavior is obliterated. . . . What is fundamentally new, what instills consciousness and mind in human behavior, is disregarded."[2] Vygotsky concluded that scientific psychology cannot ignore the facts of consciousness.

This statement alone was an unprecedented act of bravery for a young unknown psychologist. It challenged the positions of almost all leading Soviet behavioral scientists, from Pavlovians to Bekhterev and Blonsky, who rejected the category of consciousness as an "idealist superstition." Vygotsky's positive program, elaborated in a 1925 article on "Consciousness as a Problem in the Psychology of Behavior," may have appeared eclectic, but it contained in embryonic form the essentials of his future research.

Vygotsky outlined a variety of perspectives on the study of consciousness, starting with the claim that consciousness should be examined as a structure of cognitive functions such as thinking, feeling, and volition. The conscious mind thus plays the role of a regulatory and structuring apparatus.

From a physiological perspective, consciousness might be considered a reflex of reflexes. "The capacity of our body to serve as a stimulus (through its actions) for itself (for new actions)—therein lies the basis of consciousness." At this point Vygotsky relied on William James's idea that the only difference between consciousness and external experience lies in the context of phenomena. "In the context of stimuli, it is the outside world; in the context of my reflexes, it is consciousness."[3]

In analyzing the social nature of human behavior, Vygotsky claimed that "knowing others" is the basis for "knowing myself." "I am aware of myself only to the extent that I am as another to myself. . . . The individual dimension of consciousness is derivative and secondary, based on the social and constructed exactly in its likeness."[4]

Even in this early work Vygotsky singled out the phenomenon of speech as a principal force in the formation of uniquely human behavior: "In the broad sense, we can say that speech is the source of social behavior and consciousness."[5]

Although the article on consciousness was a topical challenge for the reflexologists of the 1920s, it also provides some insight into the invisible audience Vygotsky had in mind in speaking about the development of scientific psychology. Beyond Wilhelm Wundt and William James, Vygotsky showed a good acquaintance with psychoanalysis, the Wurzburg school of cognitive psychology (Oswald Kulpe), and the work of the neo-Kantian Paul Natorp, from whom Vygotsky initially borrowed the idea of the social design of personality. Later on Pierre Janet, Jean Piaget, and the Gestaltists joined the list of Vygotsky's favorite referents. He did not accept them apologetically, but rather used them as a kind of intellectual alter ego.

Throughout his career Vygotsky insisted on the developmental ("geneticheskij," from "genesis") method of study as essential for scientific psychology.[6] This point requires some terminological clarification. The terminology used by Russian psychologists and philosophers at the beginning of the century was seriously influenced, if not copied, from that of their German teachers. Kantian and Hegelian constructions were household language for Russian scholars. In this context the term "developmental" indicated not only a particular approach in child psychology, as exemplified by the work of Karl Bühler or James Baldwin, but also a general philosophy of Hegelian and Marxian mode,

which claimed that the essence of any phenomenon could be apprehended only through a study of its origin and history. For that reason
one term—development—was applied to both the individual (ontogenetic) and the historical evolution of mental functions.

Vygotsky's second thesis stated that in order to establish a scientific,
rather than a speculative, psychology one should resolve the problem
of interaction between the "lower" mental functions such as elementary
perception, memory, and attention and the "higher" ones such as
thought that are specifically human. Most of Vygotsky's contemporaries, adherents of the theory of reflexes, began with the lower functions and attempted to present higher ones as their quantitative
outgrowths. Vygotsky, as we have seen, strongly disagreed with this
strategy. He argued that psychology must center on the problem of
structural transformation of the lower functions into the higher ones.

The lower functions do not disappear in human subjects, but they
are structured and organized according to specifically human social
goals. Vygotsky used the Hegelian term "superceded" (*aufgehoben*) to
designate the transformation of natural functions into "cultural" ones.[7]

From Vygotsky's point of view, if one decomposes the higher mental
functions, one finds nothing but the natural, lower skills. This fact
secures the scientific status of behavioral theory, which needs no speculative categories of spiritual life to approach the higher functions. All
the "building blocks" of behavior seem absolutely material and can
be apprehended by ordinary empirical methods. Vygotsky stressed
that the latter statement does not mean that higher functions can be
reduced to lower ones. Decomposition shows us only the material,
but says nothing about the construction of higher functions. The principle of this construction is the kernel of the problem.[8]

Vygotsky rejected popular attempts to locate the principle of organization inside the human psyche and suggested searching for it
outside. He suggested an analogy with the tools that are interposed
between the hand and the object on which a person acts. Like material
tools, psychological tools are artificial formations. By their nature, both
are social. While technical means are directed toward the control of
the processes in nature, psychological tools master the natural behavioral processes of the individual. Examples of psychological tools
and their complexes would include signs, mnemonic techniques, and
various systems for counting.

If in elementary memory event $A$ is connected with event $B$ by the
natural ability of the human brain, in mnemotechnique this relation
is replaced by two others: $A$ to $X$ and $X$ to $B$, where $X$ is an artificial

psychological tool—a knot in a handkerchief, a written note, or a mnemonic scheme.[9]

Emphasizing the analogy with external tools, Vygotsky called his approach an "instrumental method." He was obviously attracted by the following parallel: In the external world the interaction between tool and object of action, both of which are material, results in a "product" that might be consumed materially but also brings some knowledge about the properties of the object. This "mysterious" conceptual outcome (knowledge) of a purely material interaction, theoretically cherished by Hegel and Marx, greatly inspired Vygotsky. If material interaction produces knowledge, why shouldn't the interaction between two natural processes, $A$ to $X$ and $X$ to $B$, produce a "higher" mental function?[10]

To draw this parallel further, material tools accumulate the social and practical experience of mankind in the transformation of their construction over time. Psychological tools are also nothing but a concentration of social experience. As a result Vygotsky suggested the following thesis: "In the instrumental act, humans master themselves from the outside—through psychological tools."[11]

The instrumental method in combination with a developmental approach suggested a full-scale program of research: a study of individual (ontogenetic) acquisition of psychological tools and the stages of transformation of natural psychological functions into "higher" ones; a study of the historical development of psychological tools and the corresponding development of higher mental functions; and finally a study of the most complex psychological tool, language, with respect to its formative role for human thought.

Vygotsky's program attracted a group of young psychologists that included Alexander Luria and Alexei Leontiev. Studies conducted in research institutions in Moscow and later in Kharkov and Leningrad contributed to the project.[12] Young Vygotskians were, for the most part, reluctant to engage in those fiery debates on "the correct direction for Soviet psychology" that had been raging on the pages of psychological journals. Unlike "ideologists" such as Yuri Frankfurt, Abram Zalkind, or A. Talankin, they quietly collected data, designed new experiments, and looked for educational applications. This does not mean that their leaders—Vygotsky and Luria—were exempt from the turmoil. It was absolutely impossible in those days to be detached. But what seems essential is that Vygotsky himself never used the ideological nicknames and political allegations that had infiltrated the common language of scientific discussions in the 1920s. It seems ironic that exactly the man who had the most deeply rooted epistemological basis for his theory managed to refrain from the popular methods of fighting rivals with the help of "philosophical" (actually ideological) arguments. One might guess that this restraint had a positive effect on the scientific quality of Vygotsky's program.

It turned out that only the ontogenetic aspect of mental development was studied thoroughly by Vygotsky's students and followers. In a certain sense this line of research later became a backbone of Soviet developmental and cognitive psychology. Almost all leading specialists in Soviet child psychology—Alexei Leontiev, Alexandr Zaporozhets, Peter Zinchencko, Sr., Daniel Elkonin, Peter Galperin, and Lidia Bozhovich—started as collaborators or followers of Vygotsky in his ontogenetic program.[13]

Leontiev's study of natural and instrumental memory is a classic example of the research conducted in the late 1920s within the framework of the ontogenetic perspective. In these experiments children were asked to keep in mind several colors that would be "forbidden" according to the rules of play and should not be named while answering the experimenter's questions. Colored cards were offered to the children as possible aids. The results showed that children of preschool age failed to make use of the colored cards. They made as many mistakes, naming forbidden colors, with cards as without them. Adolescents, on the contrary, made good use of the cards, separating out the forbidden ones and consulting with them before they answered. The percent of mistakes was much higher when the experiment was conducted without cards. It is interesting that for adults the performance with cards was not significantly better than without them, although in both cases it was better than in adolescents. Vygotsky explained this as a phenomenon of internalization. Adults do not cease to use psychological tools to structure their memory, but their tools are emancipated from their external forms (cards). The external sign that schoolchildren require is transformed by adults into an internal sign that is used as a means of remembering.[14]

The phenomenon of internalization—the process of transformation of external actions into internal psychological functions—was studied in two different ways. One of these, developed by Zinchenko, Zaporozhets, Elkonin, and Galperin, centered on the transformation of external actions into the mental image or function. This perspective undoubtedly had much in common with Piaget's theory of internalization of external actions, for Soviet psychologists did in fact learn a lot from Piaget while also arguing with him.[15]

Vygotsky himself was much more interested in the internalization of symbolic tools and social relations. He was greatly impressed by the French sociological school of Emile Durkheim, Maurice Halbwachs, and Charles Blondel and the related ideas of Janet.[16] The principal thesis of the French school was that the content of human consciousness consists of internalized social, interpersonal relations. From an onto-genetic perspective this means that in the process of development children begin to use the same forms of behavior in relation to themselves that others have used in relation to them.

As an example, Vygotsky suggested analyzing the development of the indicatory gesture. At first the child's gesture is simply an unsuccessful grasping movement directed at an object. In the Hegelian terms used by Vygotsky, this is the gesture "in-itself"; when the mother comes to the aid of the child, regarding the child's grasping movement as indicatory, the situation acquires quite a different character. A gesture "in-itself" is unintentionally transformed into a gesture "for others." Other people, the mother for example, introduce indicatory meaning into the child's grasping movement, and only afterward does the child himself become aware of the indicatory power of his movement. He reduces it to a gesture "addressed" to adults, not to objects. It is essential that the child is the last person who consciously apprehends the meaning of his own gesture. Only in this latter stage can the gesture be termed a gesture "for himself."

Vygotsky concludes that "the very mechanism underlying higher mental functions is a copy from social interaction; all higher mental functions are internalized social relationships."[17]

All the studies discussed so far belong to the ontogenetic perspective of Vygotsky's theory. Vygotsky, however, insisted that the same methods be used in studies on the history of human mental functions. This approach was formulated theoretically in a 1930 book by Vygotsky and Luria, *Essays in the History of Behavior*.[18] The authors outline three crucial points in the use of psychological tools: anthropogenesis, the transformation of the natural intelligence of anthropoid apes into the "instrumental" intelligence of humans; the historical development of the "primitive" mind (*pensée sauvage*) into the modern one; and the ontogenetic development of the child's intelligence into its adult form.

In order to reinforce their theoretical conjectures about the historical development of the mind with empirical observations, an expedition to remote parts of Soviet Central Asia was organized under Luria's direction.[19] The idea of the expedition was to use the unique conditions of Soviet Uzbekistan in the late 1920s to study the psychological changes that follow the rapid and radical restructuring of a region's socioeconomic and cultural system. Practically overnight a traditional, feudal Moslem society with wealthy landlords and illiterate peasants had been pronounced a Socialist Republic. Luria and his collaborators thus had an opportunity to observe different strata of a society synchronically: peasants who lived on high mountain pastures "as if nothing had happened," collective farm workers and young people who had attended short educational courses, and students admitted to teachers college after only two or three years of school. Vygotsky and Luria hypothesized that if socially determined psychological tools really play an important role in the formation of mental functions, then radical social changes that affect the structure of such tools should have an immediate influence on the forms of intelligence.

The very first experiments on the perception of geometric illusions yielded a surprise. Only the most "severe" physiological illusions, such as Muller-Lyer, occurred in almost all subjects; the more "delicate" illusions, especially ones that required perspective perception, were experienced by somewhat educated persons but were absent in illiterates. Luria got so excited that he immediately cabled to Moscow informing Vygotsky that "Uzbeks have no illusions."[20] Years later Luria still felt upset remembering this cable, for in the Soviet Union it is quite natural to "discover" political allusions in any coupling of words.

Luria and his collaborators conducted a wide-ranging pilot study that included experiments in object classification, concept formation, and problem solving. A variety of cognitive stages—roughly equivalent to those observed in child development—were revealed. Illiterate peasants failed to perform the abstract acts of classification, using instead a situational grouping. For example, they refused to distinguish similar and dissimilar objects in the group hammer–saw–log–hatchet, arguing that "they are all alike. . . . If you are going to saw, you need a saw, and if you have to split something, you need a hatchet." Even when the experimenter suggested principles of classification such as tool versus object, or weapon versus prey, the peasants refused to accept it, insisting on the practical unity of certain objects. In all the classification tests they used one and the same "method": They either grouped objects according to principles of usefulness, or included in a single group objects that could occur together in some practical situation.

In the second group of subjects—people who had attended short courses—a sort of transitional stage was observed. They accepted abstract classification but used the situational mode as well, especially when they tried to reason independently.

The third group, which included young people who had had a year or two of school training, differed significantly from the other two. The young people easily picked up the abstract notions of class, group, and similarity. The process of abstract categorization seemed to them a natural, self-evident procedure.[21]

Luria's study thus revealed the development of the relationship between social activity and communication. Vygotsky became especially interested in the differing roles of speech—the most complex psychological tool—among the groups studied. For illiterate peasants speech and reasoning simply echoed practical and situational activity. For somewhat educated people the relationship was reversed: Abstract categories dominated and restructured situational experience.

Conducting his research in the mountains of Uzbekistan, Luria could hardly have imagined the bitter fate that awaited his studies. The Vygotsky–Luria theory of cultural development was already under fire because of its apparent resemblance to the "bourgeois speculations" of Emile Durkheim. Critics hastily accused Luria of insulting the national minorities of Soviet Asia whom he, ostensibly, depicted as an inferior race unable to behave reasonably.[22] The results of the expedition were refused publication, and the very theme of cultural development was forbidden for the next forty years. Only in 1974 did Luria manage to publish his materials and thus to state the problem once again.[23]

*Vygotsky versus His Disciples*

The posthumous development of Vygotsky's ideas has taken a capricious course, seriously influenced by factors that might conventionally be labeled "external." In the early 1930s, for example, Vygotsky's theory was severely criticized for its "eclecticism" and for borrowing ideas from "bourgeois" authors. Then in 1936, two years after Vygotsky's death, the Central Committee of the Communist Party issued a decree "on pedological perversion," accusing pedologists of conducting pseudoscientific experiments that were undermining the Soviet school system.[24] The term "pedology" designated a wide range of studies and tests, roughly equivalent to the Western "educational psychology." It could be applied to the work of almost all Soviet child psychologists in the 1920s and 1930s, and Vygotsky naturally had contributed to pedological journals and participated in pedological colloquia. The decree banned all pedological activity and placed Vygotsky and others on a "black list." For that reason the disciples who wanted to develop Vygotsky's theory had to do so without naming their leader.

For the historian of psychology such circumstances create almost unsolvable puzzles. For example, in 1940 Leontiev completed his *Essays in the Development of Mind* (published in 1947), which contained a sketch of Vygotsky's cultural-historical theory.[25] Vygotsky, however, is not mentioned in the text. This fact might be attributed to Leontiev's desire to see his book published, which would have been impossible had there been clear references to his teacher. On the other hand, as later became clear, by the late 1930s Leontiev had already dissociated his "theory of activity" from that of Vygotsky.[26] It is therefore likely that Leontiev purposely avoided naming his teacher, since he disagreed with him and attributed quite a different role to the concept of cultural-historical development. Since Soviet psychologists of Leontiev's generation are more than evasive when it comes to their conduct from the 1930s through the 1950s, it is impossible to uncover the real reasons for their behavior even decades later.[27]

In the mid-1930s a group of Vygotsky's disciples and collaborators established what later became known as the Kharkov school of developmental psychology.[28] They developed Vygotsky's theory but also abandoned some of his essential ideas. This fact seems especially important because precisely in those years Leontiev, Zinchenko, Galperin, and others founded a theory of activity that was later perceived to be the exclusive and authentic elaboration of Vygotsky's program.

The demarcation between Vygotsky's legacy and the theoretical ideas of the Kharkov school occurred in the evaluation of the role of external actions in the formation of mental functions. Zinchenko once put it in a clear-cut way: "Vygotsky's principal mistake," he wrote in 1939, "occurred when he reduced the sociohistorical determination of the human mind to the influence of human culture on the individual. The development of the mind was thus restricted to the limited dialogue of human consciousness with culture, while material interaction between the human subject and reality was abandoned."[29]

Zinchenko, Leontiev, and their colleagues claimed that in order to understand the development of the human mind, psychologists must center on the individual's practical, material activity, which through internalization gives birth to intellectual functions. Vygotsky's thesis of the psychological tool as a mediating point between objects of action and mental functions was replaced by the thesis that material activity mediates between the subject and the external world. In 1956 Leontiev reiterated this thesis, simultaneously asserting that Vygotsky's emphasis on signs as psychological tools was transitory and that his theory of activity was therefore the authentic development of Vygotsky's ideas.[30]

To understand the nature of the controversy between Vygotsky and his disciples we must change our perspective of analysis and consider aspects of Vygotsky's theoretical legacy that attracted little attention until recent years. I must, once again, begin with Vygotsky's biography.

If observed in some detail, Vygotsky's career looks very different from those of his colleagues. Unlike them Vygotsky never had special psychological training. He received his doctorate in psychology in 1925, but by that time he had already become a recognized leader of a research group that included Leontiev and Luria. His dissertation, *Psychology of Art*, was hardly a student's work; it was the product of a mature scholar, equally competent in aesthetics and the behavioral sciences.[31]

Vygotsky studied humanities and jurisprudence at Moscow University from 1913 to 1917, while simultaneously attending the private Shaniavsky University to broaden his knowledge of philosophy. His penetrating erudition in the social and behavioral sciences was primarily the result of self-education and independent intellectual work, which he began very early. By 1915 Vygotsky had already completed the first sketch of his essay on *Hamlet*, which later became a first-rate tract in aesthetics.

Vygotsky was one of those rare scholars capable of conceiving the various manifestations of human culture, alienated from each other by force of the division of labor, as ramifications of "culture" in general. Poetry, children's speech, and the social categories of primitive society each had an equal right to represent the special, cultural existence that separates human beings from the rest of organic nature. Since his early work in aesthetics Vygotsky had been preoccupied with the mystery of art, which is simultaneously universal in its appeal and strictly individualistic in its production and perception.

Vygotsky did not hesitate to use symbols drawn from art in his writings. His essay "Thought and Word" bears as an epigraph a verse of Osip Mandelstam:[32]

The word I forgot
Which once I wished to say,
And voiceless thought
Returns to shadows' chamber.

Intellectual friendship tied Vygotsky to Mandelstam. The images of Mandelstam's poetry might be found, for example, on the pages dedicated to the problem of inner speech.[33] In his turn, Sergei Eisenstein, the film director best known for his *Battleship Potemkin*, learned a lot from Vygotsky and used his ideas on preconceptual thinking in his own philosophy of cinema.[34]

Vygotsky's interests ranged from literary criticism to linguistics and philosophy, and he was never bound by any professional narrowmindedness. He considered philosophical critique and epistemological reflection no less valuable for psychology than experiments and testing. It is not strange, therefore, that one of Vygotsky's first major works was dedicated to the epistemological analysis of the crisis in twentieth-century psychology. This was *The Historical Meaning of the Crisis in Psychology*, a manuscript of approximately 250 typewritten pages that was completed in 1926 but remained unpublished for more than half a century. (In the early 1960s Luria made a public promise to publish all of Vygotsky's writings including *Crisis*. But he died in 1977, before he had been able or willing to fulfill this promise. In 1981 Vasili Davydov announced that *Crisis* would appear as part of the forthcoming *Collected Papers* of Vygotsky.[35] Meanwhile numerous typewritten copies of this manuscript continue to circulate throughout Moscow's psychology community, providing on an unofficial basis some knowledge of Vygotsky's epistemological views.[36])

In this book Vygotsky pursued a number of goals and developed a variety of themes. There are some apparently self-contradictory and paradoxical statements, and on the whole the book is not easy reading. The author's position seems deliberately unclear in many instances. It seems a "scintillation" of thought, with ideas disappearing in one place and emerging in another. The philosopher of psychology Georgy Schedrovitsky attributed this to the two-tier structure of the work.[37] Vygotsky was attempting to present an epistemological critique of the crisis in psychology and, simultaneously, a concrete program for escaping that crisis. His position was therefore constantly in flux between that of philosopher and that of researcher-psychologist.

It is, from my point of view, reasonable to distinguish the central thesis of *Crisis* from a number of collateral themes. The central thesis more or less fits the intellectual atmosphere of the 1920s; the collateral themes, although elaborated to substantiate the central line of the work, turn out to be much more up-to-date in their concerns.

Vygotsky begins with the assertion—widely shared in the 1920s—that world psychology was experiencing a crisis. He cites as signs of the crisis the excessive number of different psychologies, the uncompromising struggle between natural-scientific and speculative-philosophical theories of mind, and the absence of an articulated general psychology—a body of knowledge that could serve as a concrete epistemological guide (a "methodology" in the Russian usage of this term) for the behavioral sciences. Vygotsky assumed that the elaboration of a general psychology would provide the only escape from the crisis. He pointed to the scientific method and the method of Marx as perspectives that might underlie such a general psychology.

Analyzing such trends in twentieth-century psychology as the theory of reflexes (Vladimir Bekhterev and Ivan Pavlov), Gestalt psychology, personalism (William Stern), and psychoanalysis, Vygotsky made two "collateral" statements. The first was that any given empirical fact in the behavioral sciences is already impregnated with a specific theoretical interpretation. He pointed out that psychoanalysis, behaviorism, and traditional introspective psychology not only use different concepts, but also take different phenomena as being factual. To the psychoanalyst, for example, the Oedipus complex is an obvious and common fact. That "fact," however, simply does not exist for the other schools of psychology, which consider the Oedipus complex a fantasy.

When observed from a contemporary point of view, Vygotsky's attempts to elaborate the theme of theoretically laden data obviously resemble the recent work of Paul Feyerabend, who insists that the commensurability of data obtained by different scientific schools is more than problematic.[38]

Vygotsky's second collateral statement was that the divergence of schools is accompanied by an aggressive expansion of particular psychological systems in an attempt to create a general methodology. Tracing the evolution of psychoanalysis, reflexology, Gestalt psychology, and personalism, Vygotsky revealed a uniform pattern in the development of these systems from the initial discovery to the stage of comprehensive world-views.

The development of each of these systems starts with an empirical discovery that proves to be important for the revision of existing views concerning some specific behavioral or mental phenomena. At the second stage of its development, the initial discovery acquires a conceptual form, and this concept then expands toward the adjacent problems of psychology. Even at this stage the ties between the idea and the underlying discovery are eroded; the idea appears as an abstract notion almost unrelated to the initial empirical discovery, existing, however, only because of the reputation built upon this discovery. The third stage is marked by the transformation of the idea into abstract explanatory principles applicable to any problem within the given discipline. The basic concept and subject matter of the discipline are captured by the existing explanatory principle: All behavior turns out to be a sum of conditional reflexes, or unconscious motifs, or Gestalts. At this moment the idea loses its explanatory power, since nothing is left outside it. But the inertia of expansion pushes the idea even further until the whole domain of psychology is absorbed by one explanatory principle. At the fourth stage the explanatory principle disengages itself from the subject matter of psychology and becomes a general methodology applicable to all fields of knowledge. At this moment, Vygotsky observed, the idea usually collapses under the weight of its enormous knowledge-claims.

This somewhat sarcastic sketch of the development of scientific concepts into philosophical principles was certainly not intended as an argument against the very idea of a general psychology. It was, rather, a cold-blooded diagnosis of the forms that the legitimate effort for a general psychology had taken under the social and intellectual circumstances of the twentieth century. Vygotsky emphasized the social origin of scientific methodology; in the form of general principles, scientific ideas simply return to the social cradle in which they were born. Their social nature never left them but was temporarily disguised under the "mask" of empirical facts.

Vygotsky refused to approach the crisis in psychology as a negative phenomenon that should be "overcome." Adopting the Hegelian definitions of the categories of "crisis" and "contradiction," he considered the cause of the crisis to be its power force and therefore a force for the development of psychology in general. To master the crisis is to comprehend the forces that stand behind it. Vygotsky distinguished two of the most salient forms of the crisis: the philosophical issues and the emergence of practical psychology. In philosophy the crisis was revealed in the multiplicity of general principles that had emerged as transformations of particular psychological concepts. In applied fields (technical, educational, and clinical) the demands of practice turned out to be more powerful than the a priori concepts of traditional—experimental and theoretical—psychology.

Vygotsky argued that appropriate epistemological and practical comprehension of the forces of the crisis would lead to a mastering of the discipline's development. The motto of the *Crisis* came from the New Testament: "This stone which the builders rejected was made into the head of a corner." The "stone," according to Vygotsky, was human praxis, which had certain advantages as an epistemological principle over the other explanatory principles that had emerged as transformations of particular scientific concepts. When such concepts as reflexes or the unconscious become explanatory principles, a vicious circle of object and principle immediately emerges: Reflexes as the objects of study turn out to be explained by reflexes as conceptual units. Vygotsky sought to break the circle by adopting the concept of praxis as an explanatory principle "external" to the psychological functions under investigation. The instrumental method described above is clearly nothing but an elaboration of praxis in application to behavioral studies.

The interpretation of human praxis is crucial for understanding both the controversy between Vygotsky and his disciples and the relations between Vygotsky's theory and certified Marxism. In the latter regard, a close reading of Vygotsky's work reveals that he took the writings of Marx absolutely seriously as a philosophy and also as a concrete epistemology for the political economy of the nineteenth century. At the same time he gave no sign of submission to Marxism as an ideology. He took the most sober and, at least under Soviet circumstances, most difficult position: He treated Marx as *a* theoretician, without prejudice, on a par with his treatment of Hegel, Freud, and Durkheim. This position was revealed in seemingly contradictory statements, at least for Soviet readers. On the one hand, Vygotsky stated in the *Crisis* that he was willing to approach the human psyche on the basis of having learned the whole of the Marxist method. On the other hand, he repeatedly asserted that the categories of dialectical materialism cannot be employed as the basis for a psychological theory.

These "contradictory" statements have led Soviet and American psychologists to different but equally erroneous conclusions. Americans, represented by the editors of the English translation of *Thought and Language*, decided that the references to Marx were obligatory rhetoric unessential to Vygotsky's theory. As a result, they dropped all the vaguely "philosophical" passages with references not just to Marx but to Hegel and other thinkers. Of the 318 pages in the Russian original, American readers received 153 pages with fewer words per page than in the Russian volume. "It was agreed," the translator of the book explained, "that excessive repetitions and certain polemical discussions that would be of little interest to the contemporary reader should be eliminated in favor of more straightforward exposition."[39] It seems obvious today that in pursuing a "more straightforward exposition" the editors revealed nothing but the cultural and intellectual gap between themselves and Vygotsky.

The Soviets also missed the point in their perception of Vygotsky. They were obviously shocked by statements such as: "A theory of dialectical materialism cannot be applied to the problems of psychology." If one judges this statement against the predominant motto of the 1930s to the 1950s, that classics of Marxism-Leninism are the only real founders of psychological theory, then Vygotsky's position is clearly heretical. There is no doubt that the variance from accepted Marxist rhetoric made *Crisis* a "dissident" book. The ban imposed on its publication and the general reluctance to reprint Vygotsky's works are due to the narrow-mindedness of Soviet ideological bureaucrats, who have been frightened by his unorthodox approach to Marxism.

But, more important, Vygotsky's own disciples have failed to comprehend the interpretation of human praxis suggested by their teacher, and for a long time they simply ignored Vygotsky's emphasis on the symbolic aspects of human praxis.

To get to the root of this controversy I must add a few words about the problem of praxis in general. Some of the following considerations are inspired by fairly recent achievements in philosophical anthropology, which were naturally unknown to Vygotsky. Many of them, however, seem to be an integral part of the implicit structure of his theory.[40]

It was generally accepted by both Vygotsky and his disciples that an individual achieves his "completeness" and soundness through participation in social life. It was also assumed that the individual is a "functional organ" of society in the sense of revealing the general consciousness of society in a particular form. The individual participates in social life in two ways: through the system of material production, and through the system of symbolic interaction.

Vygotsky, unlike most Marxists of his day, clearly comprehended the fact that symbolic systems, although primarily a means for the reflection of objective reality, are to a certain extent autonomous. Human activity directed to material objects is influenced by these systems. In American liguistics this reciprocal influence of the structure of language on consciousness and practical performance had been studied by Edward Sapir and Benjamin Whorf, and *Thought and Language* specifically refers to Sapir's studies.

The phenomenon of "transference" is also important for understanding human praxis. Words or gestures usurp the meaning of material reality to such an extent that participants in symbolic interaction "forget" about objects and behave as if words and signs were an ultimate reality. The magic rituals of primitive peoples and certain aspects of the art and everyday behavior of modern men offer clear examples of such transference.

The objective, material activity of mankind is determined—at least according to Marxism—by social-historical forces. But these forces cannot be immediately perceived by the individual. Material activity is presented to the individual chiefly as fragments of the process of material production and also in the form of commodities. Commodities serve as a means of universal interaction—as a "language" of objects-as-goods and people-as-consumers. But the personal traits of individual activity are reduced in the system of material production. In Marxist slang, "personal value" is overshadowed by "exchange value." In general, on the level of the reality of material production, social life is revealed as an abstract ability to exchange skills for goods. The individual is thus reduced to an objective, abstract, "partial" being: *Homo economicus.*

On the contrary, symbolic interaction involves an immediate and comprehensive image of social life as a totality. Unlike material production and consumption, language is an integral representation of social life—universal and particular at the same time. These characteristics enable language to serve as mediator between objective social-historical forces and the individual mind. The fragments of material production and consumption absorbed into the life of the individual are connected by a superstructure of symbolic representation of the social system as a whole.

If one were to use material activity as the intermediate link between the individual and the external world—as was done by Leontiev and other Vygotsky disciples—he should take the system of production and consumption (alienated labor, in Marxian terms) as an explanatory principle. The disciples, however, never developed this perspective in articulated form. We can only guess whether this might have been due to a reluctance to apply the category of alienated labor to the behavior of the Soviet people. Unwilling to use the categories of culture or praxis as explanatory principles, Leontiev and his colleagues doomed themselves to the vicious circle in which material activity as an object of study is explained through material activity as an explanatory principle.[41]

Vygotsky, in contrast, suggested focusing on the system of symbolic interaction as the meeting place of society and individual and investigating the symbolic aspects of human praxis. Thus his interest in culture as a mediating point between individual and world can by no means be treated as transient.

Vygotsky's theory of psychological tools developed in three stages. In the first stage the emphasis was on the very fact of the usage of signs as an external means for mastering the individual's natural psychological functions. This line of research was reflected in such essays as "The Instrumental Method in Psychology" and "The Genesis of Higher Mental Functions." In the second stage Vygotsky focused on the usage of various conceptual and preconceptual means as psychological tools for the development of speech and intelligence. He distinguished a number of prelogical intellectual categories used by children and also by adults in their everyday thinking and reasoning. The fifth chapter of *Thought and Language* and Luria's *Cognitive Development* are good examples of this research. In the third stage of development Vygotsky centered on the phenomenon of "inner speech," which plays a crucial role in the individual's mastering of thought. At the same time Vygotsky elaborated the relationship between the meaning and the senses of words, approaching here the "mystery" of the simultaneous universal and personal nature of language.

Historically, Vygotsky's work on inner speech appeared as a response to Piaget's book, *The Language and Thought of the Child*. Vygotsky argued that Piaget did not understand the real meaning of the child's "egocentric" speech. Such speech, according to Piaget, is noncommunicative and a relic of the presocial and egocentric stage in the development of a child's intelligence. Vygotsky, on the contrary, claimed that egocentric speech is a transient form of utterance midway between social speech (speech for others) and silent inner speech (speech for oneself).

Inner speech, in its specific role as a discourse directed to one's own self, is an extremely folded utterance. It works with semantics, not phonetics. Syntax and sound are reduced to a minimum, while the senses of words are more than ever in the forefront. Since this is speech-for-oneself, topics and subjects are omitted, and predication is predominant. In inner speech the sense of the word overbalances its meaning. According to Vygotsky, a word acquires its sense from the context in which it appears; the dictionary meaning of the word is a kernel that is immovable, while new senses may appear with new contexts. Meaning represents the socially certified and thus universal aspect of language; sense, the unique experience of a particular person.

Inner speech is to a large extent pure thought, but still embodied in a kind of language. It is a dynamic, "scintillating" entity moving to and fro between thought and language; these do not coincide, but they cannot exist separately in their mature forms. Word deprived of thought remains a "dead soul," but "voiceless thought" is also a mere shadow.[42]

Vygotsky's disciples obviously underestimated this line of research, probably regarding it as a mere reminiscence of the literary youth of their teacher. And the number of literary examples and poetic images does grow rapidly when Vygotsky approaches the subject of inner speech. This is not accidental. Vygotsky suggested that inner speech not only represents an interiorization of the social world in the form of personal consciousness, but also contains the seed of future cultural forms that are presently folded into the subjective senses of words.

What was lost by Vygotsky's disciples has been found by contemporary philosophy. In his book on the logic of "mental dialogue," Vladimir Bibler refers to Vygotsky in his discussion of the psychology of creative thinking.[43] In the concept of inner speech, Vygotsky closely approached the enigmatic problem of creative intelligence, the form of consciousness that not only absorbs the categories and clichés of culture, but also produces unique images in poetry and establishes genuinely new knowledge.

On the last pages of the Russian edition of *Thought and Language*, Vygotsky wrote that thought itself is not the last stop. "Thought does not beget a thought, but is engendered by motivation, by our desires and needs, our interests and emotions. Behind every thought the affect and volition are standing. Only they hold the answer to the last 'why' in the analysis of intelligence."[44]

One of Vygotsky's last works, *Spinoza: A Study of Passions in the Perspective of Contemporary Psychoneurology* (1933), was dedicated to the resolution of this last "why." This book is still unpublished, which means that our dialogue with Vygotsky will continue.

*Pavel Blonsky and the Failure of Progressive Education*

*There are a number of reasons for selecting Pavel Blonsky (1884–1941) for a special case study. Although he is one of the founding fathers of Soviet psychology, he is hardly known in the West. His name appears in surveys of Soviet psychology only in connection with his activity as a pedologist and with the notorious 1936 decree banning psychological testing in the Soviet Union.[1] He was, however, active at least since the 1910s as a philosopher, educator, and psychologist.*

*Blonsky is the only Soviet psychologist whose autobiography has been published in the USSR.[2] Thus we have first-hand testimony of his life and work, which can be compared with other sources to provide interesting details about what he chose to include and what to omit. He is an especially instructive case because he exemplifies the transformation of a pre-Revolutionary scholar into a loyal and active Soviet scientist and educator.*

*Last but not least, Blonsky more than once consciously borrowed concepts and ideas from John Dewey. It is instructive to trace the fate of these concepts in a social setting quite different from their native one.*

*Reformism versus Philosophy*

Pavel Blonsky was born in Kiev in 1884 to a family of Russian, Polish, and Spanish descent. As an undergraduate, he studied philosophy and social sciences at Kiev University. The period of his philosophical apprenticeship, 1902–1907, coincided with the first outburst of political activity in Russian universities, the first strikes of industrial workers, and the 1905 Revolution.

A young liberal intellectual like Blonsky naturally could not stand aloof during this momentous upheaval. His engagement with the revolutionary movement occurred spontaneously. As he related later, a scene of workers launching a strike impressed him so much that he immediately joined them, with all the typical consequences. He was incarcerated by the police, became acquainted with professional revolutionaries, and subsequently joined the party of socialist-revolutionaries. For a number of years he was active as a revolutionary agitator—a "vocation" not atypical for Russian students of the time—but he never became a professional conspirator.[3]

His political involvement was unexceptional, since in the 1900s it was as natural for Russian students to join antimonarchist groups and parties as it would be for American students of the late 1960s to oppose the Vietnam war. In pre-Revolutionary Russia, to be an intellectual was to be liberal and antimonarchist.

In spite of his revolutionary activity Blonsky's aspirations were directed neither to politics nor to Marxism, but to ancient and classical philosophy. At Kiev University philosophy was taught by Alexei Gilarov, and psychology and logic by Georgy Chelpanov, who later founded the Moscow Institute of Psychology. Blonsky vacillated for a long time before choosing an adviser. Finally he compromised: He asked Chelpanov to be his adviser, but the theme of his graduate paper, "The Philosophy of Plotinus," was elaborated under the influence of Gilarov's lectures on Plato and neo-Platonism.

Gilarov cultivated "good philosophical tastes" in his students; and this prevented Blonsky from becoming a disciple of the "tenth-rate philosophy of those days. . . . Gilarov developed a powerful critique of the giants of philosophy as well. For that reason I could become neither Kantian, nor Hegelian, nor Humean."[4]

Blonsky was reluctant to accept twentieth-century Russian philosophy, which appeared to him to be an empty husk suffering from a lack of professionalism, erudition, and exactitude. The logical consistency and power of Plato and neo-Platonism seemed incommensurable with the modern philosophy of "amateurs." Blonsky's adherence to patterns of ancient thought was not idiosyncratic; a number of Russian intellectuals at the beginning of the century were profoundly attracted by the eternal values of Greek and Roman culture:

There are eternal rocks of value
Above the stupid management of time. . . .

wrote Osip Mandelstam in 1914.

The work of such philosophers and historians of antiquity as Sergei Trubetskoj, Faddei Zelinsky, and Alexei Losev had a profound impact on the pre-Revolutionary Russian intelligentsia. Losev managed to continue his studies in the Soviet period, insisting throughout his entire life on the fundamental superiority of neo-Platonic dialectics over all later philosophical inventions.[5]

Blonsky's critique of modern "bourgeois" philosophy, which later won him a place in the Soviet establishment, was neither Marxist nor materialist. His critique of the modern degradation of philosophy as judged from the viewpoint of the subtle logic and the consistency of the classical tradition was clearly revealed in his "Essays on Early Greek Philosophy" (1914), and partially repeated in *The Reform of Science* (1920).[6] Blonsky remained immersed in the classical tradition at least until the late 1920s. In 1928 he wrote, "I am still working on the history of philosophy, especially Aristotle and Hegel."[7]

While Gilarov ushered Blonsky into the world of ancient dialectics, Chelpanov confronted him with the perspectives of modern psychology. Chelpanov's psychological seminar was a celebrated element of the curriculum at Kiev University. Blonsky remembered that to be enrolled in this seminar was a distinction in itself. There was a special entrance exam, and those who passed it felt that they had risen to the ranks of scientific nobility.[8] A student wishing to join the seminar had to learn the problems discussed in Chelpanov's *Brain and Soul*[9] by heart and also had to read German fluently. Besides holding weekly meetings with the students, Chelpanov arranged for a library stocked with current books and periodicals in philosophy and psychology where the members of the seminar could work independently. There was also a laboratory with obsolete but accessible experimental equipment.

When, in 1907, Chelpanov was invited to take a chair of philosophy and psychology at Moscow University, he recommended that Blonsky continue his graduate studies there. Blonsky entered the university not as an ordinary student but as an almost mature philosopher. His publications at that time included a book on Bishop Berkeley and an article on Eduard Hartmann.[10] Chelpanov obviously considered him a disciple and supporter; but due to the highly independent character of his thought as well as his active involvement in political affairs, Blonsky was hardly suited to the role of devoted follower. "I was a kind of prodigal son to Chelpanov," Blonsky recalled, "bringing him nothing but troubles." Blonsky confessed that Chelpanov more than once rescued him from dangerous situations that might have led him to a bad end.[11]

In the 1910s Blonsky was still preoccupied with neo-Platonism. The other lines of his career, both psychological and educational, emerged primarily as a result of sheer need. As a student, Blonsky had to find a way to support himself. The only real job he could find was teaching in a private high school. "I deliberately emphasize this point," wrote Blonsky. "My ultimate objective was to become a scholar. Teaching in the beginning was only a means for survival, probably even an annoying factor diverting me from scholarly studies."[12]

From 1908 through 1913 Blonsky taught pedagogy and educational psychology in private high schools and teachers colleges. He soon realized that if his knowledge of the subject was modest—he had never taken courses in pedagogy—the same was true of his colleagues. "Later on our common pedagogical ignorance became more and more clear to me. . . . Even now in an acrimonious mood I define pedagogy as a science any ignoramus can talk about."[13]

Blonsky calls the years 1908–1913 the "period of my pedagogical apprenticeship" and preparation for the "activity of enlightenment." He worked through the whole history of pedagogy, beginning with Johann Comenius, Johann Pestalozzi, and Friedrich Froebel, and found Lev Tolstoy, Heinrich Scharrelman, Friz Hansberg, Dmitri Pisarev, and John Dewey to be most congenial with his own point of view.

Blonsky considered the following characteristics of Russian schooling to be the principal impediments to the progress of education: dogmatism, which stresses rote learning rather than an inspiration of students' abilities; a curriculum that does not respond to the problems of everyday life and fails to take into account the child's experience; a method of instruction that ignores the stages in the development of a child's intelligence and offers him knowledge that, in principle, he is not ready to comprehend.[14]

There is a gap between the style of Blonsky's pre-Revolutionary educational writings and their content. He recalled in his memoirs that the article "Goals and Methods of the Popular School," for example, was written as a poem in a single sitting during a bout of insomnia. This poetic attitude left its mark on almost all of his educational papers of the period. They are full of reformist temper and calls for wide-ranging changes; beyond this, however, their content is modest and unoriginal. Since he considered dilettantism a prime defect of Russian education, Blonsky attempted to acquaint his colleagues with European and American educational ideas. *An Introduction to Preschool Education* (1915) and *A Course of Pedagogics* (1916) served this goal.[15]

"Goals and Methods of the Popular School" (1916) was more programmatic. In this paper Blonsky encouraged the replacement of rote learning by a "self-apprenticeship" of the child under the rational conditions of the popular school. Instead of scholastically separated subjects, he proposed a united body of scientific and practical instruction: "The school day should be a continuous flow of exercises in labor and knowledge without an artificial system of lessons."[16] Teachers should raise scientific questions in connection with the objects and events of everyday life, thus ensuring at once the rationality of learning and its orientation toward real life. People's practical, productive activity should form the logical center of the curriculum; thus mathematics, for example, should be introduced exclusively as a "technical language," a calculus for science and engineering. Blonsky's general draft for a new curriculum presupposed a gradual ascent from the more familiar phenomena of school and family to such general notions as city and country.

Blonsky's educational program greatly resembled that of John Dewey.[17] Both were equally concerned with child-centered, life-oriented problem solving and democratic education. But their attitudes toward the "embodiment" of philosophical ideas into practical forms were quite different. Treating the relationship between philosophy and education, Dewey wrote: "For philosophic theory has no Aladdin's lamp to summon into immediate existence the values which it has intellectually constructed. . . . By the educative arts philosophy may generate methods of utilizing the energies of human beings in accord with serious and thoughtful conceptions of life. Education is the laboratory in which philosophic distinctions become concrete and are tested."[18]

As for Blonsky, two poles gradually emerged in his intellectual continuum: on the one hand, the refined schemata of neo-Platonic philosophy were situated as a lost paradise; on the other hand, daily confrontations with pedagogical ignorance and obscurity provoked dreams of educational and social reform.

Blonsky's adherence to the classical tradition in philosophy went hand-in-glove with his view of the philosopher's place in society. In a 1914 essay Blonsky, with obvious sympathy, pictured the ideal philosopher as a person "who is socially well-to-do, with enormous self-consciousness, spiritually free and a universalist." From Blonsky's point of view, the proper milieu for good philosophy was an epoch of spiritual crisis marked by serious breaks in the basic parameters of life—an epoch of critique and reflection.[19]

It seems to me that even before he began to borrow from Dewey and to create the basis for Soviet progressivism, Blonsky was already doomed to failure. From the very beginning he had split his intellectual ego into the philosopher, who rejected the philosophy of his time as an offspring of decadence, and the militant, enlightened educator, intolerant of the present state of obscurity and inefficiency, who was ready to initiate educational reforms immediately.

Blonsky proposed institutional changes that had no roots in his own philosophical beliefs and developed a philosophical criticism that did not presuppose any change in the social position of the philosopher as an independent spectator and critic. He clearly did not realize that the radical social change he advocated would undermine the disengaged status of the philosopher and that his "tenth-rate philosophers" would soon become the last repository of philosophical tradition.

In contrast to Dewey's, Blonsky's search for truth was basically ambivalent. He did not consider educational reform to be a social realization of his philosophical views; and he was reluctant to direct his own critical method toward the principles of educational progressivism. Blonsky's "Goals and Methods of the Popular School" is filled with good will and liberal aspirations (and also wide and sometimes asystematic borrowings from Maria Montessori, Ernst Meumann, and John Dewey), but it contains nothing like a definite educational philosophy or socially valid suggestions. The very language of Blonsky's writings changes drastically when he leaves the ground of philosophy and turns to educational problems. Where in Dewey's studies we see continuity, in Blonsky's there is a schism.

This fact is not simply a peculiarity of Blonsky's career. Rather, it indicates the principal dissimilarity between Russian and American approaches to the embodiment of philosophical ideas in practical deeds.

In his 1929 paper on the fate of philosophy in the American setting, George Mead drew attention to the break between culture and the directive forces in the community as a characteristic of the life of the mind in America. Literature, philosophy, and art were inherited or imported from Europe, though America had separated itself decisively from that continent in its political and economic undertakings. Mead concluded that only in pragmatism, and especially in the works of Dewey, did American reality at last "meet" its own philosophy in articulated form. Dewey "occupied himself with the function of knowledge in doing. . . . And his next step was by way of the school in which he subjected his philosophy to the more severe test of actual accomplishment in education."[20] Dewey accepted a chair in philosophy at the University of Chicago with the condition that the department include education as well. One of his first steps in this new field was to establish an experimental school in which education was based on the principle that knowing is the point of doing.[21]

The close connections between the philosophy of pragmatism and progressive education are well known and sufficiently documented.[22] What is especially important for us here is the genuine embedding of philosophical ideas in educational and social practice that is revealed in this alliance.

Speaking on the characteristic features of the American mentality, Daniel Boorstin once pointed out: "The beliefs that values come out of the context and that truth is part of the matrix of experience (and hardly separable from it) become themselves part of the way of American thinking. . . . For us, fortunately, it is impossible to distinguish the history of our thought from the history of our institutions."[23] Whatever reservations we may hold about Boorstin's statement in general, in the case of Dewey it fits perfectly.

Unlike its American counterpart, Russian culture and philosophy at the beginning of the century were still predominantly elitist and divorced from the problems of everyday experience. Individual legal and civic consciousness was very weak, and the struggle for progress took the form of a battle between political parties, each with its own ideology but lacking detailed practical programs. Probably the most difficult task facing Russian society at the time was to follow the thesis that Dewey had made a cornerstone of pragmatism: to think about ends in terms of means.

Blonsky bitterly acknowledged: "We Russians are badly prepared for socially useful service. . . . It has become almost a truism that we are ready to give our lives for Russia; the problem, though, is whether we can live for it."[24]

Unfortunately, it is impossible now to judge the extent to which this inability of Russian intellectuals to think in practical and institutional terms was incurable. There were some promising signs of a growing practicality in Russian thought. Early in the century communal educational and health programs started appearing, local initiatives gradually gained ground, and legal consciousness awakened. One might say that these were seeds of a future merger of intellectual and practical forces in Russian society. Revolution, however, destroyed all these attempts, leading the country toward a quite different course.

*Pragmatism versus Utopia*

In 1913 Blonsky finished his formal education, earning a doctorate in philosophy. He was subsequently appointed associate professor at Moscow University, while at the same time he secured a position at a teachers college. With these appointments and his editorial position at the journal *The New School*, Blonsky managed for a while to develop all facets of his career simultaneously. He completed his monograph on Plotinus, wrote a book-length review of modern philosophy, and published extensively on education and school reform.[25]

In 1917, just after the Bolshevik Revolution, Blonsky took a step that decisively separated him from the pre-Revolutionary educational community. The majority of Russian teachers and university professors declared a strike to protest the Bolshevik coup d'état. Blonsky not only refused to join the action, but sent a letter to the Bolshevik newspaper *Izvestia* denouncing it and accusing his colleagues of being "antinational."[26] As a result, he lost his job at the teachers college (Moscow University was already closed), his editorial position on *The New School*, and other professional appointments.

Blonsky recalls: "I was thrown out of the 'respectable circle.' . . . The Union of High School Teachers required explanations and filed a suit against me in the court of honor. . . . My former university colleague M. M. Rubinstein wrote in a newspaper that I had stuck a knife into the back of the intelligentsia."[27] Blonsky's suffering as an outcast was not long-lived. Strikes and other overt forms of anti-Bolshevik resistance in Moscow were quickly crushed. In 1918 Blonsky was reappointed at Moscow University and also given a position in the Moscow Department of Education.

Beginning in 1919 he received promotions to a number of administrative positions within the public education system. In 1919 he was commissioned to organize the Moscow Academy of Popular Education—a teachers college of a new sort. In 1922 he joined the State Scientific Council, where in collaboration with Lenin's wife, Nadezhda Krupskaja, he developed new curricula for public school departments.

*The Reform of Science*, an impassioned record of Blonsky's criticism of modern philosophy, psychology, and education, was published in 1920.[28] Despite its sketchy style, absence of proofs, and abundance of critical temper, *The Reform of Science* remains an important testimony to the early period of Soviet behavioral science; this work is also indispensable for the understanding of the transformation of Blonsky's views. It was the first time in his career that the rebellious temperament of his educational writings invaded the pages of an apparently philosophical paper.

Blonsky termed all the main categories of philosophy and psychology "atavisms of thought"—scholarly reflections of an out-of-date *Weltanschauung*. His criticism was directed mainly against those who still used such categories as "soul," "spiritual substance," and "matter" without reservation, ignoring the substantial critique they had received from the midnineteenth century on, from both positivist philosophy and the concrete sciences.

Blonsky's positive program was sketchy at best: "Scientific psychology is a science of human behavior. . . . Psychology as a behavioral science is a biological science. . . . Scientific psychology is social psychology. . . . The human being is a *Homo technicus*. The human being is a *Homo technicus* and *Homo socialis*. From this point of view we see a key to the secret of human behavior. This key is the technical activity of mankind."[29]

Blonsky stressed the importance of the concept of technical progress and the development of industry for understanding socially determined patterns of behavior, and he praised Marxism on this ground. At the same time he expressed a hope of seeing psychology and all other fields of knowledge become exact mathematical sciences: "In essence, scientific philosophy and universal calculus are one and the same thing. . . . Any knowledge is real only so far as it is rooted in calculus. . . . Let us think as mathematicians—that should be the slogan of genuine philosophers." Returning to psychology, he wrote: "Psychology conducts research on its subject with the help of the normal methods of natural science, i.e., via the mathematical presentation of behavior as a function of many variables; and it also widely employs the comparative-evolutionary approach."[30]

Blonsky did not give any concrete examples of a mathematical approach to behavioral problems, nor did he attempt to reconcile the principles of Marxism or evolutionism with the analytical tradition of mathematics. Almost unnoticeably he had slipped from a critique of the magic words of traditional metaphysics to the creation of a metaphysics of a new sort in which key words like "God" or "matter" were simply replaced by "calculus."

The confusions in Blonsky's theoretical position seem especially interesting in comparison with the philosophy of William James. In his attack on metaphysics and "atavisms of thought," Blonsky followed almost literally James's statement that the "universe has always appeared to the natural mind as a kind of enigma, of which the key must be sought in the shape of some illuminating or power-bringing word or name. . . . 'God,' 'Matter,' 'Reason,' 'the Absolute,' 'Energy,' are so many solving names. You have rest when you have them. You are at the end of your metaphysical quest."[31] As a counterbalance to the "magic" of metaphysical thinking, James offered the pragmatic method: "If you follow the pragmatic method, you cannot look on any word as closing your quest. You must bring out of each word its cash-value, set it at work within the stream of your experience. It appears less as a solution, then, than as a program for more work, and more particularly as an indication of the ways in which existing realities may be changed. Theories thus become instruments, not answers to enigmas, in which we can rest."[32]

It seems to me that it was just this sense of the instrumentality of reason that was missing in Blonsky's battle with metaphysics. His search for a genuinely scientific method had led him to the thesis of a uniquely "correct" theory, which was so popular in post-Revolutionary Russia. He earnestly desired a method whose precision and calculuslike nature would guarantee the correctness of its application in advance. The feedback mechanisms of inquiry so vigorously defended by pragmatism left him indifferent.

In 1921 Blonsky published *An Outline of Scientific Psychology*, in which he emphasized his behaviorist position.[33] In this book and in his lecture at the First Russian Psychoneurological Congress in 1923, he argued that psychology must become a purely behavioral science and criticized the idea of taking consciousness as a subject of research.

As we have seen, Lev Vygotsky took a strong stand against this behaviorist extremism. But Vygotsky had never associated himself with the behaviorists, either Russian or American. It is more interesting that George Mead, whose own theory was called "social behaviorism," defended the study of consciousness in much the same way that Vygotsky did.[34] Mead did not hesitate to deal with the epistemological problems that inevitably emerge if one adopts a stance of radical behaviorism. Yet Blonsky's great knowledge of classical philosophy failed to protect him against the deceptive charms of the behaviorist doctrine. Once so sensitive to the inconsistencies of traditional metaphysics, he became more than tolerant of the inconsistencies of behaviorism. It seems probable that he regarded behaviorism as a means for social reform; the mentality of Blonsky the reformer here opposed that of Blonsky the philosopher and scientist.

In *The Labor School* (1919) Blonsky summarized his educational creed and established in clear-cut form the Soviet version of progressive education.[35] He started from nearly the same point as Dewey: the need to replace scholastic methods of teaching with methods that would respond to the realities of an industrialized society. "The goal of education," wrote Blonsky, "is to introduce the child to contemporary industrial culture."[36] Through labor schoolchildren were to acquire both concrete scientific knowledge and an understanding of the structure of social relations.

Blonsky assumed that since manual labor and craftsmanship belonged to obsolete modes of production, attention should be focused on machinery and industrialism: "We oppose machinery and science to manual-laborism, and industrialism to craftsmanship."[37]

Blonsky fully outlined a curriculum designed in accordance with the idea of industrialism. Social-historical subjects were to use as a point of departure the history of industry in a given town and proceed toward general laws of national industrial and social development.

In physics, Blonsky suggested beginning with machines as examples of "concrete kinematics." From involvement in real industrial production to the working principles of tools and mechanisms, and from there to theorems of mechanics—that should be the path of ascent from everyday experience to the abstract categories of science. Blonsky considered that such a sequence would guarantee adherence to the basic law of education: from sensible experience to theoretical abstraction, which in its turn must serve as a basis for further action. Dewey's principle of "learning by doing" was here applied in full strength.

In mathematics, machinery once again had to be the starting point in the curriculum. Mathematical rules and formulas were to be introduced as the tools of contemporary engineering.

Writing on biology, Blonsky suggested plant breeding and the principles of rational agriculture as starting points. Evolutionary biology, the theory of natural selection, and an outline of genetics should all be presented as a scientific basis for real agricultural problems. Medicine and the study of disease must contribute to a better understanding of the connections between human physiology and everyday experience.

In other respects the labor schools were to be child-oriented, democratic, and concerned with concrete problems of everyday life. Blonsky favorably mentioned child-centered methods of study with flexible curricula adjusted to individual aptitudes. He also endorsed "learning by doing" projects for schoolchildren to replace regular lessons featuring a "teacher asks–student answers" system.

As a general psychological framework for this curriculum Blonsky suggested paying more attention to the natural, inherited characteristics of the child and to the stages of children's development. In these questions Blonsky stuck to the pedological position, which assumed that a child's inherited, constitutional, and psychotypological characteristics should be thoroughly observed and measured in order to set adequate educational objectives at any given moment in his or her development. Pedology claimed to be the scientific counterpart to pedagogics, which was criticized by pedologists for its nonscientific character and its reluctance to employ the methods of psychoneurology.[38] Blonsky acknowledged that his pedological views were influenced by James M. Baldwin and Charles Judd,[39] while his "industrialism" and orientation toward the everyday experience came from John Dewey.

The prevailing educational policy of the 1920s was in good agreement with Blonsky's program. Industrialism, the method of projects, and the child-centered curriculum were endorsed by such influential persons as Nadezhda Krupskaja, Lenin's wife and a prominent member of the Bolshevik Party who occupied a high-ranking position in the system of state education. Victor Shulgin, a radical educational progressivist who also enjoyed favor, served as director of the Institute of Methods of School Work.[40]

But what seemed sound as doctrine hardly fit the reality of Soviet society. Blonsky's personal inability to reconcile theoretical theses with practical conditions now had a perfect social counterpart in the form of the utopian projects set in motion by the Revolution.

Let us examine the conditions in which the new progressive school system was to be established. For most of the Soviet Union, the years 1918–1922 passed under the cloud of Civil War. National industry was in ruins, and almost all civil services had ceased to exist. The crop failure of 1921 affected an area inhabited by twenty to thirty million people. Martial law had been imposed. Members of the "bourgeois classes" were deprived of their property and personal possessions and were sometimes executed merely on the basis of their family origins. The only concern people could afford was to survive physically, feeding and warming themselves and their families.

There followed the period of the New Economic Policy (NEP) in the years 1922–1928. In order to raise the production levels of food and consumer goods, small-scale private ownership was reinstated and even encouraged within certain limits. Peasants were allowed to work their private plots of land, paying agricultural taxes and selling their surplus grain in open markets. Private or cooperative workshops and tiny factories became the dominant form of business. Class antagonism, however, remained a powerful source of human hatred. Former clergymen, families of noble stock, and members of the pre-Revolutionary state bureaucracy were disenfranchised and subjected to numerous damaging restrictions, including denial of access to higher education.

Beginning in 1929, a course was taken toward industrialization. This meant the abolition of the NEP's "liberties" and the herding of peasants into collective farms. Those who refused to leave their plots of land or businesses were exiled to Siberia.

Blonsky was certainly aware of these conditions. In 1919 he published a paper "On the Most Typical Pedagogical Mistakes in the Establishment of the Labor Schools," in which he lamented the lack of educational publications and the disastrous conditions of schools and libraries.[41] He described the distress caused by the practical forms labor education had taken. He also claimed that his ideas were being misinterpreted and distorted.

Blonsky had suggested starting education by acquainting children with their immediate surroundings: school, family, and town. He still insisted on this method in a paper written in 1922, admitting, however, that "Children have classes in half-ruined buildings, wet and cold ... teachers starve ... there are no textbooks. ... Who teaches? Young, scarcely educated women without experience. Only 75 percent of them are high school graduates, and 13 percent finished only elementary school."[42] Obviously no teacher could develop any sensible educational program taking such an environment as a starting point. The real environment was therefore replaced by an imaginary, propagandistic vision of what the world would be like in the age of "fulfilled socialism."

In 1928 even Krupskaja had to confess that "the instruction in practical labor experience was not introduced." She referred to economic conditions: "Poverty did not permit us to build workshops; there was a lack of premises, a want of equipment."[43]

In 1930 , thirteen years after the Revolution, a decree of the Council of People's Commissars revealed that not only the sons and daughters of disenfranchised persons but also those of craftsmen and clerks were often expelled from school because of their nonproletarian origin.

In the early 1930s progressive education programs were sharply criticized by Soviet authorities as a "leftist deviation." The method of projects, child-centered programs, and other innovations were abolished. Even Krupskaja was forced to acknowledge her "leftist mistakes."[44] Nor did industrialism as a focus of education last long either. In 1937 a decree of the People's Commissariat of Education ordered the abolition of the teaching of labor and the liquidation of all extant schoolshops.[45] By the late 1930s all signs of progressivism had been eliminated from Soviet schools. The reigning atmosphere was one of almost military discipline, marked by scholastic teaching methods and obligatory curricula with no electives. In the 1940s the retrograde movement went so far as a return to segregated schools for boys and girls.

The principles of progressive education and the social reality in which they were to be implemented had obviously taken counter courses. Progressivism emphasized creativity and individuality in thought at a time when social circumstances dictated strong discipline and uniformity of thought; progressivism was based on the principle of democracy in education, whereas the Party leadership was proclaiming the dictatorship of the proletariat; and progressivism was committed to the idea of experimental projects that were hardly welcome in the more and more centralized system of Soviet public education, which required a stereotyped curriculum for all schools. Blonsky himself gave a clue for understanding the failure of Soviet progressivism. "I wrote *The Labor School*," he confessed, "as if the classless society of the future were already the current reality."[46]

As noted already, Blonsky may be taken to stand for the sizable proportion of the Russian intelligentsia who could not combine into a coherent whole their sober professional knowledge and their wishful social ideals. For Blonsky this schism occurred first as a "lack of communication" between his philosophical writings and his work as an educational reformer. His later interest in "mathematical philosophy" also failed to resolve this problem. In the post-Revolutionary period enthusiastic utopianism replaced liberal progressivism in Blonsky's pedagogical writings. It now became impossible to reconcile his philosophy with his educational ideas and to match those ideas with the real conditions in the schools and in society. What he produced was an "industrialism" without workshops and "democratization" for sons and daughters of legally disenfranchised and exiled people. Neglecting the real conditions of everyday life, utopian progressivism continued to insist on its ideal. Blonsky's position became not only inconsistent but truly pathetic.

Just as progressivist ideas were disappearing from the Soviet educational horizon, American progressivism celebrated its effective incorporation into the national school system. The Progressive Education Committee reported in 1937: "It is evident . . . that the tendency to be avowedly experimental is gaining ground. . . . 'Radical notions' may be safely incorporated into the instructions of a city superintendent to his corps of principals and teachers. . . . Progressive education is no longer a rebel movement; it has become respectable."[47]

Was Soviet progressivism doomed to failure from the start, or did it fall victim to social circumstances?[48] Blonsky's confession suggests the answer to this question. Soviet progressivism, although nearly an exact copy of the American version, failed to take into account one of the principal theses of pragmatism, namely, that any program is feasible only to the extent to which it is operational, bringing a feedback response from its actual social results. The classical formulation of this principle was made by George Mead: "It is impossible to so forecast any future conditions that depend upon the evolution of society as to be able to govern our conduct by such a forecast; it is always the unexpected that happens, for we have to recognize not only the immediate change that is to take place, but also the reaction back upon this of the whole world within which the change takes place, and no human foresight is equal to this. . . . What we have is a method and a control in application, not an ideal to work toward."[49]

Instead of operational hypotheses and feedback corrections, Blonsky and other Soviet progressives chose to begin with an ideal and to ignore the replies social reality sent them in response to their program.

Blonsky and his colleagues could hardly be singled out in their social blindness. They just shared a common belief in "the one and only correct theory," in a scientifically planned society, and in the passing character of current failures.

The failure of Soviet progressivism seems particularly instructive in connection with the fact that certain utopian trends also existed in American progressivism, viewed as a general social movement. Certain statements of Wilsonian liberalism, such as "to enter the war in order to end all wars forever," as well as the uncritical attitude displayed by some progressives toward developments in the Soviet Union, indicated that the American mentality was not entirely immune to the germs of utopianism.[50] Dewey himself was at first deceived by those selected aspects of Soviet life he was allowed to observe during his 1928 trip.[51] He was obviously pleased by the plans and programs of the new society, and it took him nearly a decade to realize that this "scientifically planned society" had managed to ignore scientific reason. "In the name of science," Dewey wrote in 1939, "a thoroughly anti-scientific procedure was formulated in accord with which a generalization is made having the nature of ultimate 'truth,' and hence holding good at all times and places."[52]

Within American educational progressivism a tendency toward the utopian ideal revealed itself in the attempt by radical-reconstructionists to envisage the progressive school as the nucleus of a future ideal society.[53] On his own soil, however, Dewey was much more sober than in his relation to Soviet affairs. He promptly refuted the reconstructionist program, pointing to the illegitimate confusion of the principle of rational planning with that of a utopian planned society. He also deplored indoctrination as a mode of teaching, pointing to the incompatibility of the principles of scientific pragmatism with those of indoctrination, however attractive that doctrine might seem.[54]

Here we are approaching what seems to be the kernel of Blonsky's failure. Separated from their original American context, the categories of progressive education immediately lost their original meaning and became empty linguistic forms to be filled with new Soviet content. The moral for the historian is that the social existence of ideas provides the only reliable guide for their historical reconstruction. The doctrinal form of the same ideas can be highly deceptive. Focusing on the doctrinal side of Soviet and American progressivism, one could easily overlook their principal dissimilarity, which is rooted not in a difference of educational formulas but in the antagonism of educational and social practices.

The social existence that progressive ideas gained on Soviet soil was their real existence, and this social existence preordained the utopian character of Blonsky's program. Only as actual educational practice did Dewey's theory achieve its ultimate realization. Blonsky's program had found its "embodiment" in the dramatic alienation of educational ideas from the Soviet reality of the 1920s. The seeming affinity of Soviet and American progressivism turns out to be a linguistic phenomenon only.

Blonsky himself resolved the tension between the utopianism of his program and stubborn reality by abandoning the very idea of progressive education. In 1930 he resigned from his positions connected with education and took a chair at the Moscow Institute of Psychology. He also disassociated himself from pedology, which explains the comparatively mild criticism he received when the pedologists were brought to disgrace following the decree of 1936.[55]

One searches in vain through Blonsky's later works, such as *The Development of Cognition in Schoolchildren* (1935), for a sign of his former progressivism.[56] What one finds is a very scholarly description of mental development in terms of the acquisition of logical rules, principles of cause and effect, and linguistic rules, and not one word on "learning by doing," industrialism, or child-centered processes.

# 7

## Idols and Ideals in Soviet Education

*From the 1930s through the 1950s Soviet schools were confined by a straightjacket of prescribed methods of instruction that seemed resistant to any innovations. In the late 1950s, though, both the United States and the Soviet Union became concerned with their educational programs in science. While the United States, under the spell of the first Sputnik, was hectically seeking new educational approaches, the Soviet side was quite unhappily discovering the negative effects of its rigid and outdated system. In the Soviet case, the contradictory interests of competing groups of scholars and bureaucrats resulted in a number of very different proposals for reforming that system.*

*The state bureaucracy, primarily concerned with practical skills, supported closer ties between schools and industry. This proposal was given concrete form in a 1958 state law that lasted for eight years, when it was deemed a failure and rescinded.*

*Unlike the bureaucrats, Soviet scientists worried mostly about the suppression of creativity and the rigidity of the curriculum. Gifted students were given no opportunity to set their own pace or develop their special talents. The scientists' efforts led to the establishment of special science high schools. These special schools became very popular among scholars and professional people, who turned them into university preparatory schools for their own children.*

*Humanistic scholars, meanwhile, worried that an excessive emphasis on science would create a generation of narrow-minded technocrats. They advocated a comprehensive curriculum that would include the study of human factors in scientific progress and also the art of dialectics.*

*A compromise proposal for a comprehensive curriculum based on the teaching of theoretical concepts was developed by Vasili Davydov of the Moscow Institute of Psychology. His classroom experiments showed that even the youngest students can grasp conceptual lessons. Taking issue with the empiricist methods that had dominated the school system for decades, Davydov ar-*

*gued that an understanding of the formation of theoretical concepts must be
the basic goal of education.*

*Davydov's program, although successful in an experimental setting, could
hardly be implemented throughout the school system. The achievement of excellence in theoretical science was for a long time almost the sole success of
Soviet scholarship, which was otherwise muddled in ideological matters. But
the success of a scientific elite could hardly be repeated with a whole generation of children. Davydov's proposal turned out to be another blueprint for
utopia, precise in design but impossible to execute.*

*Soviet Education at the Crossroads*

"Sputnik shock" had a well-publicized effect on the development of
American education and on science teaching in particular. Much less
publicized and less appreciated is the fact that in the late 1950s the
Soviet educational system experienced what one might call "looking-
glass shock." Soviet educators and members of the scientific establishment reviewed the effectiveness of the existing curriculum and
came to the conclusion that it was sadly deficient in the modern
sciences and failed to provide the knowledge and skills that are essential
in a period of technological revolution.[1]

One should not be deceived, however, by the similarity of the
diagnoses made by Soviet and American experts. The roots of the
problems were essentially different. To understand the Soviet situation,
one must grasp the general intellectual and social atmosphere of the
late 1950s. In 1956 Nikita Khrushchev delivered the famous speech
to the Twentieth Congress of the Communist Party in which he acknowledged the atrocities of the Stalin era and "rehabilitated" those
who had been sent to labor camps.[2] Although the speech centered
on Stalin's political mistakes and on cases of persecution of the "honest
members of the Party," it in fact challenged the entire legacy of the
Stalin period, including the policies in science, culture, and education.
It became obvious that Stalin's administration had swept many failures
under the carpet, forcibly silencing critics and substituting blatant
propaganda for serious analysis.

Indeed, the situation was far less rosy than it seemed to such American observers as Hyman Rickover.[3] The success of Sputnik masked
the fact that Soviet science was still inferior to that of the United States
in such essential fields as electronics, computer science, and molecular
biology. The blind chauvinism of the postwar years, with its pretensions
to Russian priority in almost all scientific discoveries, led to a severing
of the flow of technical information from the West and a silencing of

those Soviet specialists who were tempted to use "bourgeois" methods and ideas. A number of disciplines, including genetics, cybernetics, and non-Pavlovian physiology, were totally banned.

When Admiral Rickover astounded Congress with figures on the increasing numbers of Soviet engineers and technicians, he did not stop to note that even a "mammoth pool" of university graduates cannot counterbalance a lack of professionals in essential fields. Like the Soviet planning authorities, Admiral Rickover overlooked one fundamental principle, namely, that the effectiveness of a complex system depends decisively on the functioning of the weakest of its elements. Thousands of specialists in agricultural engineering can accomplish nothing if the principles of breeding and agricultural management are obsolete. A solid curriculum in electrical engineering does not help if there are no specialists in electronics.

In an age of technological and scientific revolution it is not enough to learn by rote the basic formulas of physics and mathematics; creativity and flexibility become the most important skills. And it was precisely the suppression of creativity and the standardization of thinking that left Soviet students unprepared for the challenge of modern technology. The Soviet delegate to UNESCO admitted in 1963 to "a certain divorce between schooling and life and the failure to prepare school graduates adequately for practical activity."[4]

While Admiral Rickover lamented the consequences of progressive education, which in his view gave unnecessary options to students, who used them to avoid science and pursue easier subjects, the Soviet system suffered from quite the opposite problem. Until 1955 there were, for example, no coeducational schools in the Soviet Union. Students of all grades wore uniforms, and all primary and high schools used the same textbooks and curricula. Uniformity and comprehensiveness were key words in Soviet education.[5]

At first glance, Soviet students had exactly what Admiral Rickover wished for their American counterparts: a clearly designed comprehensive curriculum, an emphasis on science and mathematics, and no individual electives. But in reality, all this meant that gifted students found it difficult to develop their talents since they did not fit the comprehensive model of education, while less bright students could not develop special aptitudes since they had to meet standard requirements in all subjects. Science teaching remained concentrated on school science with no immediate relevance to the problems actually being pursued in universities and research institutions.

The rigidity of the educational system was so obvious that scientists, educators, and even the state bureaucracy became anxious. As a result, in 1958 the Supreme Soviet passed a law on the development of public education. It was a characteristic example of the Sturm und Drang reformism of the Khrushchev era. The period of compulsory education was extended from seven to eight years, and one more year—an eleventh grade—was added to high school. Public schools were ordered to establish close ties with industry and to prepare their graduates for practical activity. School curricula would be redesigned to match the requirements of modern science and technology.[6]

The Khrushchev changes lasted less than eight years. In 1966 schools returned to the ten-year sequence and the "close ties" with industry were loosened because they had not had the anticipated effect. It became clear that neither schools nor industries were ready for the proposed alliance.[7]

There was, however, one part of this reform program that exceeded the limits of Khrushchev's hollow innovativeness and reflected the grassroots concerns of Soviet professionals and scientists: the creation of special high schools for students with an aptitude for science. From the very beginning the call for such schools was perceived as controversial. The establishment of schools with advanced courses in science and mathematics obviously challenged the principles of uniformity and comprehensiveness. The problem of the social attitudes of special school graduates was also troublesome. Theoretically the special schools were just another item in a long list of projects that also included schools with advanced courses in industry-related subjects such as radio engineering and chemical technology. Since physics and mathematics are essential to the entrance examinations for universities and technological institutes, however, it should have been clear from the start that the special schools would develop into preparatory schools for the future scientific elite.[8]

Scientific careers are attractive to Soviet students for a number of reasons. First, such a career carries an exemption from military service requirements, which are quite severe. Second, it offers access to the white-collar jobs and fairly intellectual atmosphere of the research institutes. Third, academic salaries are good if one can manage to earn an advanced degree. Fourth, all positions in science offer a tenure track, and nothing like professional unemployment exists in university centers such as Moscow and Leningrad.

Two more points should be noted. First, because there is no "private" business in the Soviet Union, all brainpower is channeled to state institutions. For a young person there is no choice between business or research; research wins for lack of competition. Second, unlike industrial education, which had only a few sympathizers among altruistic plant directors, the special schools had a strong lobby among scientists, including Nobel Prize winner Nikolai Semionov and academicians Jakov Zeldovich and Andrei Sakharov.

The establishment of the special schools occurred at the height of a general enthusiasm for the power of scientific knowledge. Books and journals popularizing science were being printed by the millions. Special contests—"Olympiads"—in physics, chemistry, and mathematics attracted thousands of students willing to test their ability in nonstandard problem solving. For the first time intellectual aggressiveness and an ability to compete were proclaimed virtues suitable to Soviet students.

The excitement surrounding science and its popularization only emphasized the backwardness of the ordinary school curricula. In 1962, for example, a journalist with the leading intellectual monthly, *Novy Mir*, surveyed articles from the journals of science popularization and compared them with standard high-school textbooks. He found that "between the textbooks and the problems discussed in articles . . . not only does a common ground not exist, they actually have not a single mutual aspect."[9]

The special schools obviously aimed to fill the gap between modern science and traditional education. A great deal of effort was put into them. The special schools had more flexible and more advanced curricula. A number of distinguished scientists wrote supplementary textbooks, and some of them even lectured at the schools.[10]

There was an inevitable paradox in the course of development of the special schools. Their purported function was to encourage the intellectual activity of students with aptitudes for science and thus to raise the intellectual standards of the new generation. It was assumed that students would be recruited from all social groups, since the only requirement for enrollment was an aptitude for physics and mathematics. But in reality only those who aimed for the university joined the special programs. Why should anyone spend years learning advanced mathematics if he is going next to spend a number of years as a private in the army? Motivation toward higher education, of course, was closely associated with a family's social status. In short, a majority of special school students came from families of scientists and other professionals.[11] Instead of raising the general intellectual standard of the coming generation, the special schools thus created a select class of students who entered the best universities and technological institutes and furthered the intellectual gap between the scientific elite and the general population.

While scientists exploited the new opportunities that resulted from the more pragmatic policy toward science and technology, humanists also celebrated a renaissance, although theirs had some bitter aspects. If the natural sciences had suffered during the Stalin era, the humanities had been not only ruined but corrupted. Mathematicians and physicists could find refuge in purely abstract problems, but what course could a philosopher take if an outline of dialectical and historical materialism written by Stalin was declared the apex of philosophical thought? It was a philosophical and not just a "scientific" rationale that substantiated the charges against genetics, cybernetics, and structural linguistics. The antiscientific and anti-intellectual campaigns had been waged in the name of Marxist philosophy and social thought.

In general, philosophy and the humanities as clearly ideological disciplines came to be considered the corrupted partners of the persecutors, with science as their victim. Such sentiments, widespread in the early 1960s among the technical intelligentsia, made the position of humanists especially difficult. On the one hand, they had to revive scholarship in their disciplines practically from scratch; on the other hand, they were still bound by certain ideological clichés, which at least for laymen were suspiciously akin to the ones that had dominated the Stalin era. At the same time the spectacular achievements of science provoked the belief that the humanities would soon disappear, yielding to nonspeculative methods of computer simulation and mathematical modeling.

The transition from the Stalin era immediately influenced the teaching of the humanities. Some courses in history were suspended, since they did not respond to the new official views. Historians lamented the fact that their discipline had lost its popularity; even Moscow University could not enroll decent numbers of doctoral students. While science attracted young people through the journals of popularization, historians scarcely had enough professional journals.[12]

Humanists were not happy with the proposal for special science schools. They naturally suspected that such schools would become centers of scientism, neglecting and even despising the humanities. Humanists were also concerned with the calls for early specialization made by some scientists. It seemed to them that early specialization, in whatever discipline, could only impoverish creative intelligence and turn students into narrow-minded functionaries.

With the revival of the humanities in the 1960s, which included the reestablishment of sociology, structural linguistics, philosophy of science, and other neglected disciplines, it became possible to speak of a humanist educational message. Humanists not only defended their scholarship but criticized the excessive pretensions of science and science teaching.

This humanist message was clearly expressed in a 1971 essay by the Moscow philosopher Anatoli Arseniev entitled "Science and Man."[13] Arseniev starts with the assertion that the cognitive style of contemporary science has its roots in the mechanistic scientism of the seventeenth to nineteenth centuries. Following Marx's theory of alienated labor, Arseniev suggests that in the course of this scientific and technological revolution the products of human activity were "estranged from the individual and alienated in the form of algorithms, formulas, and technological principles, becoming transformed into an objective, mechanistic entity."[14]

Modern society, according to Arseniev, regards science as a source of universal, ready-made formulas and projects that can be implemented in any place and at any time. The human aspect disappears; the process of discovery and the human origins of the scientific research that has led to the algorithms of contemporary technology are ignored. Under these circumstances, contemporary scientific ideas start to resemble ordinary commodities. The products of science are alienated from their authors, and the majority of scientists become narrow specialists working under prescribed rules.

Arseniev emphasizes that the major mistake of scientism and science teaching is the reluctance to perceive the present form of science as a transient and historically limited mode of knowledge. He argues fiercely against those who blithely trace the progress of knowledge from medieval "ignorance" to the omnipotence of contemporary science. Any epoch and any mode of culture has its own self-sufficient value. The lack of scientific experimentation in the Middle Ages does not mean that this period of history should be despised as an era of pure obscurantism. Medieval philosophy, logic, and mathematics, though they may seem alien to the contemporary scientific mentality, cannot be dismissed as unimportant or underdeveloped cultural phenomena.

Arseniev argues that since contemporary science is nothing but a single, historically limited phase in the development of human knowledge, it should not be taken as a paradigm for all forms of consciousness and rationality. Although not stated explicitly, it is clear from the general context of Arseniev's work that he considers contemporary science—Western and Soviet alike—to be a child of the capitalist system of production. Science therefore inevitably bears within itself all the contradictions inherent to capitalist society.

While refusing to speculate on what forms the scientific process might take in the future, Arseniev nevertheless bases his account on the possibility of automatization of almost all modes of production, routine scientific work included. He suggests that only the process of creative development of new knowledge should be reserved to human ingenuity. He recalls Marx's thesis that the real development of human abilities can start only after problems of material production have been solved. In respect to this desirable future, Arseniev claims that "the formal-logical and abstractive side of knowledge, which plays a decisive role in the applications of contemporary science and which used to be taken for its essence, would cease to be the goal of theoretical work and would become a task for machinery and computers rather than humans."[15]

The pursuit of objective, universally applicable scientific formulas has split the body of knowledge into a knowledge of objects and a knowledge of personal conduct. Objective knowledge has become embodied in practical common sense and modern science, while subjective knowledge has taken refuge in moral codes, art, and philosophy. Only the reunion of these alienated modes of human consciousness can provide a proper milieu for the further development of human excellence.

But how can this general message be related to the problems of education? Although this question is beyond the scope of Arseniev's paper, it does shed some light on the philosophical premises of the humanist conception of education.

Arseniev was not alone in his critique of the dehumanizing nature of science teaching. Two other philosophers—Felix Mikhailov, currently at the Moscow Institute of Psychology, and Evald Ilienkov of the Institute of Philosophy—did not hesitate to communicate their dissatisfaction with the mechanistic reasoning cultivated in Soviet schools.[16] They dismissed the thesis of inborn creativity as "undemocratic," claiming that those who failed to manifest originality and creativity in thinking are only victims of an inefficient and suppressive system of education.

Did they call for child-centered or pluralistic education? By no means. The main thesis of the philosopher-humanists was that the conceptual apparatus inculcated by the school system not only lagged behind the achievements of contemporary scientific thought but also neglected the great legacy of world philosophy. The way to improve learning was therefore to introduce training in dialectic thought, starting with its roots in Plato and concluding with Hegel, Marx, and contemporary dialecticians.

Reflection upon the cultural heritage of mankind should, they argued, become the essential tool in mastering creative intelligence. According to Ilienkov, "Personal intelligence and the ability to reason independently emerge and mature exclusively through the mastering of the cognitive culture of the epoch. Intelligence is nothing but this cognitive culture evolving into the individual mentality in the course of personal activity. There are no other constituents in the individual mind. Personal intelligence is therefore an individualized form of the cognitive treasure of society."[17]

The humanist approach opposed the idea of special educational options for the gifted. "Creative intelligence and talents of all kinds are a general norm, not the exception. . . . The absence of creativity is always a result of abnormal educational practice."[18] Since humanists believed that everybody has potential talents, they directed their efforts to the development of a comprehensive educational philosophy of creative thinking, paying little attention to students with above-average abilities. In their philosophy of education they started with the structure of creative intelligence as it emerges from world philosophy and the humanities, rejecting the individual achievements of particular groups of students as a plausible point of departure.

This version of educational philosophy has deep roots in Soviet history. Starting with the 1930s, the educated public in Russia never suffered from an abundance of cultural and intellectual options. Thus the problem of intellectual choice did not seem serious to Soviet intellectuals. The question of intellectual engagement and personal realization through such engagement—the question that has most preoccupied Western intellectuals in this century—had never been seriously considered by their Soviet colleagues. This is one reason why the principles of individualism, so cherished in American social thought, had no reverberation on Soviet soil. The possibility of intellectual choice is an absolute precondition to any kind of individualism. But when there is no room for choice, the individual instinctively seeks a bit more cultural space within the framework of the prescribed ideology and rules of conduct. Under restrictive conditions, humanistic thought is confined to permitted subjects, which it attempts to develop thoroughly. Instead of intellectual individualism, we see cultural attachment; instead of practical proliferation, intensive analysis.

For Soviet humanists who faced the problem of educational rigidity, it was quite natural to seek a solution in an officially recognized, even if unpopular, mode of culture: dialectical thought and classical philosophy. They believed that the categories of dialectical thought would be enriching for students, providing not only a corpus of valuable ideas and images but also the skills of creative reasoning. They failed, however, to propose specific educational methods. For that reason a certain discrepancy occurred between the subject of the humanists' message and its language: The questions they raised pertained directly to psychology and pedagogics, but their answers were phrased in abstract, philosophical categories that resisted transformation into practical forms.

*Bringing up Theoreticians*

One may argue that in the above story a great number of characters have appeared, but not the "stars": educators and psychologists. There is a reason for this sequence of presentation. Up until the mid-1960s Soviet educational psychologists were divided into those who were influential but retrograde and those who conducted interesting experiments but were powerless to put them into effect in the classroom. The most influential educational psychologists of the 1950s—Daniel Bogojavlensky, Natalia Menchinskaja, and E. Kabanova-Meller of the Academy of Pedagogical Sciences—were responsible for the psychological support of the rigid scholastic curriculum. The challenging experiments of Peter Galperin of Moscow University and Daniel Elkonin of the Moscow Institute of Psychology remained for a while purely research achievements with no immediate effect on the process of schooling.

In the late 1960s the picture changed. Khrushchev's educational reforms had failed to heal the troubles of the Soviet school system. At the same time the obsolete curricula and rigid methods of teaching were seriously compromised and became intolerable. At this moment Daniel Elkonin, Vasili Davydov, and their colleagues from the Moscow Institute of Psychology proposed a theory of learning that responded to the criticisms of both scientists and humanists and provided a psychological basis for a new curriculum. In theoretically elaborated form, this theory appeared in 1972 in a book by Davydov dedicated to the problem of concept formation.[19]

Davydov joined scientists in their critique of the current school curriculum, which obliterated ingenuity, suppressed talents, and lagged far behind the achievements of modern science. But at the same time, in assessing the prospects for reform, he relied largely on the humanists' thesis that dialectical thought should be one of the principal means of educational modernization. Davydov directly acknowledged the philosophical influence of Ilienkov and Arseniev; unlike them, however, he not only preached the importance of dialectics but substantiated his program in concrete methods. His proposal was courageous in that it challenged almost all existing Soviet school curricula, thus bringing into question the professional competence of most of the educational establishment.

Davydov's program touched on some issues of universal importance. To see this we need only compare his book with Jerome Bruner's *The Process of Education* (1960).[20] Bruner gave voice to the general belief of leading American scientists, educators, and psychologists that contemporary science had grown too complex and specialized to be taught as a mere sum of facts and formulas. Only the instruction of fundamental theoretical concepts and techniques could, he argued, enable students to grasp the kernel of scientific method and apply it independently. Science teaching must stop using artificial classroom simplifications and must turn closer to the paths of scientific discovery. It is the process of scientific reasoning, rather than its formal results, that should be taught.

Proceeding from other theoretical premises and using different language, Davydov moved in the same direction as Bruner. He started with a scathing critique of what he called the empiricist theory of concept formation. The traditional attitude, he claimed, based itself exclusively on the empirical, immediately observable properties of objects and processes and tried to proceed from these to abstract notions, which were then presented as true generalizations. Students were taught to rely on observable properties alone, and therefore failed to grasp the essential point of scientific methodology, which is the realization that the essence of things does not always coincide with their appearance. By abstracting common properties from a set of objects and calling them "generalizations," empiricist educators downgraded the multifaceted process of concept formation to one of classification and formal logic. This approach, Davydov conlcuded, was as out-of-date as the seventeenth-century theory of knowledge of John Locke.

Davydov gave evidence that the false idols of empiricism had dominated Soviet educational philosophy for decades, hindering the development of creative thinking and preventing the school curriculum from advancing in step with modern science.

Empiricism and the formalist method of concept formation had led to a nominalist interpretation of the process of generalization. General notions were presented merely as the common names for similar properties in essentially different and unconnected objects. For example, to introduce the concept "circle," the traditional curriculum required the teacher to point to several circular objects, such as a wheel, a plate, and the full moon, and explain that their common geometrical property is circularity. Obviously such an explanation fails to convey an adequate theoretical notion of what a circle is. Students taught in this way will understand geometrical concepts as nothing but words designating similar forms. Their notion of circle will lack connection with the essential relations that determine the circularity of such different entities as moon and wheel.

Davydov and his colleagues, after thoroughly examining the traditional curriculum, started designing experiments to test the ability of ordinary schoolchildren to cope with tasks that require conceptual problem solving. Their experiments revealed, for example, that the empiricist teaching methods prevented primary-school students from acquiring the proper notions of grammatical rules. Students were practically forced to substitute intuitive and often inadequate semantic associations for such rules. In distinguishing words with similar roots, students of the second and third grades (eight- and nine-year-olds) relied on the objective meaning of the words instead of their structure. They refused to consider the similarity of roots in such words as "chasy" (a watch) and "chasovoi" (a watchman), arguing instead that "a watch goes" while "a watchman keeps guard at one and the same place."[21]

The empiricist attitude led to a confusion of the concept of noun with the notion of an observable object. Eight-year-old students, for example, would not categorize as nouns abstractions such as "happiness" and "sorrow," since they had been taught that nouns were all related to observations. Likewise in the traditional curriculum verbs were defined as a part of speech designating movements and actions. Guided by this definition, students classified nouns such as "work" and "flight" as verbs, "because they indicate actions."[22]

Similar confusions occurred in primary-school mathematics. In the traditional curriculum, the notion of number emerged from observations of groups of objects—apples, chairs, books—arranged in pairs, triples, and so on. Students were taught to abstract the quantitative aspect of each group, thus forming the notion of number. Davydov and his colleagues set experiments in which schoolchildren who had already learned numbers and elementary arithmetical operations were asked to solve problems that required an understanding of the phenomenon of numerical relativity depending on the unit of measurement or counting. Students had to understand that the question "How many?" must always be accompanied by the definition of the unit of measurement, such as "How many chairs?" or "How many chair legs?" or "How many pairs of chairs?" Most of the students failed to solve problems that went beyond routine arithmetical excercises. They easily performed operations with numbers but were unable to use numbers and operations as mathematical "concepts" in the proper sense of this word.[23]

On the basis of his examination of the mathematics curriculum in different grades and schools, Davydov concluded that students were taught only to distinguish types of mathematical problems and to solve them with the help of known methods. When they approached a problem of an as yet unknown type, they were quite helpless because they had no experience in the independent restructuring of mathematical material.

On this point Davydov's criticism echoed the complaints of Soviet mathematicians, who had often expressed dissatisfaction with the standardization of mathematical instruction.[24] Ordinary students became accustomed to specific types of excercises but did not learn how to approach new sorts of problems, however simple they might be. Mediocre students were positively doomed, but even gifted students who showed a capacity for nonstandard thinking were hurt by being forced to comply with the comprehensive curriculum.

In his criticism of traditional methods Davydov also commented on such ideologically sensitive matters as history, noting that high-school graduates were not at all prepared for independent historical analysis and were quite ignorant of the categories of historical thought. The history curriculum looked like a chronological table embellished with verbal pictures of events. Students were served ready-made formulas of the past—often one-sided and theoretically obsolete—rather than the skills that would allow independent analysis.[25]

Davydov's positive educational program was based on an explicit philosophical and psychological premise. He claimed that theoretical, not empirical, thinking must be an exclusive goal of education and that the everyday experience of a child contributes nothing but confusion to the process of learning. The empiricist curriculum must therefore be replaced by theoretical definitions of objects and processes as they appear in scientific thought. "For a child guided only by immediate experience of the surrounding world, this theoretical approach is a novelty . . . that cannot emerge by itself. In a course of study it is essential to distinguish in the student's mind the properties of things that are given in immediate experience and the properties that appear with the help of theoretical reflection."[26]

Within the framework of theoretical knowledge, objects are transformed into scientific idealizations. To teach the technique of this transformation—that is, how to think theoretically—is the foremost task of education. The first step in this direction is to establish school subjects that can serve as means of theoretical inquiry. Davydov rejected the empiricist thesis of continuity, which stated that the school curriculum must start with everyday experience and gradually transform it into scientific notions. From the very beginning, he argued, students must learn to analyze objects as representatives of abstractions. The acquisition of theoretical concepts would liberate students from the repetitiveness of the present curriculum, which returns to the same notions every other grade in order to push them a bit further.

To answer the predictable skepticism concerning the ability of primary-school students to deal with abstract concepts, Davydov pointed to a series of experiments he had conducted with Daniel Elkonin and other colleagues, in which they had proved that seven- and eight-year-old students are quite able to form theoretical concepts with the proper assistance of a teacher.[27]

Such assistance must include the introduction of outward actions that enable the student to distinguish, and objectivize in the form of a model, relations that can stand for the general principles being taught. The psychologist's task is thus to develop a technique of outward operations and graphical models that can help the student ascend from sensible models to purely mental actions. Various techniques of this kind had been developed by Elkonin and Galperin, following Lev Vygotsky's notion of the internalization of external conduct into mental actions. Davydov's project connected the method of internalization with the concept of theoretical learning.

For example, according to the experimental program developed by Davydov and his colleagues, eight-year-old students started to learn about the morphology of words with the help of schematic diagrams. Suggesting the word "book" for morphological analysis, the teacher transformed it into the plural, "books." Students were encouraged to draw a frame around the variable part "s," which signifies plurality, and to indicate what meaning each morphological unit bears in itself. Working with different words, students were taught to make a structural analysis of their morphology, to present this analysis in a schematic form, and to associate variations of meaning with the structural properties of words. Eventually concrete morphemes were replaced by purely symbolic models that represented only an ordering of morphological units and their conceptual meaning.[28] The students thus mastered a form of linguistic analysis that enabled them to work with any word even if they had never encountered it before. Gradually the overt activity of analysis and modeling became condensed and internalized in the form of mental actions. These mental actions are nothing but a conceptual knowledge of morphology and the ability of linguistic analysis.

To develop a new mathematical curriculum Davydov started with the concept of value. Although this concept underlies all school mathematics, it is traditionally introduced only after such particular notions as whole and fractional numbers. An experimental program for first-graders acquainted them with the relations of values, such as volume, length, and weight, by representing these relations in the form of long and short lines. Eventually the lines were replaced by symbols such as $a$ and $b$. Students learned to use the signs for more ($>$) and less ($<$) and to write simple forumlas such as $a > b$ or $a = b$. Arithmetical operations such as summation and extraction were also taught in algebraic form, without concrete numbers. The concept of number was then introduced on the basis of a theoretically comprehended concept of value and value relations. Students learned to see in numbers a representation of the relations between given values when one of them is taken as a measure: $a/b = N$, where $a$ is any object presented as a value, $b$ is a measure, and $N$ is a number. The conceptual approach to mathematics helped Davydov's students to avoid most of the failures that beset students in ordinary schools.[29]

The effectiveness of Davydov's experimental curriculum challenged the well-established thesis of Jean Piaget that the natural limits of a child's intelligence preclude the mastering of abstract notions before adolescence. Davydov had proved that with specially designed curricula and an appropriate educational technique eight-year-olds can master the skills of theoretical reasoning.[30] In this Davydov disagreed not only with Piaget but also with Bruner, who used the Piagetian idea of the unchangeable character of the stages. While Bruner advocated the adjustment of curricula and methods of instruction to particular stages of intellectual development, Davydov's experiments opened a quite different perspective. He showed not only that theoretical concepts could be learned by eight-year-olds but that cognitive development itself may take another pace if appropriate methods of instruction are introduced.

Davydov believed that only theoretical concepts could give students an adequate knowledge of science and humanities. He also linked the basic concepts of modern science with dialectical philosophy, claiming that they both appeared as a reaction against empiricist doctrines. "Hegel," wrote Davydov, "was the first philosopher-educator who deliberately developed a method of instruction based on the dialectical theory of mind."[32] In Hegel's educational writings Davydov sought and found an endorsement for his own proposals. The theoretical approach creates idealized "objects" or models and analyzes observable phenomena with the help of these models. Theoretical discourse— scientific as well as dialectical—starts with the construction of such models and idealizations. Science, philosophy, and education have, therefore, essentially one and the same goal: the mastering of the technique of theoretical concept formation.

Throughout the 1970s new and original curricula in mathematics, the Russian language, literature, biology, physics, the visual arts, and music were developed by Davydov's group. They also elaborated various components of educational activity, set up criteria, and worked out indices of learning. In their paper, "A Concept of Educational Activity for Schoolchildren" (1981), Davydov and A. K. Markova outlined the major achievements of this program and pointed out the controversial moments.[33] First, and quite predictably, it turned out to be impossible to restructure the process of cognitive development without touching the sphere of motivation. Second, the data obtained so far showed no direct link between object-oriented activity and mental development. Davydov and Markova concluded: "A person need not become submerged in activity. With regard to learning, this means that mental development cannot be derived directly from the logic of the development of educational activity."[34] For each type of educational activity a personalized form should be found and an appropriate learning technique designed. Therefore, the focus of the psychological program of Davydov's group shifted toward problems of motivation and personal reflection and the construction of individualized programs of educational activity.

The last fact, however, did not challenge Davydov's basic educational credo that a curriculum oriented toward theoretical concept formation should become comprehensive.

It was quite natural that Davydov and his collaborators should emphasize the importance of theoretical concepts as the most underdeveloped and at the same time the most promising part of the science curriculum. But when they envisaged theoretical training as the *exclusive* content of comprehensive education, they obviously went beyond reasonable limits. Taking Davydov's project literally, one should learn nothing but theoretical concepts.

What would happen to graduates who received exclusively theoretical courses of instruction? Entering life, they would experience a terrible shock in discovering that politics, ideology, and practical decision making do not obey the rules of conceptual thinking. The mode of thinking that Davydov proposed for comprehensive instruction can in reality be used only by members of the scientific elite involved in fundamental research. There is an obvious gap between such forms of reasoning and the ones required for dealing with everyday social realities. If the division of labor and professional opportunities did not change drastically, what would this army of theoreticians do? Davydov's students would be welcome in Goethe's Pedagogical Province or in Hermann Hesse's Castalia, but scarcely in the Soviet Union.[35]

Two traditions seem clearly to stand behind Davydov's exaggeration of theoretical scholarship. One belongs to the history of Soviet psychology at the point where the disciples of Lev Vygotsky started to focus on the psychology of concept formation to the neglect of the field of preconceptual thinking. The preconceptual means of reasoning that dominate everyday intelligence, beliefs, and ideologies were kept outside the scope of Soviet psychology for decades. Davydov, despite his reformist temper, did not deviate from this tradition, treating the phenomenon of preconceptual reasoning as a mere obstacle on the road to purely theoretical intelligence.[36]

The second tradition that contributed to the exaggeration of theoretical learning derives from the social experience of Soviet intellectuals. In the Soviet Union theoretical scholarship has always played the role of a refuge harboring those who sought relief from political turmoil and the changing requirements of Communist ideology. Since these requirements more than once caused a collapse of social disciplines and practical projects, Soviet scholars slowly learned that the most abstract and analytical subjects are the most secure. Their experience told them that excellence could be more easily achieved in mathematics, with its relatively stable corpus of recognized principles, than in sociology, a subject laced with minute twists of ideology. Theoretical achievements have a good chance of being transmitted to the next generation, thus bringing the scholar satisfaction, but with a practical project one can never be sure whether it will be destroyed by the next shift in social attitude.

In short, fundamental studies proved to be more rewarding both intellectually and personally. But the limits of theoretical scholarship were just an extension of its virtues. Theoretical knowledge had to remain elitist, and theoreticians could not dream of social recognition for their achievements. In this respect Davydov's project looks like an outright utopia, for it gives no clues about how to reconcile the existing elitism of theoretical scholarship with the comprehensiveness of the proposed curriculum. Davydov and his philosopical advisers just picked up the valuable experience of the theoreticians and extended it, illegitimately, to the whole of society.

One might only guess that Davydov was actually quite aware that his call for comprehensiveness was a hollow one and that he simply used it as a tactical slogan to engender support for the idea of theoretical learning. The developments of the last few years seem to support the latter point of view. The psychological studies of cognitive development triggered by the program in theoretical concept formation have obviously overshadowed the task of designing a comprehensive curriculum. Nevertheless, only the future will show whether Davydov's program is a high-quality research project under the guise of an educational utopia or a genuinely utopian project.

# Notes

## Introduction

1. Michael Cole and Irving Maltzman, eds., *A Handbook of Contemporary Soviet Psychology* (New York: Basic Books, 1969); Josef Brozek and Dan Slobin, eds., *Psychology in the USSR: An Historical Perspective* (White Plains, NY: International Arts and Sciences Press, 1972).

2. James Wertsch, ed., *The Concept of Activity in Soviet Psychology* (New York: Sharpe, 1981), 3.

3. See John McLeich, *Soviet Psychology: History, Theory, Content* (London: Methuen, 1975).

4. Raymond Bauer, *The New Man in Soviet Psychology* (Cambridge, MA: Harvard University Press, 1968), 9.

5. See Luciano Mecacci, *Brain and History: The Relationship between Neurophysiology and Psychology in Soviet Research* (New York: Brunner & Mazel, 1979). See also my review in the *Journal of the History of the Behavioral Sciences* 19 (1983), 259–262.

6. Levy Rahmani, *Soviet Psychology: Philosophical, Theoretical and Experimental Issues* (New York: International Universities Press, 1973); Mecacci, *Brain and History*; Ted Payne, *S. L. Rubinštejn and the Philosophical Foundations of Soviet Psychology* (Dordrecht: Reidel, 1968); Alexander Luria, *The Making of Mind: A Personal Account of Soviet Psychology* (Cambridge, MA: Harvard University Press, 1979). Scholars writing on Soviet psychology have used a number of different systems of transliteration for names. This practice has inevitably caused confusion, for names like Rubinstein might also appear as Rubinshtein or Rubinštejn. In this book the following system has been adopted. Generally accepted spellings such as Vygotsky have been honored. Then, if there are translations authorized by the author, I have used the spelling in those translations. This is the case for Luria, Zaporozhets, Shpilrein, and some others. In all other cases I have tried to use a standard transliteration scheme, as in the cases of Bekhterev or Nebylitsyn, and to return to their common form non-Russian names such as Bernstein, Rubinstein, or Kannabich.

## Chapter 1: Four Generations of Psychologists

1. On Russian natural sciences in the pre-Revolutionary period see Alexander Vucinich, *Science in Russian Culture, 1861–1917* (Stanford: Stanford University Press, 1970). On Russian philosophy of the same period see Vasili Zenkovsky, *A History of Russian Philosophy* (London: Routledge & Kegan Paul, 1967), and Nikolai Lossky, *History of Russian Philosophy* (London: George Allen & Unwin, 1952).

2. Elena Budilova, *Borba Materializma i Idealizma v Russkoi Psikhologicheskoj Nauke* (Moscow: APN, 1960); Anatoli Smirnov, *Razvitie i Sovremennoe Sostojanie Psikhologicheskoj Nauki v SSSR* (Moscow: Pedagogika, 1975); Artur Petrovsky, *Istorija Sovetskoj Pskihologii* (Moscow: Prosveschenie, 1967).

3. *Voprosy Filosofii i Psikhologii* (1889–1918).

4. *Vestnik Psikhologii, Kriminalnoj Antropologii i Gipnoza*, later merged with the other periodicals edited by Bekhterev.

5. *Novye Idei v Filosofii*.

6. On the relations between experimentalists and psychologist-philosophers see Nikolai Lossky, *Vospominanija* (Munich: Wilhelm Fink, 1968), 120; Alexander Lazursky and Semen Frank, "Programma Issledovanija Lichnosti," *Russkaja Shkola* (January 1912). Ivan Pavlov, Vladimir Bekhterev, Nikolai Lossky, and Alexander Vvedensky participated in the joint meeting of the philosophers and physiologists organized by the Petrograd Philosophical Society; see *Psikhiatricheskaja Gazeta* no. 6 (1917).

7. On the perspectives of the biologization of psychology see Georgy Zeleny, "Sovremennaja Biologija i Psikhologija," *Novye Idei v Filosofii* 9 (1913), 40–66.

8. See Pavel Blonsky, *Moi Vospominanija* (Moscow: Pedagogika, 1971), 62–63.

9. See Georgy Chelpanov, "Otchet o Dejatelnosti Pskihologicheskogo Seminarija pri Moskovskom Universitete," *Pskihologicheskie Issledovanija* 1 (1914).

10. For a biographical note on Chelpanov and a bibliography of his work see *Enciklopedicheskij Slovar Granat*, vol. 45, part 3 (1929), 677–679.

11. On the establishment of Moscow Institute of Psychology see Georgy Chelpanov, "Zadachi i Organizatsija Moskovskogo Pskihologicheskogo Institute," in *Trudy Vtorogo Vserossijskogo Siezda po Experimentalnoj Pedagogike* (St. Petersburg, 1913).

12. Because of the war and Revolution only few issues of *Psikhologicheskoe Obozrenie* were published.

13. Georgy Chelpanov, "Ob Exparimentalnom Metode v Psikhologii," *Novye Idei v Filosofii* 9 (1913), 12–39.

14. German psychologists Narciss Ach, Osvald Kulpe, and Karl Marbe, who worked at the Wurzburg Institute of Psychology, developed a method of systematic introspection that revealed the existence of imageless thoughts. Alfred Binet, a French psychologist, invented one of the first systems of mental tests, the Simon–Binet scale.

15. See T. W. Wann, ed., *Behaviorism and Phenomenology* (Chicago: University of Chicago Press, 1964).

16. See Vladimir Preobrazhensky, "Nekotorye Zakony Illuzij," *Trudy Otdelenija Fizicheskih Nauk Obschestva Lubitelej Estestvoznanija* 7, no. 2 (1905).

17. The fabulous utopianism of the first years after the Revolution was excellently depicted by Andrei Platonov in his novel *Chevengur* (Ann Arbor: Ardis, 1978). On the collectivization of spouses see *Socializatsija Zhenschin* (Petrograd, 1918) and Lev Navrozov, *The Education of Lev Navrozov* (New York: Harpers Magazine Press, 1975), 245.

18. On the situation in Soviet science and philosophy in the 1920s see David Joravsky, *Soviet Marxism and Natural Science, 1917–1932* (London: Routledge & Kegan Paul, 1961); Loren Graham, *The Soviet Academy of Science and the Communist Party, 1927–1932* (Princeton: Princeton University Press, 1967).

19. Petrovsky, *Istorija Sovetskoj Psikhologii*, 46–46.

20. For a record of the activities of the Moscow Psychological Society from 1918 through 1922 see *Mysl* no. 3 (1922), 186–187.

21. Lossky, *Vospominanija*, 218.

22. Raymond Bauer, *The New Man in Soviet Psychology* (Cambridge, MA: Harvard University Press, 1968), 52. Bauer's book although written in 1952, remains the most penetrating study of the history of Soviet psychology. See also Levy Rahmani, *Soviet Psychology* (New York: International Universities Press, 1973).

23. P. Efrussi, *Uspehi Psikhologii v Rossii* (Petrograd, 1923), 20.

24. Ibid., 22.

25. Ibid., 26. See also Konstantin Kornilov, "Psychology in the Light of Dialectical Materialism," in *Psychologies of 1930*, Karl Murchison, ed. (Worcester, MA: Clark University Press, 1930), 243–278.

26. See Ivan Pavlov, *Izbrannye Proizvedenija* (Moscow, 1949), 337–353, 553.

27. Petrovsky, *Istorija Sovetskoj Psikhologii*, 54–57.

28. Alexander Luria, *The Making of Mind* (Cambridge, MA: Harvard University Press, 1979), 17.

29. See Bauer, *The New Man in Soviet Psychology*, 67–92.

30. Alexei Gastev, *Poezija Rabochego Udara* (Moscow, 1926), 8. See also Richard Schultz and Ross McFarland, "Industrial Psychology in the Soviet Union," *Journal of Applied Psychology* 19 (1935), 265–308.

31. Alexei Gastev, *Vosstanie Kultury* (Kharkov, 1923), 22. See also Bauer, *The New Man in Soviet Psychology*, 81.

32. Aron Zalkind, *Ocherki Kultury Revolutsionnogo Vremeni* (Moscow: Rabotnik Prosveschenija, 1924), 100–103.

33. Pavel Blonsky, *Reforma Nauki* (Moscow, 1920), *Ocherk Nauchnoj Psikhologii* (Moscow, 1921), *Pedologija* (Moscow, 1925).

34. Pavel Blonsky, *Izbrannye Sochinenija*, vol. 1 (Moscow: Pedagogika, 1979), 35.

35. Lev Vygotsky, *Mind in Societyy* (Cambridge, MA: Harvard University Press, 1978). See also Luria, *The Making of Mind*, 38–57.

36. Blonsky, *Reforma Nauki*, 28.

37. A well-argued critique of the concept of the planned society is given by Karl Popper in *The Poverty of Historicism* (Boston: Beacon Press, 1957).

38. For a detailed account of the struggle between mechanists, dialecticians, and Mitin's bolshevizers see Joravsky, *Soviet Marxism and Natural Science.*

39. Aron Zalkind, "Psikhonevrologicheskij Front i Psikhologicheskaja Diskussija," *Psikhologija* 4, no. 1 (1931), 19.

40. "Itogi Diskussii po Reaktologicheskoj Psikhologii," *Psikhologija* 4, no. 1 (1931), 1–12.

41. *Psikho-Nevrologicheskie Nauki v SSSR. Materialy Pervogo Vsesojuznogo Sjezda po Izucheniju Povedenija Cheloveka* (Moscow, 1930).

42. Boris Ananiev, "O Nekotoryh Voprosah Marxistsko-Leninskoj Rekonstrukcii Psikhologii," *Psikhologija* no. 3–4 (1931), 332.

43. Bauer, *The New Man in Soviet Psychology*, 103–109; Alexander Luria, "Krizis Burzhuaznoj Psikhologii," *Psikhologija* no. 1–2 (1932); Issak Shpilrein, "O Povorote v

Psikhotekhnike," *Psikhofiziologija Truda i Pskihotekhnika* no. 4–6 (1931). See also Petrovsky, *Istorija Sovetskoj Psikhologii*, 226–237.

44. See Bauer, *The New Man in Soviet Psychology*, 116–127.

45. On the moral atmosphere in Soviet science in the period of the purges see Mark Popovsky, *Manipulated Science* (New York: Doubleday, 1979).

46. Dmitri Uznadze, *The Psychology of Set* (New York: Consultants Bureau, 1966).

47. See the special issue of *Soviet Psychology* 18, no. 2 (1979/1980), dedicated to the work of the Kharkov school.

48. The life, career, and scientific views of Sergei Rubinstein were recounted in the monograph of Ted Payne, *S. L. Rubinštejn and the Philosophical Foundations of Soviet Psychology* (Dordrecht: Reidel, 1968). Unfortunately the author paid no attention to the campaign against Rubinstein that had been launched in the late 1940s and seriously influenced his further career. There is also a regrettable misprint, namely the date of Rubinstein's election as a member-correspondent of the Academy of Science. The actual date is 1943. In 1953—the date given in Payne's book—Rubinstein was in disgrace.

49. Sergei Rubinstein, "Problemy Psikhologii v Trudah K. Marxa," *Sovetskaja Psikhotekhnika* no. 1 (1934).

50. See Sergei Vavilov, *Nauka Stalinskoj Epohi* (Moscow: Politizdat, 1950); Loren Graham, *Science and Philosophy in the Soviet Union* (New York: Knopf, 1972), 13–14, 195–256, 324–354.

51. "Vyshe Znamia Sovetskogo Patriotizma v Pedagogicheskoj Nauke," *Sovetskaja Pedagogika* no. 4 (1948), 9.

52. On the anti-Semitic campaign of the late 1940s and early 1950s see Gerald Israel, *The Jews in Russia* (New York: St. Martin's Press, 1975), 193–213; Isaac London, "Days of Anxiety," *Jewish Social Studies* 15 (1953), 275–292.

53. "Russian Psychoanalytical Society," *International Journal of Psycho-Analysis* 10 (1929), 562.

54. The attack against Rubinstein was launched by Victor Kolbanovsky in the Party journal *Bolshevik* 17 (1948), 50–56.

55. P. Plotnikov, "Ochistit Sovetskuju Psikhologiju ot Bezrodnogo Kosmopolitizma," *Sovetskaja Pedagogika* no. 4 (1949).

56. Leonid Zankov, "Puti Pskihologicheskogo Issledovanija i Preodalenie Burzhuaznyh Vlijanij," *Sovetskaja Pedagogika* no. 5 (1949), 67.

57. Plotnikov, "Ochistit Sovetskuju Psikholgiju," 13.

58. Mark Mitin, *Filosofskie Nauki v SSSR za Dvadzat Piat Let* (Moscow: Znanie, 1943), 28–29.

59. Boris Teplov, *Sovetskaja Psikhologicheskaja Nauka za Tridzat Let* (Moscow: Znanie, 1947), 13, 16–19.

60. *Nauchnaja Sessija Posviaschennaja Problemam Fiziologicheskogo Uchenija Akademika Pavlova* (Moscow and Leningrad, 1950). See also Luria, *The Making of Mind*, 219–221; Payne, *S. L. Rubinštejn*, 52–67.

61. See Anatoli Smirnov, "Sostojanie Psikhologii i ee Perestroika Na Osnove Uchenija I. P. Pavlova," *Sovetskaja Pedagogika* no. 8 (1952), 61–87; "Materialy Soveschanija po Psikhologii," *Izvestija Akademii Pedagogicheskih Nauk SSSR* 45 (1953).

62. A representative collection of papers of psychologists mentioned above may be found in Michael Cole and Irving Maltzman, eds., *A Handbook of Contemporary Soviet*

*Psychology* (New York: Basic Books, 1969). See also Josef Brozek and Dan Slobin, eds., *Psychology in the USSR: An Historical Perspective* (White Plains, NY: International Arts and Sciences Press, 1972).

63. Esras Asratian, "Some Vital Problems in the Development of I. P. Pavlov's Teaching," *Soviet Psychology* 5 (1967), 7.

64. Jeffrey Gray, ed., *Pavlov's Typology: Recent Theoretical and Experimental Developments from the Laboratory of B. M. Teplov* (New York: Macmillan, 1964); *Problemy Differentsialnoj Psikhofiziologii* (Moscow: Prosveschenie, 1969).

65. Vladimir Zinchenko and Valentina Gordon, "Methodological Problems in the Psychological Analysis of Activity," in *The Concept of Activity in Soviet Psychology*, James Wertsch, ed. (New York: Sharpe, 1981); Vladimir Zinchenko and Merab Mamardashvili, "Problema Objektivnogo Metoda v Psikhologii," *Voprosy Filosofii* no. 7 (1977).

66. Alexander Zinoviev, "Problema Stroenija Nauki i Logike i Dialektoke," *Dialektika i Logika. Formy Myshlenija* (Moscow: ANSSR, 1962). Evald Ilienkov, *Dialektika Abstraktnogo i Konkretnogo v "Kapitale" Marxa* (Moscow: ANSSR, 1960).

67. Anatoli Arseniev, Vladimir Bibler, and Bonifatij Kedrov, *Analiz Razvivauschegosia Poniatija* (Moscow: Nauka, 1967); Alexander Zinoviev, *Foundation of the Logical Theory of Scientific Knowledge* (Dordrecht: Reidel, 1973); Evald Ilienkov, *Ob Idolah i Idealah* (Moscow: Politizdat, 1968); Felix Mikhailov, *The Riddle of the Self* (Moscow: Progress, 1980); Merab Mamardashvili, *Forma i Soderzhanie Soznanija* (Moscow: Vysshaia Shkola, 1968); Eric Soloviev, *Existentialism i Nauchnoe Poznanie* (Moscow, 1966); Mark Turovsky, *Trud i Myshlenie* (Moscow: Vysshaia Shkola, 1963).

68. The yearbooks *Sistemnye Issledovanija* (Moscow: Nauka) were published starting in 1969.

69. Ludwig von Bertalanffy, *General Systems Theory* (New York: Braziller, 1968).

70. Nelli Nepomniaschaja, "O Metode Sistemnogo Issledovanija Psikhologicheskogo Razvitija Detej," *Voprosy Psikhologii* no. 6 (1973); Vladimir Lefebvre, *The Structure of Awareness* (Beverly Hills: Sage, 1977); Vitali Dubrovsky et al., *Problemy Sistemnogo Inzhenerho-Psikhologicheskogo Projektirovanija* (Moscow: MGU, 1971); Zinchenko and Gordon, "Methodological Problems in the Psychological Analysis of Activity."

71. Georgy Schedrovitsky, *Problemy Metodologii Sistemnogo Issledovanija* (Moscow, 1964); translated in *General Systems* 11 (1966).

72. Georgy Schedrovitsky et al., *Razrabotka i Vnedrenie Avtomatizirovannyh Sistem v Projektirovanii* (Moscow: Strojizdat, 1975).

73. Vasili Davydov, *Vidy Obobschenija v Obuchenii* (Moscow: Pedagogika, 1972).

74. Vasili Davydov, "Seven-Year-Old Thinkers? Why Not?" *USSR: Soviet Life Today* no. 11 (Washington, DC: Embassy of the USSR, 1964).

75. Vasili Davydov and Leonid Radzikhovsky, "Teorija L. S. Vygotskogo i Dejatelnostnyj Podhod v Psikhologii," *Voprosy Psikhologii* no. 1 (1981), 68–80; Vladimir Zinchenko, "Idei L. S. Vygotskogo o Edinitsah Analiza Psikhiki," *Psikhologicheskij Zhurnal* 1 (1981), 118–133.

76. Two new periodicals have been established recently: *Psikhologicheskij Zhurnal* (*Psychology Journal*) in 1980 and *Vestnik Moskovskogo Universiteta. Psikhologija* (*Proceedings of Moscow University: Psychology*) in 1977.

*Chapter 2: Personalities and Reflexes*

1. "Visceral physiology" is the study of organs in the cavities of the body, such as the stomach or liver, particularly in contrast to "neurophysiology," which concerns the functions of the brain and nervous system.

2. For a first-hand account of Pavlov's research style and habits see Boris Babkin, *Pavlov: A Biography* (Chicago: University of Chicago Press, 1949). Babkin had spent several years in Pavlov's laboratory before the Revolution and left an interesting memoir.

3. The word "conditional" undoubtedly preserves the meaning of Russian term *uslovnye* much better than the more common translation "conditioned." Stephen Toulmin argued against the latter usage in his brilliant essay, "The Mozart of Psychology," *The New York Review of Books* September 28, 1978. Although I admire Toulmin's article in general, I disagree with his version of those circumstances that led to the wrong translation of the term *uslovnye*.

4. Ivan Pavlov, *Izbrannye Proizvedenija* (Moscow, 1949), 142.

5. Ibid, 151.

6. The specific "scientistic" narrow-mindedness of Pavlov clearly revealed itself in the following episode reported by Babkin. While a graduate student, Babkin decided to concentrate on the history of medicine and informed Pavlov of his decision. In response, Pavlov burst out: "History of medicine! How absurd! This is utter nonsense— all medical history leads to the same things." In a while Babkin changed his mind and turned to experimental physiology. Pavlov's reaction was absolutely unambiguous: "It seems that Babkin is a serious man, since he has decided to leave this nonsense— the history of medicine—and become a physiologist." (Babkin, *Pavlov*, pp. 79, 83.)

7. Ivan Pavlov, *Conditioned Reflexes* (Oxford: Oxford University Press, 1927), 17.

8. Ibid., 26.

9. Ivan Pavlov, *O Fiziologii i Patologii Vysshei Nervnoi Dejatel'nosti* (Moscow: Znanie, 1949), 4. My italics.

10. For a comprehensive account of this approach see Jeffrey Gray, ed., *Pavlov's Typology: Recent Theoretical and Experimental Developments from the Laboratory of B. M. Teplov* (New York: Macmillan, 1964).

11. Ivan Pavlov, *Lectures on Conditioned Reflexes*, vol. 2 (New York: International Publishers, 1941), 93.

12. Ivan Pavlov, *Psychopathology and Psychiatry* (Moscow, 1961), 275.

13. Pavlov, *Lectures on Conditioned Reflexes*, vol. 2, 113.

14. *Pavlovskie 'Klinicheskie Sredy'* (Moscow, 1949), 190.

15. Pavlov, *Lectures on Conditioned Reflexes*, vol. 2, 93.

16. Pavlov, *Psychopathology and Psychiatry*, 276.

17. A similar appeal to hypothetical neurophysiological structures was made by Konrad Lorenz when he tried—in vain—to save the concept of chain reflexes as a basis for instinctive behavior. See Teodora Kalikow, "Konrad Lorenz's Ethological Theory, 1939–1943," *Philosophy of the Social Sciences* 6 (1976), 15–34. See also Alex Kozulin, "Atomism vs. Structuralism in the Behavioral Sciences," *Boston Studies in the Philosophy of Science* (Dordrecht: Reidel, forthcoming).

18. See Ivan Pavlov, *Polnoe Sobranie Trudov*, vol. 3 (Moscow, 1949), 474.

19. Ivan Pavlov, *Izbrannye Proizvedenija* (Moscow, 1949): on Gestalt psychology see pp. 487–495; on Pierre Janet, pp. 465–470.

20. Lawrence Kubie, "Pavlov, Freud and Soviet Psychiatry," *Behavioral Science* 4 (1959), 29–34.

21. One of Pavlov's former students, Yuri Frolov, pointed out that it was Edward Thorndike whom Pavlov honored most and to whom he "gave priority in research in the field of nervous activity." See Yuri Frolov, *Pavlov and His School* (London: Kegan, Trench, Traubner, 1937), 11.

22. Viktor Kandinsky (1849–1889) was a Russian psychiatrist who suffered from schizophrenia and managed to leave an excellent description of his own experience (Kandinsky–Clerambault syndrome).

23. The "Wednesdays" had begun in the early 1920s as weekly colloquia chaired by Pavlov. In the late 1920s and in the 1930s the colloquia were dedicated mainly to the problems of higher mental processes and clinical psychology. For the years 1933–1935 there are stenographic records of the meetings. In my translation I try to preserve the original flavor of Pavlov's oral delivery.

24. *Pavlovskie 'Klinicheskie Sredy'* (Moscow, 1949), 188. According to the classification of mental disorders based on the observations of Peter Ganushkin, which were famous in Pavlov's days, psychasthenia belongs to the group of asthenic conditions, which could be either a sign of inborn psychotic personality or a result of psychoneurosis. It is characteristic of psychasthenics to be unnecessarily scrupulous, repetitive, and diffident and to have no vivid imagination. Many of the peculiarities of Pavlov's life confirm the conjecture on the psychasthenic nature of his personality.

25. Ibid., 190.

26. Ibid., 189.

27. Babkin in his memoirs emphasizes that Pavlov was sensitive only to so-called realistic art and would not tolerate symbolic themes.

28. H. Koshtojanz, "I. P. Pavlov kak Estestvoispytatel," *Pod Znamenem Marxizma* no. 4 (1936).

29. *Signal'nye Sistemy Cheloveka* (Leningrad, 1965); L. Pervov, *Osobennosti Osnovnyh Nervnyh Processov i Signal'nyh Sistem pri Isterii* (Moscow and Leningrad, 1960); Mark Burno, *Pskihopatii* (Moscow: Znanie, 1975); Eugene Boiko, *Mozg i Psikhika* (Moscow, 1969)

30. Robert Tucker, *The Soviet Political Mind, Stalinism and Post-Stalin Change* (New York: Norton, 1971), 157.

31. Boris Teplov, *Sovetskaja Psikhologicheskaja Nauka za Tridzat Let* (Moscow: Znanie, 1947).

32. It must be noted that there was an idealistic element to the profession of physician in Russia. The majority of physicians were terribly underpaid, worked in difficult conditions, and spent half their time traveling to remote villages. Because of all this an aura of gratitude and confidence enveloped them—an aura that reinforced their high professional and moral standards.

33. On the "irreducible" nature of the legacy of the humanists see Leonid Batkin, *Italjanskie Gumanisty: Stil Zhizni, Stil Myshlenija* (Moscow: Nauka, 1978).

34. Babkin, *Pavlov*, 89.

35. Vladimir Bekhterev, *Vnushenie i ego Rol v Obschestvennoj Zhizni* (St. Petersburg, 1903).

36. Vladimir Bekhterev, "Objective Investigation of Neuropsychical Activity," *Proceedings of the International Congress of Psychiatry and Experimental Psychology* (Amsterdam, 1907); Vladimir Bekhterev, *Objektivhaja Psikhologija* (St. Petersburg, 1907–1912; German and French translations published in 1913).

37. Babkin, *Pavlov*, 90–91.

38. See Vladimir Bekhterev, "Ot Mraka k Svetu," in *Schit*, Leonid Andreev, Maxim Gorky, and Fedor Sologub, eds. (Moscow and Petrograd, 1916).

39. Igor Guberman, *Bekhterev: Stranitsy Zhizni* (Moscow: Znanie, 1977), 113.

40. Vladimir Bekhterev, "Primenenie Metoda Associativnogo Motornogo Reflexa pri Simulatsii," *Russij Vrach* (1912); published in German in *Zeitschrift für Neuropatologie und Psychiatrie* 13, no. 2.

41. Guberman, *Bekhterev*, 132.

42. Vladimir Bekhterev, "Ubijstvo Yuschinskogo i Dannye Psikhologopsikhiatricheskoj Ekspertizy," *Vrach* (1913). On the Beilis case see Maurice Samuel, *Blood Accusation: The Strange History of the Beilis Case* (New York: Knopf, 1966).

43. Vladimir Bekhterev, "Mne Otmschenie i As Vozdam" and "Ot Mraka k Svetu," in *Schit*, Leonid Andreev, Maxim Gorky, and Fedor Sologub, eds. (Moscow and Petrograd, 1916).

44. Anatoli Lunacharsky, *Vospominanija i Vpechatlenija* (Moscow, 1968), 317–318.

45. Vladimir Bekhterev, *General Principles of Human Reflexology* (New York: International Publishers, 1932), 81.

46. See Alexander Schniermann, "Bekhterev's Reflexological School," in *Psychologies of 1930*, Karl Murchison, ed. (Worcester, MA: Clark University Press, 1930).

47. This paper was translated into English and published in a special issue of *Soviet Psychology* 8 (1969), 50–63, dedicated to Bekhterev's school.

48. See Raymond Bauer, *The New Man in Soviet Psychology* (Cambridge, MA: Harvard University Press, 1968), 49–92; Elena Budilova, *Filosofskie Problemy v Sovetskoj Psikhologii* (Moscow: Nauka, 1972), 83–89.

49. Boris Ananiev, "O Nekotoryh Voprosah Marxistsko-Leninskoj Rekonstrukcii Psikhologii," *Psikhologija* no. 3–4 (1931), 325–344. Originally the term "Menshevik" meant a member of the minority faction of the Russian Social Democratic Party, which opposed the more radical majority faction, the Bolsheviks. By the late 1920s, however, it had become a political epithet used by radical communists to label "moderate" Party members.

50. Ananiev abandoned reflexological ideas in the 1930s, survived the toughest period, and eventually became chairman of the psychology department at Leningrad State University.

51. Boris Ananiev, in *Reflexologija ili Psikhologija: Materialy Discussii* (Leningrad, 1929), 33.

52. Boris Ananiev, in *Reflexologija i Smezhnye Discypliny* (Leningrad, 1930), 77.

53. Ananiev, "O Nekotoryh Voporsah," 332.

54. For a highly insightful criticism of the utopian aspect of the planned society see Karl Popper, *The Poverty of Historicism* (Boston: Beacon Press, 1957).

55. See A. Emery, "Dialectics vs. Mechanics, a Communist Debate on Scientific Method," *Philosophy of Science* 2 (1935), 9–38.

56. Boris Ananiev, "Psikhologija Pedagogicheskoj Otsenski," *Trudy Instituta po Izucheniju Mozga* 4 (1935).

*Chapter 3: Nikolai Bernstein*

1. Nikolai Bernstein, *The Coordination and Regulation of Movements* (London: Pergamon Press, 1967), 127. This volume is an abridged translation of a collection of articles, written over a period of years and published in Russian in 1966 under the title *Ocherki po Fiziologii Dvizhenij i Fiziologii Aktivnosti*. Unfortunately the English version is a word-for-word translation that does not reflect the quality of Bernstein's literary style and sometimes even distorts his argument.

2. Nikolai Bernstein, *Obschaja Biomekhanika* (Moscow: VCSPS, 1926). During the 1920s and early 1930s Bernstein and his collaborators published much of their research in German professional journals; see *Pflügers Archiv* 217 (1927), *Arbeitsphysiologie* 3 (1930) and 6 (1933).

3. Figure adapted from Bernstein, *Ocherki*, 44. See also Bernstein, *Coordination*, 20.

4. Nikolai Bernstein, "Problema Vzaimootnoshenija Koordinatsii i Lokalizatsii," *Archiv Biologicheskih Nauk* 38, no. 1 (1935); reprinted in Bernstein, *Coordination*, 20–21.

5. The concept of reflex circle appeared for the first time in Bernstein's article "Fiziologija Dvizhenij," in *Fiziologija Truda*, Konradi, Slonim, and Farfel, eds. (Moscow, 1934), 441–449. John Dewey in his article "The Reflex Arc Concept," *The Philosophical Review* 3 (1896), foreshadowed the idea of circular reflexes.

6. Proprioceptors are receptors in muscles that are sensitive to compression. Bernstein sometimes used "proprioception" as a general term for all feedback impulses flowing from moving parts of the human body.

7. George Miller, Eugene Galanter, and Karl Pribram, *Plans and Structures of Behavior* (New York: Holt, 1960).

8. Bernstein, *Coordination*, 23. The first sketch of a mathematical theory of movement was published by Bernstein in *Zeitschrift für angewandte Matematik und Mechanik* 7 (1927), 476. Only at the end of his life did Bernstein witness the development and appreciation of the ideas of mathematical biomechanics; see Israel Gelfand et al., *Models of the Structural-Functional Organization of Certain Biological Systems* (Cambridge, MA: MIT Press, 1971).

9. See Karl Pribram, *Languages of the Brain* (Englewood Cliffs, NJ: Prentice-Hall, 1971), 246.

10. Bernstein, *Coordination*, 50–57.

11. Nikolai Bernstein, *O Postroenii Dvizhenij* (Moscow: Medgiz, 1947).

12. Bernstein, *Ocherki*, 97–101.

13. Figure adapted from Bernstein, *Ocherki*, 237.

14. See Nikolai Bernstein, "Nazrevshie Problemy Reguliatsii Dvigatelnykh Aktov," *Voprosy Psikhologii* no. 6 (1957); reprinted in Bernstein, *Coordination*, 129–130.

15. Alexei Leontiev, *Problemy Razvitija Psikhiki* (Moscow: MGU, 1972), 300, 378. Recently Vladimir Zinchenko has attempted to employ some of Bernstein's ideas within the framework of revised version of Leontiev's theory; see Vladimir Zinchenko and Valentina Gordon, "Methodological Problems in Analyzing Activity," in *The Concept of Activity in Soviet Psychology*, James Wertsch, ed. (New York: Sharpe, 1981).

16. On the Pavlovian Session see *Nauchnaja Sessija Posviaschennaja Problemam Fiziologicheskogo Uchenija Pavlova* (Moscow, 1950), and Ted Payne, *S. L. Rubinstejn and the Philosophical Foundations of Soviet Psychology* (Dordrecht: Reidel, 1968), 52–67.

17. On the design of prosthetic appliances see Nikolai Bernstein, "K Biomekhanicheskoi Teorii Postroenija Protezov Nizhnih Konechnostei," *Trudy Instituta Protezirovanija* no. 1 (1948). On sport physiology see Nikolai Bernstein, ed., *Issledovanija po Biodinamike Khotby, Bega, Pryzhka* (Moscow, 1940). On the training of astronauts see Lev Chkhaidze, *Koordinatsija Proizvolnyh Dvizhenij Cheloveka v Uslovijah Kosmicheskogo Poliota* (Moscow: Nauka, 1965).

18. *Filosofskie Voprosy Fiziologii Vysshei Nervnoi Dejatelnosti i Psikhologii* (Moscow, 1963).

19. Esras Asratian, "Some Vital Problems in the Development of I. P. Pavlov's Teaching," *Soviet Psychology* 5 (1967), 7.

20. See Elena Budilova, *Filosofskie Problemy v Sovetskoj Psikhologii* (Moscow: Nauka, 1972), 233–245.

21. Miller, Galanter, and Pribram. *Plans and Structures of Behavior.*

22. Ludwig von Bertalanffy, *General Systems Theory* (New York: Braziller, 1968), 208–209.

23. Bernstein warned against the careless application of cybernetic concepts to biopsychological phenomena in his *Ocherki*, 249.

24. Philip Bassin, *Problema Bessoznatelnogo* (Moscow: Medizina, 1968), 248.

25. Philip Bassin, "Otkrytoe Pismo E. A. Asratianu," *Voprosy Filosofii* no. 4 (1971).

26. Ekaterina Shorokhova, "Prinzip Determinizma v Psikhologii," *Metodologicheskie i Teoreticheskie Problemy Psikhologii* (Moscow: Nauka, 1969).

27. Nikolai Bernstein, *Ocherki po Fiziologii Dvizhenij i Fiziologii Aktivnosti* (Moscow: Medizina, 1966).

28. See Lev Chkhaidze and V. Velikson, "Certain Aspects of the Mathematical Modelling of the Dynamics of Biokinematic Chains," *Biophysics* 20 (1975), 143–147; Israel Gelfand et al., "Issledovanie Poznoj Aktivnosti," *Biofizika* 9 (1964), 710–717.

29. Alexander Asmolov, "Problema Ustanovki v Neobikheviorizme," in *Verojatnostnoe Prognozirovanie v Dejatelnosti Cheloveka*, Josif Feigenberg and Eugene Zhuravliov, eds. (Moscow: Nauka, 1977), 60–111.

30. Alex Kozulin, "Sistemnyi Podhod v Izuchenii Detskoi Psikhiki," in *Sistemnye Issledovanija Ezhegodnik* (Moscow: Nauka, 1977), 250–260.

31. Bernstein, *Ocherki*, 278–279.

32. Pribram, *Languages of the Brain*, 51.

33. See Josif Feigenberg, "Probabilistic Prognosis and its Significance in Normal and Pathological Subjects," in *A Handbook of Contemporary Soviet Psychology*, Michael Cole and Irving Maltzman, eds. (New York: Basic Books, 1969).

34. L. Gurova, "Alerting Reactions in Schizophrenics," *Soviet Psychology* 12, no. 4 (1974).

35. Josif Feigenberg and Vladimir Levi, "Verojatnostnoe Prognozirovanie i Eksperimentalnye Issledovanija Ego pri Patologicheskih Sostojanijakh," *Voprosy Psikhologii* no. 1 (1965), 42–54.

36. Emma Rootman and Alex Kozulin, "Reflection of the Information Analysis of Stimuli and Motor Preparedness in Different Components of Sensory Evoked Potentials," *Agressologie* 16 (1975), 131–135.

निष्कर्ष

37. See William Estes, "Probability Learning," in *Categories of Human Learning*, A. Melton, ed. (New York: Academic Press, 1964); Daniel Kahneman and Amos Tversky, "On the Psychology of Prediction," *Psychological Review* 80 (1973), 237–251.

38. See Samuel Sutton et al., "Evoked Potential Correlates of Stimulus Uncertainty," *Science* 150 (1965), 1187–1188; Samuel Sutton and D. Paul, "Evoked Potential Correlates of Response Criterion in Auditory Signal Detection," *Science* 177 (1973), 362–364.

39. E. Bazhin, J. Meerson, and I. Tonkonogy, "Ob osobennostjah Verojatnostnogo Prognozirovanija pri Nekotoryh Psikhopatologicheskih i Neiropsikhologicheskih Sindromah," *Schizofrenija i Verojatnostnoe Prognozirovanie* (Moscow: CIUV, 1973).

40. Rebekka Frumkina and A. Dobrovich, "Disorders in the Probability Organization of Speech Behavior in Schizophrenia," *Soviet Psychology* 12, no. 4 (1974).

41. Rebekka Frumkina, ed., *Prognoz v Rechevoi Dejatelnosti*, (Moscow: Nauka, 1974), 201–227.

42. The results of these experiments were partially published by Alex Kozulin et al., "Vlijanie Vvedenija Semanticheskoi Informatsii na Bessoznatelnye Ustanovki u Pogranichnyh Bolnyh," in *Problemy Psikhoterapii: Alkoholism i Nevrozy*, Vladimir Rozhnov, ed. (Moscow: CIUV, 1976). Since the data were distributed binomially, I estimated the variance, which proved that the performances of normals and schizophrenics are statistically different.

*Chapter 4: The Problem of the Unconscious*

1. *Sotsializatoija Zhenschin* (Petrograd, 1918), 4–5. See also Lev Navrozov, *The Education of Lev Navrozov* (New York: Harpers Magazine Press, 1975), 245–246.

2. Alexander Bogdanov, *Krasnaya Zvezda* (Leningrad and Moscow: Kniga, 1925), 9. See also Leland Feltzer, ed., *An Anthology of Pre-Revolutionary Russian Science Fiction* (Ann Arbor: Ardis, 1982).

3. Bogdanov, *Krasnaya Zvezda*, 108.

4. See Alexandra Kollontai, *Love of Worker Bees* (London: Virago, 1977); Russian edition published in 1923.

5. See Alexander Luria, *The Making of Mind* (Cambridge, MA: Harvard University Press, 1979), 28–37.

6. Karl Levitin, *Mimoletnyi Uzor* (Moscow: Znanie, 1978), 44–55. Levitin reproduces portions of Luria's memoirs that he had tape-recorded. These portions partly overlap *The Making of Mind*, which was published exclusively in English, but they also contain some interesting variants.

7. Alexander Luria, "Psikhoanaliz Kak Sistema Monisticheskoy Psikhologii," in *Psikhologija i Marxizm*, Konstantin Kornilov, ed. (Moscow and Leningrad, 1925), 79; English translation in *Soviet Psychology* 16 (1977/78), 6–45.

8. Ibid., 66.

9. "Russian Psycho-Analytical Society," *International Journal of Psycho-Analysis* 9 (1926), 294–295.

10. Alexander Luria, "Krizis Burjuaznoi Psikhologii," *Psikhologiya* no. 1–2 (1932), 72.

11. Alexander Luria, *The Nature of Human Conflicts* (New York: Liveright, 1932).

12. Levitin, *Mimoletnyi Uzor*, 54.

13. Bernard Bykhovsky, "O Metodologicheskih Osnovaniyah Psikhoanaliticheskogo Ucheniya Freuda," *Pod Znamenem Marxizma* no. 11–12 (1923), 159.

14. Ibid., 169. See also Lawrence Kubie, "Pavlov, Freud and Soviet Psychiatry," *Behavioral Science* 4 (1959), 29–34.

15. *Pravda* June 14, 1925.

16. Wilhelm Reich, "Psychoanalysis in the Soviet Union," in Reich, *Sex-Pol*, Lee Baxandall, ed. (New York: Random House, 1972), 86; German edition published in 1929.

17. Schmidt published Luria's early book on psychoanalysis in 1923 using his position of head of the State Publishing House. See Levitin, *Mimoletnyi Uzor*, 48.

18. See the various reports on the membership and activities of the Russian Psychoanalytical Society in the *International Journal of Psycho-Analysis* 3–14 (1922–1933).

19. Artur Petrovsky, *Istorija Sovetskoj Psikhologii* (Moscow: Prosveschenie, 1967), 90.

20. Bernard Bykhovsky, "Geneonomicheskie Vzgliady Freuda," *Pod Znamenem Marxizma* no. 9–10 (1926).

21. Petrovsky, *Istorija*, 90.

22. Reich, "Psychoanalysis in the Soviet Union," 81.

23. *International Journal of Psycho-Analysis* 9 (1928), 399.

24. An article based on this book was eventually published in German: Dmitri Uznadze, "Bergsons Monismus," *Archiv für Geschichte der Philosophie und Sociologie* 30 (1926).

25. See Jean Piaget and M. Lambercier, "Essai sur un effet d'Einstellung survenant au cours de perceptions visuelles successives," *Archives de Psychologie* 30 (1944), 139–196; also Dmitri Uznadze, *Psikhologicheskie Issledovanija* (Moscow: Nauka, 1966), 141, and *The Psychology of Set* (New York: Consultants Bureau, 1966).

26. Uznadze, *Psikhologicheskie Issledovanija*, 150.

27. Ibid., 152.

28. For a history of phenomenological psychology in the United States and Western Europe see Henrik Misiak and Virginia Sexton, *Phenomenological, Existential and Humanistic Psychologies* (New York: Grune & Stratton, 1973); also Herbert Spiegelberg, *Phenomenology in Psychology and Psychiatry: A Historical Introduction* (Evanston, IL: Northwestern University Press, 1972).

29. Uznadze, *Psikhologicheskie Issledovanija*, 150.

30. Dmitri Uznadze, "K Voprosu ob Osnovnom Zakone Smeny Ustanovki," *Psikhologija* no. 9 (1930).

31. Philip Bassin, *Problema Bessoznatelnogo* (Moscow: Medizina, 1968), 222–223.

32. On the transformation of behavioristic concepts see Sigmund Koch, "Epilogue," in *Psychology: A Study of a Science*, Sigmund Koch, ed., vol. 3 (New York: McGraw-Hill, 1959).

33. In his review of the studies in language and intelligence conducted by Georgian psychologists, Revaz Natadze unwittingly revealed that the concept of set was not a genuine source of these studies but was just attached to them as a label. See Revaz Natadze, "Studies on Thought and Speech Problems by Psychologists of the Georgian SSR," in *Recent Soviet Psychology*, N. O'Connor, ed. (New York: Pergamon, 1961).

34. *Eksperimentalnye Osnovy Psikhologii Ustanovki* (Tbilisi, 1961).

35. Philip Bassin, A. Prangishvili, and A. Sherozija, eds., *Bessoznatelnoe* (Tbilisi: Metzniereba, 1978).

36. Ibid., vol. 1, 58.

37. Ibid., vol. 1, 145.

38. Ibid., vol. 1, 27–28.

39. Ibid., vol. 1, 239.

40. Ibid., vol. 2, 562.

*Chapter 5: Lev Vygotsky*

1. A first-hand account of this meeting can be found in Alexander Luria's memoir, *The Making of Mind* (Cambridge, MA: Harvard University Press, 1979), 38–39.

2. Lev Vygotsky, "Soznanie kak Problema Psikhologii Povedenija," *Psikhologija i Marxizm*, Konstantin Kornilov, ed. (Moscow and Leningrad, 1925); English translation reprinted in *Soviet Psychology* 17 (1979), 5–35, here p. 7.

3. Ibid., 19, 32.

4. Ibid., 30.

5. Ibid., 29.

6. On the developmental method in psychology see Lev Vygotsky,"The Genesis of Higher Mental Functions," in *The Concept of Activity in Soviet Psychology*, James Wertsch, ed. (New York: Sharpe, 1981).

7. Lev Vygotsky, *Psikhologija Podrostka* (Moscow and Leningrad, 1931), 348.

8. Lev Vygotsky, "The Instrumental Method in Psychology," in *The Concept of Activity in Soviet Psychology*, James Wertsch, ed. (New York: Sharpe, 1981).

9. Ibid., 138.

10. Lev Vygotsky, *Mind in Society* (Cambridge, MA: Harvard University Press, 1978), 54.

11. Vygotsky, "The Instrumental Method," 141.

12. On the development of Vygotsky's research program in the works of his disciples see the Vygotsky memorial issue of *Soviet Psychology* 5, no. 3 (1967).

13. See Michael Cole, ed., *Soviet Developmental Psychology: An Anthology* (New York: Sharpe, 1978).

14. Alexei Leontiev, "Studies in the Cultural Development of the Child," *Journal of Genetic Psychology* 40 (1932), 52–83. See also Vygotsky, *Mind in Society*, 40–45.

15. A lucid example of the polemics between Soviet psychologists and Piaget is presented in the afterword of Daniel Elkonin and Peter Galperin to the Russian translation of John Flavell's book, *The Developmental Psychology of Jean Piaget: Genticheskaja Psikhologija Jean Piaget* (Moscow: Prosveschenie, 1967).

16. The recent interest in the work of Vygotsky and Luria among American psychologists and philosophers is combined, ironically, with an overwhelming neglect of those who preceded and to some extent inspired the Vygotsky–Luria program. The appropriate works of Pierre Janet, Maurice Halbwachs, and Charles Blondel on the historical determination of the development of psychological functions are still mostly unavailable in English, and their concepts and ideas are still beyond the intellectual focus of American psychologists. See, however, Maurice Halbwachs, *The Collective Memory* (New York: Harper & Row, 1980).

17. Vygotsky, "Genesis of Higher Mental Functions," 157–164.

18. Lev Vygotsky and Alexander Luria, *Etiudy po Istorii Povedenija* (Moscow, 1930).

19. Luria's recollections of this expedition are included in *The Making of Mind*, 58–80.

20. Karl Levitin, *Mimoletnyi Uzor* (Moscow: Znanie, 1978), 43.

21. Alexander Luria, *Cognitive Development* (Cambridge, MA: Harvard University Press, 1977), 53–79.

22. On the accusations against Luria and Vygotsky see Michael Cole, "A Portrait of Luria," in Luria, *The Making of Mind*, 208–214.

23. Alexander Luria, *Ob Istoricheskom Razvitii Poznavatelnyh Processov* (Moscow: Nauka, 1974); an abridged version of this book was published in English under the title *Cognitive Development*.

24. On the decree against pedology see Raymond Bauer, *The New Man in Soviet Psychology* (Cambridge, MA: Harvard University Press, 1968), 116–127.

25. Alexei Leontiev, *Ocherk Razvitija Psikhiki* (Moscow, 1947).

26. On his disagreement with some aspects of Vygotsky's theory see Leontiev's introduction to Lev Vygotsky, *Izbrannye Psikhologicheskie Issledovanija* (Moscow, 1956); see also Leonid Radzikhovsky, "Analiz Tvorchestva L. S. Vygotskogo Sovetskimi Psikhologami," *Voprosy Psikhologii* no. 6 (1979), and Vasili Davydov, "The Category of Activity and Mental Reflection in the Theory of A. N. Leontiev," *Soviet Psychology* 19 (1981), 3–29.

27. Vygotsky was scientifically "rehabilitated" in the mid-1950s. Since then three volumes of his writings have been published: *Izbrannye Psikhologicheskie Issledovanija* (1956), *Razvitie Vysshih Psikhocheskih Funkzij* (1960), and *Psikhologija Iskusstva* (1965; 2d ed., 1968). The first two volumes were printed in a miserable number of copies and immediately sold out. No new printings have been undertaken. This has led to a very peculiar situation in which the books of the officially recognized founder of Soviet cognitive and developmental psychology are still for all practical purposes unavailable to Soviet students.

28. See the special issue of *Soviet Psychology* 18, no. 2 (1979/80), dedicated to the Kharkov school.

29. Peter Zinchenko, "Problema Neproizvolnogo Zapominanija," *Nauchnye Zapiski Kharkovskogo Pedinstituta Inostrannyh Jazykov* 1 (1939), 153.

30. Alexei Leontiev and Alexander Luria, "Pskihologicheskie Vozzrenija Vygotskogo," in Vygotsky, *Izbrannye Psikhologicheskie Issledovanija*.

31. *Psikhologija Iskusstva* had been written between 1915 and 1922, but it was published only in 1965. In those early years Vygotsky considered himself primarily a literary critic and was also under the spell of the psychoanalytic theory of catharsis. In the second Russian edition (1968) an essay on *Hamlet* was published as a supplement. Unfortunately, in the English version of *Psychology of Art* (Cambridge, MA: The MIT Press, 1971), the essay on *Hamlet* was omitted. There are serious grounds for considering this essay a masterpiece, in some respects even more valuable than the main text, which reflects many transient influences.

32. The essay "Thought and Word" was included in Vygotsky's book *Thought and Language*. Vygotsky reproduced an early, unpublished version of Mandelstam's poem, a sign of their close friendship.

33. Lev Vygotsky, *Myshlenie i Rech* (Moscow, 1934), 317. Unfortunately these images were omitted in the English version of *Thought and Language* (Cambridge, MA: The MIT Press, 1962).

34. On the fruitful cooperation between Vygotsky, Luria, and Eisenstein see Vjacheslav Ivanov, *Ocherki po Istorii Semiotiki v SSSR* (Moscow: Nauka, 1976), 28–29, 66–67.

35. In 1982, when this chapter was already finished, *Crisis* was at last published: Lev Vygotsky, *Sobranie Sochinenij*, vol. 1 (Moscow: Pedagogika, 1982), 291–436.

36. Recently some Soviet psychologists have ventured to discuss the problems raised in *Crisis*. See Mikhail Jaroshevsky and G. Gurgenidze, "L. S. Vygotsky—Issledovatel Problem Methodologii Naukii," *Voprosy Filosofii* no. 8 (1977), 91–106; Vasili Davydov and Leonid Radzikhovsy, "Teorija L. S. Vygotskogo i Dejatelnostnyj Podhod v Psikhologii," *Voprosy Psikhologii* no. 1 (1981), 68–80; Vladimir Zinchenko, "Idei L. S. Vygotskogo o Edinitsah Analiza Psikhiki," *Psikhologicheskij Zhurnal* 1 (1981), 118–133. See also Alex Kozulin, "Vygotsky and Crisis," *Studies in Soviet Thought* 26 (1983), 249–256.

37. This point of view was presented by Georgy Schedrovitsky at the colloquium on the theoretical legacy of Vygotsky held at the Moscow Institute of Psychology in April 1979.

38. See Paul Feyerabend, *Against Method* (New York: Schocken/NLB, 1978).

39. Translators' preface to Vygotsky, *Thought and Language*, p. xii. The bias of these omissions was brilliantly criticized by Stephen Toulmin in his essay, "The Mozart of Psychology," *The New York Review of Books*, September 28, 1978.

40. In my paper "Psychology and Philosophical Anthropology: The Problem of Their Interaction," *Philosophical Forum* 15 (1984), I discuss in some detail the relationship between Vygotsky's theory and the problems of twentieth-century philosophical anthropology.

41. This vicious circle of objects and explanatory principles has been analyzed by Erik Judin, *Sistemnyi Podhod i Printsyp Dejatelnosti* (Moscow: Nauka, 1978).

42. The problem of inner speech is discussed in *Thought and Language*.

43. Vladimir Bibler, *Myshlenie kak Tvorchestvo* (Moscow: Politizdat, 1975), 158.

44. Vygotsky, *Myshlenie i Rech*, 314.

*Chapter 6: Pavel Blonsky and the Failure of Progressive Education*

1. The term "pedology" designates a wide range of studies and tests, (roughly equivalent to the range of American "educational psychology") that had been developed in the 1920s and 1930s. The 1936 decree of the Central Committee of the Communist Party "abolished" pedology and disbanded all pedological institutions.

2. Pavel Blonsky, *Moi Vospominanija* (Moscow: Pedagogika, 1971).

3. Ibid.

4. Ibid., 60.

5. See Alexei Losev, *Antichnyi Kosmos i Sovremennaja Nauka* (Moscow, 1927), and *Istorija Antichnoi Estetiki*, vols. 1–6 (Moscow: Iskusstvo, 1963–1980).

6. Pavel Blonsky,"Etudy po Istorii Rannej Grecheskoj Filosofii," *Voprosy Filosofii i Pskihologii* 5 (1914), 471–496, and *Reforma Nauki* (Moscow, 1920).

7. Pavel Blonsky, *Izbrannye Pedagogicheskie i Psikhologicheskie Sochinenija*, vol. 1 (Moscow: Pedagogika, 1979), 32.

8. Blonsky, *Moi Vospominanija*, 62.

9. Georgy Chelpanov, *Mozg i Dusha* (Moscow, 1900).

10. Pavel Blonsky, *Problema Realnosti u Berkeley* (Kiev, 1907), and "Eticheskaja Problema u Ed. Hartmann," *Voprosy Filosofii i Psikhologii* no. 88 (1907), 272–308.

11. Blonsky, *Moi Vospominanija*, 65. In 1923 Chelpanov was fired from the Moscow Institute of Psychology, which he had established in 1912. One would search the pages of Blonsky's recollections in vain looking for an account of this episode. There is no indication that Blonsky ever tried to help his former professor. It was Gustav Schpet, a Russian follower of Husserl and a specialist in aesthetics, who helped Chelpanov to survive the 1920s.

12. Blonsky, *Izbrannye Sochinenija*, vol. 1, 32.

13. Ibid., 33.

14. Ibid., 40–41.

15. Pavel Blonsky, *Vvedenie v Doshkolonoe Vospitanie* (Moscow, 1915), and *Kurs Pedagogika* (Moscow: Zadruga, 1916).

16. Pavel Blonsky, *Izbrannye Sochinenija*, vol. 1, 43.

17. See John Dewey, *The School and Society* (Chicago: University of Chicago Press, 1899); Russian translation, 1907.

18. John Dewey, *Democracy and Education* (New York: The Free Press, 1966), 329. On Dewey's educational program and the American Progressive Education movement see Lawrence Cremin, *The Transformation of the School* (New York: Vintage Books, 1964); Vince Hines, "Progressivism in Practice," in *A New Look at Progressive Education*, James Squire, ed. (Washington: ASCD, 1972), 118–164.

19. Blonsky, "Etudy po Istorii Rannej Grecheskoj Filosofii," 495.

20. George Mead,"The Philosophies of Royce, James, and Dewey in Their American Setting" (1929), in *Selected Writings* (Indianapolis: Bobbs-Merrill, 1964), 388.

21. See Katherine Mayhew and Anna Edwards, *The Dewey School* (New York: Atherton, 1966).

22. See Cremin, *Transformation of the School*; Morton White, *Social Thought in America* (New York: Viking, 1949); D. Rucker, *The Chicago Pragmatists* (Minneapolis: University of Minnesota Press, 1969).

23. Daniel Boorstin, *America and the Image of Europe* (New York: Meridian, 1960), 59, 61.

24. Blonsky, *Izbrannye Sochinenija*, vol. 1, 69.

25. Pavel Blonsky, *Filosofija Plotina* (Moscow, 1918), and *Sovremennaja Filosofija*, 2 vols. (Moscow, 1918/1922). These books were actually written in 1913–1917.

26. *Izvestia*, no. 208, 1917.

27. Blonsky, *Moi Vospominanija*, 146.

28. Blonsky, *Reforma Nauki*.

29. Ibid., 31, 34.

30. Ibid., 18, 21, 28.

31. William James, *Pragmatism and Other Essays* (1907; reprinted in 1966 by The Free Press), 26.

32. Ibid.

33. Pavel Blonsky, *Ocherk Nauchnoj Psikhologii* (Moscow, 1921).

34. George Mead, "The Genesis of the Self and Social Control" (1925), in his *Selected Writings*, 267–293; Lev Vygotsky, "Consciousness as a Problem in the Psychology of Behavior" (1925), *Soviet Psychology* 17 (1979), 5–35.

35. Pavel Blonsky, *Trudovaja Shkola* (Moscow, 1919).

36. Blonsky, *Izbrannye Sochinenija*, vol. 1, 97. It is highly instructive to compare Dewey's *The School and Society* and Blonsky's *The Labor School*.

37. Blonsky, *Izbrannye Sochinenija*, vol. 1, 91.

38. Under the label of "pedology" numerous, sometimes conflicting approaches to child development and education had been united. Undoubtedly a strong interest in the inherited characteristics of children's behavior and in the possibilities for testing these characteristics seriously influenced all pedological studies, but this could hardly be called its subject matter. In a collection of papers on *Pedology and Education* (Moscow, 1928), for example, speculations on the "psychophysiology of the proletariat" by Aron Zalkind were published side by side with studies of "collective reflexology" by Vladimir Bekhterev and the psychoanalytical studies of Lev Vygotsky.

39. James Baldwin, *Mental Development in a Child and the Race* (1896); Charles Judd, *Genetic Psychology for Teachers* (1903).

40. On Soviet education in the 1920s see Sheila Fitzpatrick, *Education and Social Mobility in the Soviet Union, 1921–1934* (London: Cambridge University Press, 1979); Maurice Shore, *Soviet Education* (New York: Philosophy Library, 1947).

41. Blonsky, *Izbrannye Sochinenija*, vol. 1, 165–180.

42. Pavel Blonsky, "Nachalnaja Shkola v Promyshlennom Rajone," *Na Putiah k Novoi Shkole* no. 2 (1922), 13, 34.

43. Nadezhda Krupskaja, *Voprosy Narodnogo Obrazovanija* (Moscow, 1928), 11.

44. See Raymond Bauer, *The New Man in Soviet Psychology* (Cambridge, MA: Harvard University Press, 1968), 100–102; Fitzpatrick, *Education and Social Mobility.*

45. Decree No. 393, *Sbornik Prikazov i Rasporiazhenij po Narkomprosu RSFSR* (Moscow, 1937).

46. Blonsky, *Izbrannye Sochinenija*, vol. 1, 35.

47. Cremin, *The Transformation of the School*, 276.

48. See William Brickman, "Soviet Attitudes towards John Dewey as an Educator," in *John Dewey and the World View*, Douglas Lawson and Arthur Lean, eds. (Carbondale, IL: Southern Illinois University Press, 1964), 64–136. Brickman, however, makes some factual mistakes in his paper. He claims, for example, that Blonsky died during the purges of 1930s, which is not true.

49. Mead, *Selected Writings*, 3.

50. For a critique of the utopian aspects of the American progressivism see David Noble, *The Paradox of Progressive Thought* (Minneapolis: University of Minnesota Press, 1967). For an account of the post-Revolutionary developments in Russia viewed by a left-wing American progressive see Waldo Frank, *Dawn in Russia* (New York: Scribners, 1932).

51. John Dewey, *Impressions of Soviet Russia and the Revolutionary World* (New York: The New Republic, 1929).

52. John Dewey, *Freedom and Culture* (New York: Putnam, 1939), 87.

53. George Counts, *Dare the School Build a New Social Order?* (New York: John Day, 1932); Harold Rugg, *American Life and the School Curriculum* (Boston: Ginn & Co, 1936); Theodore Brameld et al., *Design for America* (New York: Hinds, Hayden & Eldredge, 1945).

54. The discussion on the aims and limits of reconstructionism may be found in the journal *The Social Frontier* of 1935. See also John Dewey, *Experience and Education*

(New York: Macmillan, 1938); Mary Mix, "Social Reconstructionism, Past and Present," in *A New Look at Progressive Education*, James Squire, ed. (Washington: ASCD, 1972).

55. The decree of the Central Committee of the Communist Party of July 4, 1936, on pedology included the following directives: "To abolish the positions of pedologists in schools and to withdraw all pedological textbooks. . . . To stop teaching pedology in all teachers colleges. . . . To criticize in the press all existing theoretical works of living pedologists." See *Direktivy VKP(b) i Postanovlenija Sovietskogo Pravitelstva o Narodnom Obrazovanii* (Moscow: APN RSFSR, 1947), 192–193. Although the decree was officially directed against pedology alone, in fact all fields of applied psychology and testing suffered from its consequences; see Bauer, *The New Man in Soviet Psychology*, 116–127.

56. Pavel Blonsky, *Razvitie Myshlenija Shkolnika* (Moscow: Uchpedgiz, 1935).

*Chapter 7: Idols and Ideals in Soviet Education*

1. See Nigel Grant, *Soviet Education* (Harmondsworth, England: Penguin, 1972), 96–103.

2. For the text of Khrushchev's speech see Bertram Wolfe, *Khrushchev and Stalin's Ghost* (New York: Praeger, 1957).

3. Admiral Rickover, in his attack on American schools, claimed that Soviet education was far ahead in science teaching and in the overall training of scientists and engineers. See Hyman Rickover, *Education and Freedom* (New York: Dutton, 1959), and *American Education—A National Failure* (New York: Dutton, 1963).

4. S. G. Shapova, ed., *Polytechnical Education in the USSR* (UNESCO, 1963), 377.

5. On the uniformity and comprehensiveness of Soviet education see Urie Bronfenbrenner and John C. Condry, Jr., *Two Worlds of Childhood: U.S. and USSR* (New York: Russell Sage, 1970), 28–51.

6. On the sources and content of Khrushchev's educational reforms see "Strengthening the Ties of School with Life, and Further Developing the System of Public Education," *Soviet Booklet* 44 (London: Soviet News, 1958); George Bereday et al., eds., *The Changing Soviet School* (Boston: Houghton Mifflin, 1960), 86–99; Joan Pennar, Ivan Baralo, and George Bereday, eds., *Modernization and Diversity in Soviet Education* (New York: Praeger, 1971), 41–47.

7. "Desiatiletnjaja, Trudovaja, Politekhnicheskaja," *Uchitelskaja Gazeta* August 15, 1964.

8. On the special schools see Grant, *Soviet Education*, 90; Bereday et al., *The Changing Soviet School*, 374–378; John Dunstan, *Paths to Excellence and the Soviet School* (Windsor: NFER, 1978), 116–176.

9. S. Vladimirov, "Kto Ikh Nauchit?" *Novy Mir* no. 11 (1962), 219.

10. See Bruce Vogeli, *Soviet Secondary Schools for the Mathematically Talented* (Washington, DC: NCTM, 1968).

11. On the social status of students of the special schools see Victor Zorza, "Class Struggle Looming in Russia," *The Guardian* July 2, 1966.

12. The situation in Soviet social sciences and the humanities and the devastation caused by Stalin's policies were discussed during the All-Union Congress of Historians in 1962. See *Vsesouznoe Soveschanie Istorikov* (Moscow, Nauka, 1964).

13. Anatoli Arseniev, "Nauka i Chelovek," in *Nauka i Nravstvennost* (Moscow: Politizdat, 1971), 114–158.

14. Ibid., 130.

15. Ibid., 148.

16. For the philosophical and educational views of Mikhailov and Ilienkov see Felix Mikhailov, *The Riddle of the Self* (Moscow: Progress, 1980); Evald Ilienkov, *Ob Idolah i Idealah* (Moscow: Politizdat, 1968).

17. Ilienkov, *Ob Idolah i Idealah*, 158.

18. Ibid.

19. Vasili Davydov, *Formy Obobschenija v Obuchenii* (Moscow: Pedagogika, 1972).

20. Jerome Bruner, *The Process of Education* (Cambridge, MA: Harvard University Press, 1960); Russian translation, 1962.

21. Davydov, *Formy Obobschenija*, 114.

22. Ibid., 114–122.

23. Ibid., 155–158.

24. A. Khinchin, *Pedagogicheskie Statji* (Moscow, 1963).

25. Davydov, *Formy Obobschenija*, 163–167.

26. Ibid., 95.

27. Vasili Davydov, "Seven-Year-Old Thinkers? Why Not?" *USSR: Soviet Life Today* no. 11 (Washington, DC: Embassy of the USSR, 1964).

28. Davydov, *Formy Obobschenija*, 380–383. See also A. K. Markova, *The Teaching and Mastery of Learning* (New York: Sharpe, 1979).

29. Davydov, *Formy Obobschenija*, 385–394.

30. Ibid., 389–390.

31. Bruner, *The Process of Education*, 33–54.

32. Davydov, *Formy Obobschenija*, 341.

33. For the English version of this paper see Vasili Davydov and A. K. Markova, "A Concept of Educational Activity for Schoolchildren," *Soviet Psychology* 21 (1983), 50–76.

34. Ibid., 57.

35. In his novel *Wilhelm Meister*, Goethe depicted a Pedagogical Province inhabited by artists and scholars. A similar utopian community of refined intellectuals appears under the name of Castalia in Hermann Hesse's novel *Magister Ludi*.

36. For Davydov's views on Vygotsky's theory of learning see Vasili Davydov, "The Problem of Generalization in the Works of L. S. Vygotsky," *Soviet Psychology* 3 (1967).

# Index

Pavlovian school, 3, 16, 20, 26, 28,
  62–63, 71–73, 103
Pavlovian Session of the Academy of
  Sciences, 26, 70, 98, 163
Payne, Ted, 4
Pedology, 17, 121, 131, 136, 169–171
  decree against, 22, 110, 121
Pestalozzi, Johann, 124
Petrovsky, Artur, 11, 93
Phenomenology, 10, 29, 96–98, 166
Philosophical Society, Petrograd, 7, 11,
  14
Philosophy
  and education, 30, 32, 125–126,
    144–145, 151
  in post-Stalin era, 29–30, 142–143
Piaget, Jean, 19, 25, 28, 30, 74, 104,
  107, 119, 151, 167
Pisarev, Dmitri, 124
Plato, 122, 144
Popper, Karl, 15, 66
Pragmatism, 126, 129–130, 134–135
Praxis, 115–117
Preobrazhensky, Vladimir, 6, 10
Pribram, Karl, 28, 72, 75, 98
Psychasthenia, 47–48, 161
Psychoanalysis, 3, 17, 22, 46, 83–96,
  98–101, 104, 114
Psychoanalytical Society, Russian, 25,
  84, 88, 92, 94
Psychological Society, Moscow, 6,
  10–11
Psychology
  academic degrees in, 33
  child and educational, 17–18, 30–32,
    37, 107 (*see also* Pedology;
    Developmental psychology)
  crisis in, 113–115
  industrial and engineering, 15–16, 22,
    28–30, 37
  institutional structure of, 33–38
Psychology of activity, 23, 29, 70, 99,
  111
Psychoneurological Institute, 6–8,
  53–54
Psychophysical problem, 9–10
Psychotechnic, 16. *See also* Psychology,
  industrial and engineering

Radlov, Ernest, 6
Rahmani, Levy, 4
Rank, Otto, 92
Ravich-Scherbo, Inna, 29
Reactology, 14, 20, 86, 94, 96

Reductionism, physiological, 7, 43,
  71–72
Reflex, 7, 9, 18, 52, 63, 65–66, 68,
  70–72, 88, 91, 96, 103–105, 114–115
  arc, 64, 71
  associative, 51–54, 56, 59, 64
  circle, 28, 65, 69, 72, 163
  conditional, 20, 41–49, 53, 59, 62, 64,
    71–72, 160
  therapy, 17
  unconditional, 42–43, 71
Reflexology, 21, 46, 51, 53–54, 56–59,
  61, 94, 96, 103–104, 114, 171
Reich, Wilhelm, 91, 93–94
Revolution, 9, 11, 13–15, 56, 127
Ribot, Teodul, 6
Rickover, Hyman, 138–139
Rossolimo, Georgy, 6
Rubinstein, M. M., 128
Rubinstein, Sergei, 4, 23–27, 36, 38,
  49, 158

Sakharov, Andrei, 141
Sakharov, Leonid, 19
Sapir, Edward, 117
Sapir, Isay, 20
Scharrelman, Heinrich, 124
Schedrovitsky, Georgy, 30–31, 113,
  169
Schizophrenics, behavior of, 75–77,
  79–81
Schmidt, Otto, 92, 166
Schmidt, Vera, 92, 94
Schnierman, Alexander, 20, 25
Schools, special science, 137, 140–142
Schopenhauer, Arthur, 10
Schpet, Gustav, 6
Science
  popularization of, 7, 141
  in school curricula, 31–32, 125, 131,
    137–141, 144, 147
Semashko, Nikolai, 91
Semionov, Nikolai, 141
Set, psychology of, 22, 27, 73–74, 83,
  95–100, 166
Severtsov, Alexei, 12
Sexual revolution, 84–85, 91
Shemiakin, F., 20
Sherozia, A., 99
Sherrington, Charles, 48
Shevarev, Peter, 9
Shif, Zhozefina, 19
Shik, Mark, 74
Shpilrein, Isaak, 16, 20–22, 25, 27

## DATE DUE

GAYLORD                                    PRINTED IN U.S.A.